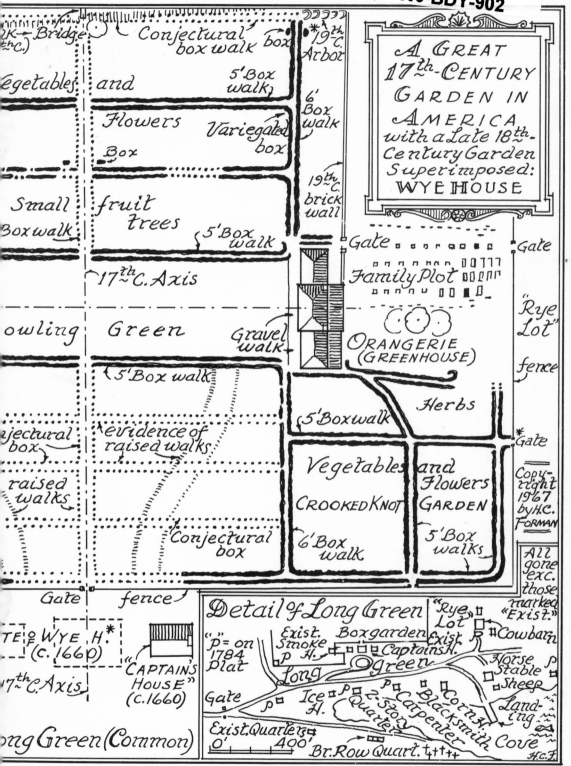

OLD BUILDINGS
GARDENS
AND FURNITURE
IN
TIDEWATER MARYLAND

OLD BUILDINGS
GARDENS
AND FURNITURE
IN
TIDEWATER MARYLAND

By

H. CHANDLEE FORMAN
Ph.D. (Fine Arts), A.I.A.

———

Drawings and Photographs
by Author Except Where Noted

———

TIDEWATER PUBLISHERS
A DIVISION OF BAY COUNTRY PUBLISHING CORPORATION

CAMBRIDGE   MARYLAND

1967

Library of Congress Catalog Card Number: 67-17538

Manufactured in the United States of America

To My Son

Richard Townsend Turner Forman

Other Books by Dr. Forman

Jamestown and St. Mary's: Buried Cities of Romance

Early Nantucket and Its Whale Houses

The Architecture of the Old South

Early Manor and Plantation Houses of Maryland

Virginia Architecture in the Seventeenth Century

The Turner Family of "Hebron" and Betterton, Maryland

Tidewater Maryland Architecture and Gardens

Editor of

Underhill's Old Houses on 'Sconset Bank, Nantucket

Six Quaker Clockmakers

The Singing Day and Other Poems

Contents

Acknowledgments

These persons or organizations, among others, graciously loaned or gave photographs or drawings:

Mr. J. Reaney Kelly
Mr. James C. Wilfong, Jr.
Mrs. E. Herman Cohn
Mrs. Sylvia Bothé
Mrs. Robert A. Gibney
Mr. Robert Bartlett Dixon
Miss Elizabeth H. Bartlett
Mr. Joseph Haislip
Mr. Francis E. Engle
Dr. Elizabeth Merritt
Mr. H. Robins Hollyday
Mrs. Hugh P. LeClair

Col. and Mrs. Miodrag Blagojevich
Admiral and Mrs. William Warlick
Mr. Harrison Weymouth, Jr.
Mr. James T. Wollon
Mr. H. Osborne Michael
Maryland Historical Society
St. Paul's Church, Centreville
Library of Congress
Historic American Buildings Survey
  (HABS)
Frances Benjamin Johnston Collection
Henry Francis du Pont Winterthur Museum

These persons or organizations, among others, kindly assisted with some of the textual material or helped in one way or another:

The late Mr. Samuel Sutton
The late Mr. and Mrs. Robert G. Henry
Commander Harold Manakee
Mr. James C. Wilfong, Jr.
Mr. Townsend Scott, IV
Mr. Charles Todd
Mr. Edward Plumstead
Capt. and Mrs. John B. Brown
Mr. Bryden Bordley Hyde
Mr. Brice Clagett
The late Mr. Guy Weatherly
Mr. and Mrs. Morgan Schiller
Mr. William Elder
Mr. Churchill Murray
Mrs. George D. Olds, 3rd

Mr. and Mrs. E. Bayly Orem
Mrs. Caroline Lippincott Forman
Mr. J. Donnell Tilghman
Mr. and Mrs. Robert E. Aldrich, Jr.
Mr. Richard Goldsborough
Mr. and Mrs. Theodore Dorman
Mrs. John Jeffries
Mr. John Wesley Cooper
Col. and Mrs. Laurence Cobb
Mrs. Maynard Barney
Mr. and Mrs. J. Spence Howard, Jr.
Mrs. Howard Short
Mrs. Frank W. Mish, Jr.
Rev. Edward B. Carley
Historic Annapolis, Inc.

The following organizations gave grants-in-aid for archaeological and historical research on St. Mary's City, some of which material is herein published for the first time:

American Philosophical Society, Philadelphia, Pa.
American Council of Learned Societies, Washington, D.C.

OLD BUILDINGS
GARDENS
AND FURNITURE
IN
TIDEWATER MARYLAND

I.

A Glimpse of Early Maryland

I.

A Glimpse of Early Maryland

Making a Record of a Civilization

THIS is the second volume of the planned three-volume "Tidewater" series—this one having been written at Easton, Maryland; Nantucket, Massachusetts; and Tegucigalpa, Honduras. What a way to spend a life—making on paper a record of a peculiarly Maryland civilization, already eight- or nine-tenths obliterated; and also giving attention to Virginia, New England, and other regions. In *Tidewater Maryland Architecture and Gardens*[1] the writer pointed out how one spark or one building contractor was the reason for the disappearance, or the hopelessly changing, of innumerable old buildings in the Free State.

Showing an awareness of the fast vanishing heritage of Maryland, one writer gave examples of the work of the Historic American Buildings Survey in Prince George's County, and asked: "Where are they now?"[2] Can measured drawings of a structure combat the power of the bulldozer? Those old places, he declared, are compelling evidences of our early culture. Once gone, nothing can bring them back. In Maryland we do not have the cathedrals, castles, catacombs, and villages of more ancient civilizations. In the 300 and more years since the founding of Maryland, not one original flimsy or temporary settler's house—or even an American Indian abode—has survived the ravages of time.

In 1936 and soon after, the Historic American Buildings Survey made some photographs and a few drawings of sixty-five early Prince George's County buildings. Nine of those structures had disappeared in the following fifteen years: *The Cedars* (Fig. 193), a Maryland governor's home, was reduced to its brick foundations in 1951[3]; *Elverton Hall* (Fig. 185)—God bless that interesting dwelling of Federal Style before its owner sent it skyward with dynamite in 1950; *Hatton's Mansion* (Fig. 189), with its towering two-storey chimney-pent,[4] enjoyed a complete isolation that eventually resulted in its neglectful

1

undoing; *Westwood* near Cheltenham was destroyed; *Friendship* was perhaps situated too close to a main thoroughfare to survive the wave of commercialization; *Grovehurst* (Fig. 188) vanished completely from the face of the earth without a single trace of its whereabouts; *Parthenon Heights,* marked by teakwood paneling, was bulldozed to make room for a shopping center; *Gladswood* received the losing end of a whim by government officials to convert it to "hash" on the grounds of the Patuxent Wildlife Refuge; and lastly, *Poplar Neck* could not stand the weight of an added fifteen years and was swallowed up by another governmental operation.

Since 1951 many more of the remaining fifty-six buildings in Prince George's County have disappeared. When one considers all the other counties of the State, how many recorded structures of the Historic American Buildings Survey have gone forever, or have been hopelessly changed? Finally, estimate the never-to-be-recorded, forgotten early examples of Maryland architecture that have ceased to exist since 1936. No survey can save them now.

Future generations of Marylanders living in their picture-window "ranch" houses or "drug-store colonials," or even in underground caves and shelters, may possibly learn about the kind of habitations their ancestors built by viewing the records of the Historic American Buildings Survey or architectural books and photographs.

In *Early Manor and Plantation Houses of Maryland* (1934),[5] the writer made the first published survey of early buildings in the Free State, and that material, having been collected since 1931, formed the basis and guide for much of the work of the Historic American Buildings Survey in 1936 and later. As editor of the national records of that Survey in the Library of Congress, Washington, in 1936, he combed through and sometimes rewrote the manuscript material, or had corrections made to the measured drawings and photographs, sent in from all the States, including Maryland, and the overseas possessions. In retrospect, that was a very pleasant experience, working with Dr. Leicester Bodine Holland, then chief of the Fine Arts Division of the Library of Congress, and with Miss Virginia Daiker, who has had faithful charge of the Survey records in the Library for a number of years. In 1948 the writer warmly dedicated his volume, *The Architecture of the Old South,*[6] to Leicester Holland.

Since 1931, this writer has been making a survey of, and recording, early Maryland buildings of all kinds and conditions, and has compiled the oldest, most complete set of records in this field. In 1952 a small survey of some public and semipublic buildings was made on the Eastern Shore of Maryland and had many references to *Early Manor and Plantation Houses of Maryland* as source material, but it did not cover even one quarter of the public buildings on the Eastern Shore; and besides, the block floor plans lacking interior partitions were woefully inadequate for a record.

From 1961 to 1963 the writer made the first measured drawings of Eastern Shore of Maryland structures ever put on the sheets of the Historic American Buildings Survey—like the *Wye House Orangerie* (Fig. 46) and the *Wye Town Corn House.* During the summer of 1964 the Survey sent a small group of draughtsmen to Annapolis to make records of the early edifices there. Also in that year, an amateur group began a further survey—thirty-three years after the author started his own survey in a professional manner. It is the fashion, and will be for a long time to come, to make historic house inventories in Maryland.

INDIAN CULTURE GONE BUT NOT FORGOTTEN

It was previously mentioned that not one American Indian dwelling has endured above the soil of Maryland. In short, Marylanders are forever deprived of knowing their Indian physical background in the way that the city of Rome is reminded of its Roman past. The extent of Indian culture can be estimated by historic references, scientific excavations of ruins, and archaeological collections that have been made.

It must be remembered that Indians in Maryland lived in wigwams, which were dwelling-houses—not in tents, as school children are taught to believe.

Catching Crabs on Shores of "Cedar Point."
Copy by H.C.F. of an 1854 Sketch by Wm. E. Bartlett
showing him & his family about 1846.

Figure 1

For instance, near Snow Hill, Worcester County, the Indians inhabited a "Town of Whigwhams." In general they were a skillful and dexterous people, with a graceful and courtly manner. The whites in Maryland often used their products and utensils, as we shall see.

All through the inventories of the white settlers of the Free State runs the word "canoe" or "canow"—the Chesapeake log canoe. In 1638, four years after the founding of St. Mary's City, the first capital, one canoe was left by John Bryant; in 1642, "1 canow" by Leonard Leonardson; and in 1658, "a Canow" by John Dernall.

When he died in 1647, Gov. Leonard Calvert of *East St. Mary's* left "a little Tomahawke." Then there were "trading" fishhooks and "trading" axes kept in the house by other colonists in the 17th century. The early housewife used "Indian wooden bowls." Eleven of them, for example, were left (1675) in the St. Mary's County dwelling of William Baker, and two were in Captain William Lewis' home. Three "indian Basketts" hung or sat in the domicile of Richard Lusthead of Mattapany, and two in Robert Ridgely's Milk House in St. Mary's City.

The Maryland colonists often ate Indian food and wore Indian clothes. The Kitchen at *Cedar Park* (1736), Anne Arundel County, held 146 baskets of Indian corn. In 1682 Robert Ridgely stored twenty-six barrels of Indian corn, and in 1723 Edward Smith of Annapolis left 100 bushels, valued at one shilling sixpence a bushel. Sometimes corn was called maize; Justinian Snow (1639) of St. Mary's County, left half a pound of "mase" when he died. The pumpkins belonging to Richard Cox in 1647 originated as an Indian food. One can be sure, too, that the settlers used plenty of Indian gourds, like a gourd of sugar.

Throughout Maryland mortars and pestles were used for grinding foods; but the Indian could not claim to have invented them, because the word "mortar" comes from the Anglo-Saxon, *mortere,* and "pestle" from the Latin, *pestillum.*

Wrapped up in Indian fashion by wild animal coverings, the early pioneer used bearskins, as the "one Bare-skin" in the house of William Lewis in St. Mary's City, in addition to raccoon, muskrat, beaver, deer, buckskins, and others. He also used them on floors and on beds for warmth. In 1648, Thomas Allen owned "one deare skin with feathers in it"—evidently a handsome covering. Leonard Leonardson and his family had two raccoon "matchcoats." In 1642 Thomas Adams died possessing an old "beaver hatt."

Beavers were also used as currency. Sterling was scarce, and tobacco formed a standard monetary unit. The amazing number of tobacco houses in the Free State proves that the weed was a large industry. Long clay pipes (Fig. 28) discovered in the early homes are evidence that smoking was common.

Further, some of the wooden or clay cooking and dining utensils used by the whites were probably of Indian origin, such as the "wooden dishes, platters, bowls & pales" of Christopher Martin and Joseph Edlo, or the "earthern panns" owned by them, or the "Indian bowles" in the 1709 kitchen of Samuel Layfield of Somerset County. Even as late as 1764 a wooden bowl was in Joseph Cox Gray's home in Dorchester County.

The white man had the wampum of the Indian. For instance, beads used in making them were found in John Dernall's hut when he died in 1658. There is little doubt that the influence of Indian culture on the early Anglo-Saxon civilization of Maryland was considerable.

REGARDING PRIMITIVE CONSTRUCTIONS

A few Maryland examples of unusual or primeval building have been recorded by the writer. Many of them have disappeared completely, like the several thatched-roof huts set on crotches and raftered with a covering of brush at Kent Fort. This was the Virginia trading post (1631) of William Claiborne, which later became part of the land of Maryland. Early Virginia had hundreds and perhaps thousands of *crotcheted* or *cruck* buildings, which were medieval in style.[7] In describing the *Church of 1607* at Jamestown, Capt. John Smith declared that it was set upon "crotchets," covered with rafters, rushes, and earth. This meant that the building was supported or hung upon pairs of bent or curved tree trunks placed together in the shape of a Gothic pointed arch and spaced one "bay" apart. A "bay" is a standard unit, generally about sixteen feet, although sometimes it could vary. The buildings called "crotcheted" at Kent Fort probably closely followed English precedent and were like the cruck church described here.

Next, in the *Archives of Maryland* there is a reference to "The Thatcht house" in 1656 in Kent County. In the first few years after settlement there must have been literally thousands of thatched roofs. Being unsuitable for the severe American winters and subject to fire and dampness, they were discontinued. But in Cecil County on *Augustine Manor* there once stood an old cow shed with thatched roof.

Far superior to thatch or wood as a roofing material was the early Maryland "Pantyle," that curious S-shaped clay tile, first found in the Free State on the site of the *Palace of St. John's* (1638) in St. Mary's City, the early capital, and the clay shingle tile, first discovered in the foundation of the *Secretary's Office* in that settlement.[8] Roofing clapboards, put on horizontally, but never used today, were better than thatch, and remnants of them still lie on the roofs of *Cedar Park,* constructed about 1690, in Anne Arundel County, and *Resurrection Manor* (1652) in St. Mary's County.

Possibly the rarest and most unique roof known in Maryland and perhaps in the United States is on the west side of an *Old House Ruin* in Southern Maryland: an up-and-down clapboard roof (Fig. 208). Unfortunately for the tenants, that covering was never leakproof, because the rain dripped between the clapboards—even though they were nailed tightly together and tarred in the overlaps. The roof, at least 200 years old, was preserved by a later, higher roof which had been built over it.

The wooden chimney was an extremely flammable piece of construction. As described in *The Architecture of the Old South,*[9] at one time Maryland formed a landscape of wooden chimneys. They were usually termed "Welsh" or "Welch" chimneys, because in the 17th century more of them survived in Wales than elsewhere in Great Britain. Thus, in Maryland in 1653 one Paul Simpson was to have had built for him by Thomas Wilford of the County of Northumberland, England, a fifteen-foot, square dwelling with a "welch Chimney." In 1659 in Calvert County, James Hall constructed at Hebden's Point a timber-framed house and had set up the "Posts of the Welch Chimney"—a reference indicating wattle-and-daub, a kind of basketry daubed with mud or plaster, may have been set between posts.

In Kent County the Courthouse of 1698 was to have had a wooden chimney, as was the Courthouse of the same year built on the Gunpowder River, Maryland.

Before its destruction about 1913 there stood in Dorchester County near Reids Grove a windowless, plank-log, one-room cabin, called *Jack Lord's cottage* (Fig. 2) with a kind of wooden chimney called "catted." The fireplace and flue were made of clay and straw worked together in rolls and laid between wood posts—a type of construction occasionally found in Virginia outhouses through the end of the 19th century.[10]

At any rate, as far as Jack Lord was concerned, he had to go outside whenever it rained in order to stop up holes in the clay made by the water. His cottage must have been a late descendant of a primitive domicile once widely prevalent in Maryland.

Another type of wooden chimney, in the fashion of cribbing, is shown (Fig. 220) at *Mt. Pleasant* in Baltimore County.

The "Welsh" stairs in Maryland must have been a primitive and steep means of access to an upper floor. Perhaps it approximated the English "stee" or ladder to the loft.

One of the oldest structural forms in the Free State was *puncheoning,* the medieval method of setting punches or puncheons, sometimes called quarters, upright in the ground so that the space between them was about the same as the thickness of the puncheon. The interstices between the wooden posts were

Figure 2

usually filled with wattle-and-daubing. "Post and pan" was an old English term for such posts and basketry coated with clay or plaster. The earliest recorded example in Virginia seems to have been at Berkeley in 1619 where most of the buildings had "punches" set in the earth. A Maryland example was used in the Courthouse of Charles County (1675), which was repaired in 1697—the new twenty-foot-square room was not to be timber-framed, but to have "Posts in the ground of Locust."[11]

Another early Maryland type of construction is puzzling, but no doubt in time the matter will be clarified. At *St. Luke's Church* (1730–32) in Church Hill, Queen Anne's County, there was ordered to be constructed a twenty-foot-long house with a "Bastard frame," to be weatherboarded with clapboards and roofed with feather-edge shingles.

About the year 1801 William E. Bartlett[12] of *Wakefield,* Talbot County, a future Baltimore druggist, accompanied his mother in a carriage to visit an uncle in Caroline County. Years later he wrote that "after we got over the Choptank River at Dover Ferry, we had to travel through a marsh for the distance of near a mile, when we reached fast land, and drove under a pretty large spreading oak . . . Near by," he continued, "stood a hut (Fig. 3), made of long poles stood on end, forming a base of about ten feet in diameter, and cone-like top. The poles were covered with clay, having a hole for a door, and opening near the top for the escape of smoke. A poor white family inhabited this miserable looking hut."

A Caroline County round hut of long poles covered with clay, occupied about 1801, by a poor white family. Copy by A.C.J of an 1854 drawing by Wm. E. Bartlett ~

Figure 3

This type of circular structure of poles and clay represents the oldest form of habitation in Great Britain—the Neolithic or New Stone Age conical house of timber poles, with hole for a doorway. It was also the kind of prehistoric hut used in various parts of Europe and elsewhere. And here was one at our own front door—Caroline County.

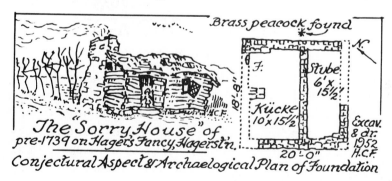

The "Sorry House" of pre-1739 on Hager's Fancy, Hagerstn. Conjectural Aspect & Archaelogical Plan of Foundation

Figure 4

In present-day England such structures are still being erected by charcoal burners, who must camp out beside their stacks of charring logs to see that they are not set afire. But in 1816 Benjamin Henry Latrobe made a watercolor of a charcoal burner's hut on Sugar Loaf Mountain in Maryland, similar to the one in Caroline County. The usual facing material was wattle-and-daub, which has been described as wickerwork of twigs or branches plastered with clay. In his drawing Bartlett depicted some of the fencing around that little boothy as posts interwoven with branches. Clay might not stick well to upright poles; but when the poles were woven with branches, the clay would adhere easily.

Other primitive abodes were the tree house (Fig. 220) which is reported to

Fig. 5. A(top). Edward Lloyd (d. 1796), builder of *Wye House* mansion (1784), his wife Elizabeth Tayloe Lloyd, and their daughter Anne, painted in 1771 by Charles Willson Peale. B(bottom). Detail from left portion of portrait showing Palladian-style villa with colonnades and pavilions. Courtesy, Henry Francis du Pont Winterthur Museum.

have stood at "Barrett's Delight" near Loch Raven; the rammed-earth or "adobe" hut which was said to be near Landover, Prince Georges County, in the 1930s;[13] or the 18th-century houses in Snow Hill believed to have been similar to "booths"—that is, market or fair stalls, or temporary shelters.

One of the most important structures of this kind was the pre-1739 *Sorry House* (Figs. 4 & 232) of Jonathan Hager, the founder of Hagerstown. The *Sorry House* foundation was excavated in 1953 by Mrs. Frank Mish, Jr., and the writer. A "sorry" house is what the name implies: poor, cheap, mean, or miserable. Of Maryland-German architecture, Hager's hut had two rooms, one fireplace, and probably casement windows with quarrels or panes (Fig. 11) held in wood strips.

THE NAMES OF MORE MARYLAND ROOMS

The rooms of early Maryland buildings were shown in *Tidewater Maryland Architecture and Gardens*[14] to be named differently from those in use today: the "Hall" was never the passageway, but the Great Hall or Great Room, now the Living Room; and the space over a particular room was designated by the word "chamber," as hall chamber, parlor chamber, porch chamber, and the like. A chamber was not called "bedroom."

Since the publication of the above work in 1957, we have found references to actual "passages" in the Maryland records. For example, the New House of 1683 owned by Samuel Tovy of St. Mary's County contained one room (Hall), a closet, a *passage,* and an upper room. In the early days the hall and the passage were different areas in a building.

Aside from those standard names for rooms, there were many others. Let us begin with the smallest dwellings, such as Guy Mirck's cot of 1682: it contained an Outward Room, an Inner Room, a Buttery—not named for butter, of course, but for bottles,—a Kitchen and a Loft. Actually Mirck had a three-room residence, where the Outward Room served for living and dining and the Inner Room as a bower or bedchamber.

Another of the same year and same classification was John Hillen's containing Hall, "Kitching," Entry, Store, Cellar, and Loft. It is interesting that the term, "Entry," was employed, instead of the more usual word, Porch. The Store was often a separate outhouse and may have been in this case.

Perhaps one of the smallest lodgings on record was Stephen Marty's cottage of 1683 in St. Mary's County, having Hall, Bed Chamber, and the Quarter outbuilding for servant or slave. A similar cubicle belonged to John Gathor of Anne Arundel County who had in 1703 only a Lower Room, a Chamber, and at some distance, a Mill House.

In those days it was sometimes customary to name a room for a person, such as the owner or his wife; in James Bodkin's tiny hut of 1683 there were only "His Lodging Chamber" and the "Kitchin Room," besides the Mill House.

In 1684 one of Capt. James Neale's homes in Charles County apparently contained only a Hall, a "Studie," and a "New Room"—probably an addition. Likewise, Arthur Young's cottage of 1711 in Calvert County had but three rooms: Kitchen, Hall, and "Ye Lodging Roome." This last area, as we shall see in the next chapter, had a mint of money lying in it, probably much to the discomfiture of guests.

Perhaps the smallest residence in the Free State belonged in 1652 to Henry Potter of St. Mary's County. This "dwelling house," about ten feet long, was on a plantation owned by him. The following year Paul Simpson possessed a fifteen-foot-square house.

The medium-sized Maryland home had four to seven rooms. Several examples are cited here: In 1682 Henry Stocket had the usual Hall and Kitchen, but also an "Inward Chamber" and an "Outward Chamber Upstairs," a Loft over the Kitchen, and in addition, "Ye Schoole House." In Kent County Thomas Soule's cottage of 1674 held five rooms, namely, Hall, Bed Chamber, "the inner room of the bed chamber," probably for children, "the outer room," and the "inner chamber above staires." In addition there were a shed and an area "Under the Staires," as well as Milk House, and Quarter, each with its own shed and loft.

One of the most important of the middle-sized homesteads was *Cedar Park* (Fig. 150) in Anne Arundel County. At first (*c.* 1690) it had seven rooms in addition to an outside kitchen and a store. There were the usual Hall and Parlor, with the appropriately named Chambers above them, and a front Porch and Porch Chamber. In the seventh room the writer discovered the ancient name for what he called "supra-attic" in his *Tidewater Maryland Architecture and Gardens.* This was the tiny "Peake Room," located *over the Porch Chamber,* since there were no spaces for windows in the other two gables. Another name for it was the "Upper Loft."

A house of similar size was Benjamin Solley's (1675) in St. Mary's County: Hall and Hall Chamber, Kitchen and Kitchen Chamber, a "New Lower Room" —corresponding to a Parlor,— a "New Upper Chamber," a Buttery, Cellar, and, curiously, an "Iron Loft," presumably for the storage of iron, although that plantation also had a Store.

Other rooms with unusual names in the average-sized habitation were the "Children's Room" and "Stone Kitchen" at Col. Walter Smith's (1711) in Calvert County, and the plain "Room" and "Room Chamber" at Joseph Cox Gray's (1764) in Dorchester County. Emeus Mansell's in 1683 in St. Mary's County contained not only a "Cydr Room," but also a "Great Chimneyed Hall" besides its regular Hall. Since the word chimney meant fireplace in those days, the regular Hall evidently had no means of heating, while the "Great Chimneyed Hall" did have.

It is estimated that the large early Maryland home had eight rooms or more. In the 17th century it was well represented by Philemon Lloyd's *Wye House* (Fig. 36B) of about 1660 in Talbot County and by Robert Ridgely's home of 1682 in St. Mary's City. Lloyd had some rooms named for colors, thus: Hall, New Room—implying an addition or parlor,—Upper Chamber, the "Blew Chamber," "Studdy Chamber," and "Black Chamber."

Next in Lloyd's home was the area called "In the Staire Case"—referring to a stair in a case or box, as was common in the 17th century. Then came a room for the mistress of that great plantation: "Madam Lloyd's Room," followed appropriately by the "Nursery," "Closet," "Kitchin" and "Kitching Loft," the closet for "Linnen," and the Store.

Ridgely's great house contained—besides the customary Hall and Hall Chamber, Parlor and Parlor Chamber, and Kitchen,—"Mrs. Ridgely's Chamber," the "Chamber over Mrs. Ridgely's Room," "Closett," "Nursery and 2 Closetts," and "Nursery Loft." In addition, there were a Cellar, Wash House for laundry, a Quarter and Loft, Milk House, and Store. It seems the Linen Closet was always simply called "Linnen."

Another fairly large domicile, the *Slicer-Shiplap* or *Edward Smith House* (1723) in Annapolis, had some rooms described by their outlook or orientation.

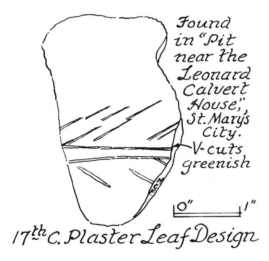

Found in "Pit near the Leonard Calvert House," St. Mary's City.
—V-cuts greenish

17ᵗʰ C. Plaster Leaf Design

Figure 6

Thus we find a Hall, Dining Room, Parlor Chamber—an inference that there was a Parlor beneath it,—Back Room, "Room fronting Capt. Gordon's," "Small Chamber fronting Capt. Gordon's," as well as Kitchen, Kitchen Back Room, and Garret. By the way, the Hall in this building was not the main cross-passage-way, but a tiny room next to the Dining Room large enough for a small table and chairs, but nothing more.

Comparable to *Slicer-Shiplap* inn was Roger Boyce's dwelling (1774), *Quinn* or *Sweet Air* (Fig. 253), in Baltimore County where there is the usual Hall or Great Room, as well as "The Passage," the "Passage Chamber" at the head of the stairs, the "Passage Upstairs," the Hall Chamber, "Mrs. Boyce's Room," and the Chamber over the "Inner Room." Further, there were the usual Kitchen, Cellar, and then another Hall called the "Old Hall,"—plus the "Brick Passage," the Back Room, Quarter, and Smith's Shop.

By 1798 the "porch" on a house had become known as the "Piazza." At *Sweet Air* or *Quinn,* for example, the piazza was fifty-three feet long and two storeys high.

A room with an unusual name was located between a dwelling-house and kitchen outhouse at "Coles Harbor" (1726) on the site of the future city of Baltimore: this was the "Middle Lodging Room." Also there was "a passage from one to ye other," probably meaning that a passage ran alongside this guest room from the house to the kitchen.

Romao Cosden's home of 1683 in Calvert Town contained a "White Lymed Room," a "Room over ye Cellar," and a Stable. It is strange that the room over the cellar was not identified.

The "Landing" and "Yard," as well as the "Logg House," were mentioned at Henry Ward's six-room domicile of 1684 in Cecil County.

John Dernall (1685) had, curiously, "ye Chappell Room so-called," as well as six other rooms, not including "servants at home quarter"—for slaves were usually called servants. Again, John Norwood (1674) in Anne Arundel County had an "Out Room," besides "Kitchen outroomes" and "on the drawer's head."

OUTHOUSES RARELY DEPENDENCIES

Other types of outbuildings have been found in addition to those listed in *Tidewater Maryland Architecture and Gardens* (1957). In the first place the reader should be cautioned against always calling an outhouse a "dependency." A dependency is an outhouse, but an outhouse is not necessarily a dependency. To qualify as a dependency, an outbuilding *must* be part and parcel of a formal design in which the main building is the dominant motive, in this way.

Figure 7

In *The Mansions of Virginia*,[15] Thomas T. Waterman correctly defined dependencies as the minor or flanking buildings of a *composition*. Note that there has to be a formal composition or design. The two original pavilions of the *Wye House* mansion in Talbot County, as revealed in the "Old Plat" of 1784 (Fig. 35), were dependencies, before the curtains or hyphens were built to join them to the main house.

Tobacco houses dotted the early Maryland landscape, and tobacco became valuable enough to be used as currency. In the 17th century, for instance, a fifteen-foot-long dwelling-house cost 300 pounds of tobacco to construct. Tobacco outbuildings were generally much larger than the habitations. In 1652 Gov. Robert Brooke, of "Della Brooke Manor," owned two "great houses full of tobacco: the one 100 feet in length, the other 90; both 32 feet in breadth."[16] In 1676 every tobacco grower had to have a "good tight tobacco house with a good lock and key."

One of the items that was valued at the time of Samuel Tovey's death in 1683 was "tobacco hanging," referring to the weed drying in the outhouse built for it. Likewise, one William Smithfield bequeathed (1648) "his crop of tobacco as it is hanging in the [out] howse."

In Kent County in 1655 a "walplate tobacco house" was constructed—meaning that it was not flimsily built, but had wooden plates on which rafters were set securely. Another Maryland tobacco outhouse, fifty feet long, was to have rived ("ryve") sticks on which to hang the weed.

Besides the usual Milk House or Dairy, Hen House, Smoke or Meat House, Corn House, Ice House, Barn, Stable, Coach House, and Quarter House, often there were a Store House, a Weaving or Loom House, a School House, an Ash House, a Wash House—today called a Laundry,—a Mill House, and a Well House. At *Merryman's Delight* in Baltimore County was a Turkey House. According to an old plat hanging in the Maryland Historical Society, *Taylor's Mount* in 1779 had the following, in addition to the usual outhouses: Dry Well House, Blacksmith's Shop, Servants' Lodges, Poultry House, and a Free Men's Lodge. In 1639 at "Snow Hill Manor" the Quarter was called the "outhouse necessary for servants lodging," but at *Taylor's Mount* it was designated "Negro Quarters."

The kitchen was frequently a separate outhouse, as described at "Coles Harbor" on the site of Baltimore City: "one Kitchen about 20 feet long and 15 foot broad with a brick chimney and brick oven in it."

On "West St. Mary's Manor" in 1762 were a Granary, a Log Stable, a Shed 12' by 8' in size; at *Sweet Air* or *Quinn* (1774) there were, among other outhouses, a Smith's Shop, and (1798) a brick Office adjoining the house, a Spring House "over the spring within a few yards of the dwelling house," a brick Kitchen sixteen feet square, a Poultry House, and rarest of all, a brick Cabbage House. Other unusual outhouses included the Salt House, the Bathing House (Fig. 239)—even the *Paca House* in Annapolis had a Cold Bath House,—the Tool House, the Root Cellar with pyramidal roof, and the Gardener's House.

The post-Revolutionary plantations seem to have had the most sophisticated kinds of outhouses. "Harlem," in Baltimore, for example, had a Pavilion on top of a mound, with an ice vault under it; a complete Greenhouse with two hot beds and twelve movable frames, a brick Gardener's House, a Dairy laid with marble, and a Pigeon House.

The Necessary House was too insignificant to be listed as a man's possession. Sometimes it was called "privy," as in the diary of Mrs. Forman, wife of Gen. Thomas Marsh Forman.

Another type of outhouse commonly found on Maryland plantations, especially on the Eastern Shore, is the Windmill. In the first two centuries of white settlement the Free State must have been a landscape of mills of all kinds—something most of us have forgotten. On the Miles River in Talbot County, for instance, we have learned of the former existence of a "post mill" called "Gossage's (Fig. 66) on "Big Dundee," and another at "The Anchorage" farm. There was a post mill near Woolford in Dorchester County. The *Honga Windmill* (Fig. 134) at Lake Cove in the latter county was of the Dutch type, with movable cap so that the blades could be turned into the wind.

Mr. William E. Bartlett, a Baltimore druggist, in 1854 made a drawing of a post mill (Fig. 8) on his Eastern Shore property, *Wakefield*. "At the age of fourteen years," he wrote, "I have attended the wind mill. My brother John when about 16 years of age was grinding one day when he ran an arm off and otherwise injured the mill." His sketch shows John running an arm off. William and the boys' parents are nearby. There appears to be the top of a sailboat on a creek beyond the mill.

At the left of the drawing is shown a Quarters at *Wakefield,* and thereby hangs a tale. About 1805 a tenant by the name of John Orem, his wife, and several children lived in that little outhouse, all maintained on an income of sixty dollars a year. "A happier family surely could nowhere be found," wrote Mr. Bartlett. Orem had the use of a dwelling at *Wakefield* and a garden, and had board at the main house, except on "first days," meaning Sundays, when he ate in his own cottage. "Himself and family always seemed to have enough.

Post Mill at Wakefield, Talbot County, about 1805.
John Bartlett, then 16, was grinding one day when he
ran an arm off & otherwise injured the mill. Copy by H.C.J.
of an 1854 sketch by Wm. E. Bartlett.

Figure 8

How small a sum of money is capable of satisfying a contented mind. I never saw anything like discontent in this humble family." Tell that to the Welfare State planners today. Sixty dollars a year are not enough, because a family is still considered pauperized at $3,000. per annum—even though they own a new automobile, new television, and new laundromat. But as Mr. Bartlett indicated, happiness does not depend on money.

PLANTATION HELP

In Maryland, as in the majority of the English colonies in America, a legalized system of indenture and servitude flourished—even in the pre-slavery era.

Worker tenants on early Maryland manors and plantations were both whites and negroes, servants and slaves. In 1685 Philemon Lloyd had, among his possessions at the "Plantation on Lloyd Insula," negroes, cows, goats, bulls, shoats, and steers; and at the "Lower Plantation on Lloyd Insula," negroes and cattle. He had one "Denby a Negro" and "Sempe Human's wife, a negro," each appraised at twenty pounds sterling. But John Foreman, "an Englishman," was not as valuable, for he was appraised at only ten pounds sterling.

In 1711 in Dorchester County William Smith made an accounting of his people under the heading, "Servants and Slaves":

"Robert Bozell, white servant, 3 years to serve.

Hercules, a white boy, two years to serve.

Negro Ned, aged about 25 years.

Negro Jenny, a woman, aged about 21 years."

Edward Smith, innholder owner of the *Slicer-Shiplap House* (1723) in Annapolis, listed a white servant, Mary, who had three and a quarter years to serve, a mulatto man who was a convict called Briston, a negress named Tone with a five-months'-old child, and a negro boy of twelve called Kildair.

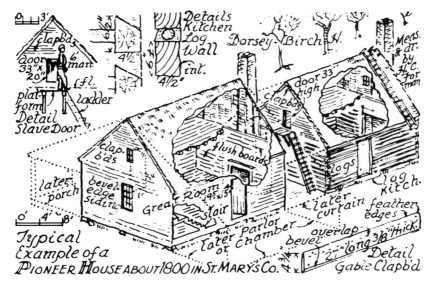

Figure 9

At Richard Galloway's *Cedar Park* in 1736 twenty-four negroes were named as his property, described by age, thus: "1 Boy Sam 14 yrs old, a Legacy," or "a woman named Hagar, blind, with a four months' old child." In the Store there were three pairs of negroes' shoes, valued at eighteen pence; and in the "Stock" was a parcel of negroes' bedding.

At the *Dorsey-Birch Cottage* (Fig. 9) in St. Mary's County the writer recently found perhaps the smallest outside doorway for humans in the Free State: 2'-9" high and 20" wide at the top of a steep ladder, for slave or servant wishing to enter the kitchen loft. Even that little trap door must have been an improvement over the entrance holes in the typical round mud huts of Central Africa.

On September 11, 1855, a ship captain, Canot, was purported to have published an account in Baltimore describing the branding of Africans before their embarcation for America. William E. Bartlett, Baltimore druggist, quoted page 107 of that account:

"Two days before embarcation, the head of every male & female is neatly shaved; and, if the cargo belongs to several owners, each man's Brand is impressed on the body of his prospective Negro. This operation is performed with pieces of silver wire, or small irons fashioned into the merchant's initials, heated just hot enough to blister without burning the skin. When the entire cargo is the venture of one proprietor, the branding is always dispensed with. The Negroes are naked except for a britch cloth."

Bartlett, a Quaker, then wrote a poem declaring that he would not have a slave till his land or fan him when he slept or tremble when he awoke and that he had never owned a slave and never would own one.

It was in Talbot County where *Wakefield,* Bartlett's home place, stands that Frederick Douglass (1817–95), most noted American negro of his time, was born.

The pernicious institution of slavery flourished also in New Hampshire, where negroes' conduct was regulated by law in 1714; in Rhode Island, where there was a slave mart; and in Connecticut and Massachusetts. In fact, blacks were imported into New England from the West Indies from the year 1638 onward.

The English had slavery in New York beginning in 1665—the Dutch, having been there before them, were good teachers in that respect. There was

Figure 10

the same kind of bondage in Delaware, New Jersey, and the Southern Colonies; also in Florida and Louisiana. William Penn, Quaker founder of Pennsylvania, in 1718 died a slaveholder. At the same time even the Mother Country, Britain, practiced slavery in the 18th century in a minor form on the great estates, if the existing iron slave rings with the property owners' names (Fig. 10) are an indication.

It was not until 1772 when Chief Justice Mansfield gave his important decision that no man could be held as a slave in England that 14,000 to 15,000 slaves were set free there.

THE PARTS OF EARLY BUILDINGS

In considering this subject in *Tidewater Maryland Architecture and Gardens,* we noted that dormers were called "dormants" or "lutarn windows," hipped roofs were "pyramids," and so on. Since that volume was published, new finds have been made in the ancient building vernacular. First, there are terms applied to houses: repair work was spoken of as "reparation," like the "reparations" made in 1639 at *Snow Hill Manor* in St. Mary's County. "Reparation nailes" are repair nails.

In figuring the amount of glass for windows, the early builder or joiner wrote of it as so many lineal feet, thus: "28 foote of glasse for windows" at *Snow Hill Manor.* When a dwelling was to have leaded windows, it was specified to be "glazed with Lead and Glass." To "glaze" a structure meant to give it glass windows.

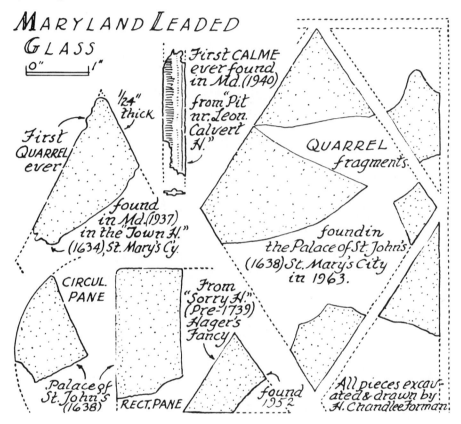

Figure 11

A few pieces of leaded glass, of various shapes, have been drawn for this book (Fig. 11) and are rectangular, triangular, circular and diamond-shaped. Such a pane is called a quarry or quarrel.

It is interesting that in 1714 the vestry of *St. Paul's Church,* Kent County, ordered "Moulds for the Glazier" to be made—thereby perhaps inferring that the small leaded panes were formed in molds.

At this point it is appropriate to correct a statement about glass made both in *The Architecture of the Old South* (1948) and in *Tidewater Maryland Architecture and Gardens* (1957) that the *Third Haven Meetinghouse* (1682–84), Easton, preserves some of its original sliding sash. There is no original sash remaining there; the few old sash with wide muntins (Fig. 14) may be as old as 1797, the year when the addition on the south side of the meeting-house was built; the remaining sash are relatively modern.

In this State no whole hinged casement with leaded glass of early date has yet been discovered; but the writer has been able to make a reconstruction drawing of twin, fixed, leaded windows (Fig. 12) of 1667–1700 at *Holly Hill*, Anne Arundel County, even though all the lead calmes or strips have been lost and only one pane, rectanguler in shape, remains for inspection and study. Since there was never a way to open or shut these windows, there was no ventilation; they were nailed to the rebates or recesses of the frame— the nail holes are still in evidence. The lead calmes were strengthened by lead ribbons wrapped around vertical wood bars or stays on the inside, as the drawing shows. The interior of the window frame was decorated, top and sides, by a simple cyma molding.

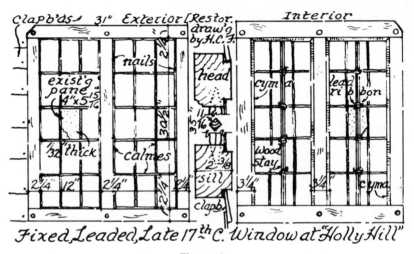

Fixed Leaded, Late 17th C. Window at "Holly Hill"

Figure 12

The "guillotine" window seems generally to have been introduced into Maryland homesteads about 1700, but leaded windows persisted throughout the Free State for at least five decades after 1700. *Old Wye Church* (Fig. 71B), for example, built during 1717–21, had leaded windows in 1745.

We know that lead weights and pulleys were placed in the *Capitol* building windows in Williamsburg in 1723, and were probably beginning to be used in Maryland at that time. At *St. Martin's Chapel,* or *Church,* built in 1756 in Worcester County, the sash were not to have the dangerous notch-and-catch contrivances of the "guillotine," but to be double-hung, that is, with lead weights and pulleys. This *Chapel* had "Single Crown or good Northward Glass," which means hard glass shaped with a crown, and of single thickness. The expression, Northward, evidently means substantial enough to withstand strong and bitterly cold winds.

Early Maryland homes had hardware of wood, wrought iron, and brass. In *Jamestown and St. Mary's: Buried Cities of Romance*[17] we discussed several types of old hardware, such as the stock lock or rim lock, usually fastened on the inside of doors. The original *Wye House* in 1685 kept fourteen stock locks and twenty-two pairs of hooks and hinges in the Store—as well as six latches, some iron padlocks, and twenty-four hasps.

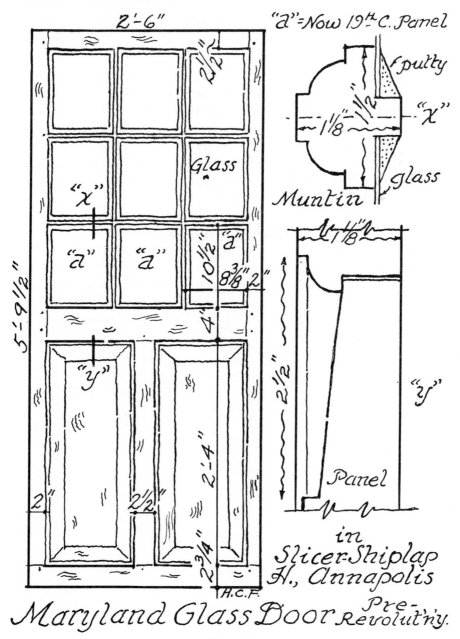

Maryland Glass Door *Pre-Revolut'ny.*

Figure 13

The goods of John Cockshutt in 1642 included nine cupboard locks, three door spring-locks, five latches, six pairs of hinges and an odd hinge, a stock lock, a pair of "SS"—whatever they were,—and twelve pairs of "dufftaels," a kind of hinge. The "spring-locks" were spring stock locks with a throw or bolt.

The repair list for *Snow Hill Manor* in 1639 included four stock locks, lead solder—probably for the calmes or lead strips of the casement windows,— hasps, and fourteen pieces of "crosse garnish" for the doors. These were cross-decorations in the form of iron T hinges.

When the reader meets with certain old terms concerning courthouses and prisons, he may find some unfamiliar names. The word "cage" makes one think of a modern bank, but in the early days it meant a prison. The robber went to a "cage." Then occasionally one runs across the term "pitch," only to find that it referred not to the slope of a roof, but to the vertical height of a building, usually in the first storey from the "grunsells" or ground sills to the wall plate, on which rest the rafters or joists. Thus, the *Joppa Town Courthouse* of 1709 had a thirteen-foot pitch.[18] But a different way of measuring a height was used in the *Talbot Courthouse* of 1711, where the thirteen-foot pitch measured from the level of the earth to the wall plate.

The *Joppa Courthouse* had a pair of stairs with rails and "bannisters"— which are balusters. For some reason the early joiner could not say baluster, so always called them "banisters." Further, this courthouse was "overjetted" one foot on each side, which has nothing to do with the jet age, but indicates that the structure had "jetties" or overhanging floors. The origin of the jetty, it seems, was due to the method of placing joists flat, thereby causing an unstable or dancing floor, which the jetty, when built, counteracted. Such joists were termed "galloping joyce."

Figure 14

Many courthouses, like churches, had pairs of "folding doors"—or double-doors, having two leaves. Of the same order were "folding" shutters and "folding" casements.

At the *Calvert County Courthouse* we find that in 1675 the ceiling was repaired with clapboards—evidently one could look right up into the roof. The "cage" was not very large: only twelve feet square. A new pair of stairs was to be built—described as "half pac'd Large Staires," one with easy treads or half-steps.

While most 17th-century buildings in the State had small porches, generally enclosed with walls, the *Cambridge Courthouse* of that time did have a large porch at the end of the building with rails and balusters.

Today one thinks of baseboards as being the skirting boards around a room, but in the *Brick State House of 1676* in St. Mary's City, the first capital, "baseboards" were placed at the gable-ends: in other words, they were barge or verge boards along the rakes of the roofs. In 1680 the *Talbot Courthouse* at York on Skipton Creek had twelve "archytryve windows." The word "architrave" means the parts that surround a door or window, like jambs, lintel, and their moldings. In the *Talbot Courthouse* of 1711 were "Lights over the [front] Door, worked with Archytrive on ye sd Door Case." The doors of the building were "folding wainscott doors," that is, double-doors, panelled, and the ones downstairs were to be "bolectioned"—having a raised or bulbous molding on them. On *St. Luke's Church* of 1730–32 in Church Hill were more elaborate doors, each being of the folding variety, with two half gates in them—evidently wickets,—and with iron hinges, locks, and bolts.

"Mundillions," as the carpenters pronounced them, were S-shaped or block-shaped brackets on a box cornice; that is, modillions.

It seems to have been the custom for courthouses to have glass in the transom-windows, but shutters were usually below the transom-bars. The arrangement allowed for the lower part of the windows to be closed in bad weather and for enough light to come through the glass casements of the upper windows for men to work inside. Thus, the *Oxford Courthouse* of 1709 had "wooden shutters for the lower part of the windows, and glass for the upper." Even *St. Luke's Church,* mentioned above, had "Two Third Parts of ye windows . . . Glazed and ye Lower third part . . . with panelled shutters with Iron hinges."

In connection with churches and meetinghouses, we find other unusual terms. The "circle" means the apse, as for instance: "a Circle to be at the East End [of the Church] for Communion" in *St. Paul's* (1711–14) in Kent County. The "arch" sometimes referred to the proscenium arch in front of the chancel, though at times it meant the rounded or barrel vault over the nave, as, for example, "The arch in the roof of said House to be finished workmanlike," or "The roof on the inside to be Arched the whole inside."

A curious reference was made in 1714 to the above *St. Paul's Church* where the carpenter was paid for "smoothing & nailing the Arch peses [pieces] in the Ceiling & Striking the Scaffold pieces"—which obviously means that the rafters and collar beams had a series of smaller wooden pieces to make a more rounded angle for the barrel vault. The floor of the church had tiles, ten inches square and two inches thick.

An "alley" was an aisle, and sometimes it was spoken of as a "lane," thus: "Two lanes, a Cross lane" were the three aisles in *St. Luke's Church,* Church Hill. Ordinarily the "alleys" were laid with well-burned bricks at ground level, while the floors of the box pews, up one step, were put down with good "quarter'd Pine Plank." The pulpit was usually raised about five feet from the wood floor and had "Steps, rales, Bannisters [balusters], and Canopy." But *St. Luke's Church* was to have pews paved with free stone. Perhaps worshippers brought their own floor cushions or foot warmers.

Eastern Shore Episcopal churches were generally laid out with regular and uniform-sized box pews, as at *Green Hill Church* (1733; Figs. 116 & 117). But at *St. Paul's Church* in Kent County it was stipulated that "anyone who wanted may lay two pews adjoining into one for the advantage of more room"—a case where small box pews were enlarged.

Then, too, the gallery often had "seats" or "benches," thereby dispensing with the luxury of pews, as in *St. Paul's* of Kent; but *St. Luke's,* cited above, and *Spring Hill Church* (Fig. 117, bottom left) contained box pews in the gallery.

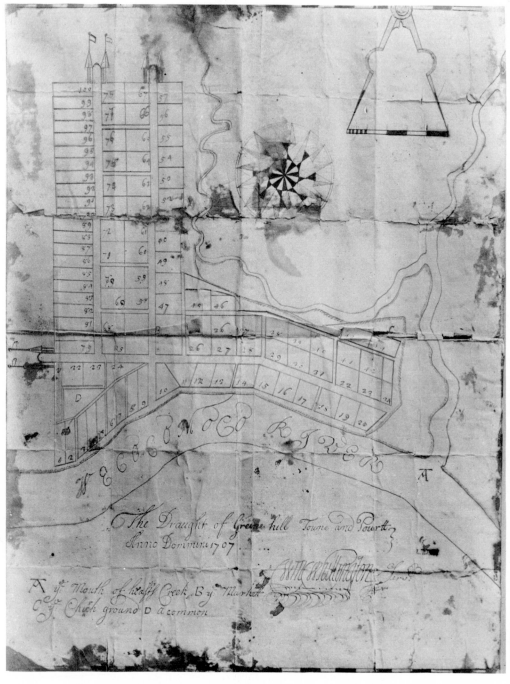

Fig. 15. Plat of Green Hill Town and Port in 1707, showing the Wicomico River, a house on lots 1 and 2, and three city gateways with flags—probably mere symbols. A, "Mouth of heast's Creek"; B, "Market"; C, "Church ground"; D, "A common." Author photo.

There was sometimes a "Clerk's pew" and a "Vestry pew." The front of the ordinary pew, that is, the woodwork along the aisle, usually had "quarter Round Raised work"—referring to a quarter-round panel molding with raised panels, as may still be seen at *Green Hill Church.*

On the western edge of the roof at *St. Luke's Church,* Church Hill, was planned a "Cupella" which was to contain a 180-pound bell. But when the time came to build there, a "pent house" or covered passage, comprising an open framework to support a bell, was constructed against the west gable-end.

The builders of those days would not have been content with the short and flimsy wooden shingles used today. On *St. Martin's Chapel,* for example, they placed cypress shingles two feet long and one inch thick; and the "good well joynted Cypress shingles" that were laid on the roof of *St. Luke's Church* were not sufficient weatherproofing, because they had to have tar over them to "defend" the roof from the weather.

Maryland churches were not all painted white as we "modern Victorians" of today would like to believe. That also holds true for homesteads and other kinds of structures. The doors and windows at *St. Martin's Chapel* were primed with linseed oil and red ochre as a first coat, with a lead color as a second. The cove cornice and barge boards had two coats of "Train oil and red Okre." The body of the church and the ceiling were plastered and whitewashed.

The front folding doors of churches usually held good stock or rim locks, but the other doors were fastened on the inside by wooden bars which fitted through iron staples set in the jambs. *St. Paul's Church* in Kent County had a "Cross bar on the inside" of two doors, one of the folding doors having a lock. Two staples to the door at the west end of the church had to be mended.

JOINERS OR ARCHITECTS?

It was in Annapolis, the second capital of Maryland, that the rise of the professional architect occurred in the late 18th century. Before that time, it seems, those who performed architectural services in the Province were called "joiners" or "carpenters"— artisans who finished woodwork in buildings,—or "undertakers," for construction work.

These men were builders with little or no academic training; nevertheless, the term "architect" means "master-builder," one who plans buildings and supervises their construction.

In 1770 in Queen Anne's County, one James Coursey was called "House-Joiner." Such a man performed "carpenter's, joyner's, and turner's work"— turning objects on a lathe,—as well as construction masonry, and other work on buildings, such as glazing and painting. The artisan, William Elbert, who made a contract with the vestry of *Old Wye Church* at Wye Mills to construct a fane in 1717 was termed "Carpenter" in the articles of agreement. In 1729 the building contract for *St. Luke's Church,* Church Hill, Queen Anne's County, was given to the Rev. John Lang, called the "undertaker."

After the middle of the 18th century in more cosmopolitan areas than

Church Hill and Wye Mills the inhabitants evidently demanded the services of a better qualified expert than a down-country "joiner" for certain elegant or sophisticated buildings. For the first time in the public records the term "architect" was employed.

Robert Key of Annapolis referred to himself in the 1770s as a carpenter and joiner, but others called him "architect." Although the relatively small sum which he received from Edward Lloyd, owner of the *Wye House* mansion (1784), for work on that homestead does not warrant the assumption that he planned the whole job there, it is entirely possible that he was the designer. At any rate he made there several alterations and additions "about the Green House," and "Mansion House," and so on. For some twenty-eight years Key performed services for members of the Lloyd family on their properties in Annapolis and on the Eastern Shore.

Others of the same period who were called "architect" in the records were William Noke, Joseph Horatio Anderson (d. *c.* 1781), and William Buckland (d. 1774)—the first known great master-builder in the Province.

Noke, a county sheriff, was associated with Anderson on *St. Anne's Church, Annapolis,* and other works. Buckland, whose portrait by Charles Willson Peale hangs in Yale University, was noted in Virginia for his interior of *Gunston Hall.* In Annapolis he is generally credited with the *Hammond-Harwood House,* the *Brice House,* and *Strawberry Hill,* now gone, as well as other construction. Both he and his assistant, John Randall, were famous for their fine woodcarving, a kind of joinery. Some of it resembles the work of Grinling Gibbons, a 17th-century English master woodcarver of soft woods, sculptor, decorator, and chief figure in the naturalistic Anglo-Netherlandish school of carving.

Occasionally when an architect was hired to do a job, a superintendent or clerk-of-the-works was employed, as in the case of the *Chase-Lloyd House,* Annapolis, where Edward Lloyd was billed for thirty pounds sterling on account of one Allen Quynn's "overlooking" the building work.[19]

MORE GARDEN DESIGNS IN MARYLAND

Gardens are the result of a particular culture and are an outward sign of a special grace.[20] The English gardening tradition was strong in the Colony from the beginning, but seems to have been represented largely by small knot gardens or kitchen gardens or a combination of both. A "knot" is a square or oblong parterre designed symmetrically on two axes at right angles. The open kind of knot was usually designed in boxwood or rosemary with colored earths or sands; closed ones had the spaces filled with flowers. Probably the crooked knot garden (End Papers) beside the *Wye House Orangerie* is an example that has come down to us from the 17th century. The type persisted in the *Hard Bargain* garden (Fig. 197) of the 18th century which had four solid squares of box—of which three remain—penetrated by curved path-ways.[21] A reconstruction of a knot about 1700 (Fig. 169) was accomplished at *West St. Mary's Manor.*

When William Eltonhead died in 1658 in Calvert County he left "one Sun-dyall" in his estate; it is reasonable to assume that the timekeeper was located in the middle of the Eltonhead garden.

In 1684 in Cecil County, one Henry Ward left a domicile with "Kitchen" and "Yard," which must have been the kitchen garden or herb garden. Such plots were filled with vegetables, small fruits and herbs sufficient to supply a household for most of the year.

A deed received in 1671 by Daniel Curtis for his plantation in Somerset County included "Courtyards" and "Closes," terms not to be taken too literally because they were of ancient English usage and in Maryland formed stock items, among others, in a deed of transfer.

The fencing around these early gardens were of several types. Pales or paling, sometimes called palisades or "pallizadoes," were common. The pales or pickets usually were stout, sometimes being four inches thick. At "Coles Harbor" (1726) on the site of Baltimore City was a "pail'd garden in good repair." Other fences were of wattle or basketwork, or of latticework painted with colors, or of post-and-rails. The fencing on *Carmel* plantation (Fig. 123), Worcester County, in 1774 had 800 "panels," probably referring to sections of a rail fence. A cornfield, bounded by "3,000 fence logs," was probably surrounded by an old-fashioned "worm" fence.

Sometimes brick or stone walls were used, according to the availability of the material. *Rousby Hall* of the early 18th century in Calvert County had an enclosing wall of brick around the main house, garden, and some outhouses for purposes, it has been said, of protection from the Indians; *Make Peace* (*c.* 1663) is reputed to have had a similar kind of wall for defense. The stone walls about *Trentham* (Fig. 237) in Baltimore County are an excellent example of how a plantation was subdivided into compartments for various uses.

Probably the largest 17th-century garden extant in the country is at "Wye House" (End Papers and Fig. 37) in Talbot County which was laid out on a symmetrical axis behind the home of the first Edward Lloyd. Constructed about 1660, only a portion of the original homestead still stands above ground.

The 18th-century garden, no matter how small, was usually balanced on an axis and had "falles" or grass terraces. Even little *Rousby Hall* had two "falles" immediately in front of it. *Quinn* or *Sweet Air* has a garden on the south side of the house with three terraces some 150 feet in length, measuring from the front doorway. There were also a large kitchen garden and yard paled in, and three apple orchards. The garden at *Ratcliffe Manor* (Fig. 56) was apparently an allée of boxwood extending down three "falles," with large loops of box near the mansion. At *Hampton* in Baltimore County the garden (*c.* 1800) has a row of four "falles" with grass ramps leading from one to another and with boxwood parterres on either side of the central path on the three lowest terraces.

Two small gardens of the early 18th century are at *Cornwaleys' Crosse Manor* and *Holly Hill*. The former (Fig. 16) comprises only a long, narrow allée of old boxwood, leading down to the water, with what appear to be half-circles of younger box added at intervals. The garden may be as early as the date of the so-called manor house (1710–30), which forms the gambrel-roof nucleus of the present structure. In the 1930s we "discovered" an original oil painting on canvas (Fig. 17) in *Holly Hill* showing a plat or survey of that plantation in Anne Arundel County, along with an inset view in false perspective of the house and garden.[22] The painting depicts a forecourt comprising a knot garden with four squares separated by walks and bounded by pale fences with pickets set closely together. A small gateway with finials on the posts and a gate with downward bow on the top rail are centered on the garden. Also small square dependencies are located at the corners on the inside of the front fence; and there is a small gate at the rear, next to the abode.

The type of garden at *Holly Hill* might incline one to assign the forecourt to the original 17th-century portion of the homestead; but the configuration of the paths, one of which disappears behind the wing of early 18th-century date, suggests that the garden was probably designed at the time when the wing was built.

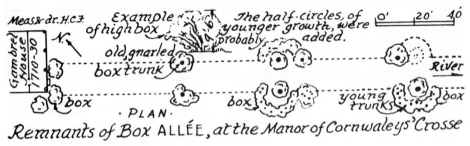

Figure 16

Most of the original Annapolis gardens have disappeared. In 1797, Richard Sprigg's *Strawberry Hill* garden was considered the finest in that city, and had a cold bath house, spring, and running stream. The *Governor's House* or *Edmond Jenning's Mansion* had a garden which was not extensive, but which had a central walkway terminated by a small, green mount beside the Severn River. It has been pointed out that the "Terrace" at "Wye House" was a kind of mount, on which one could take the air and enjoy the scenery. Sometimes there was a bosquet or grove of trees behind or adjacent to the garden, as once existed at *Harlem* in Baltimore.

A good example of the long and narrow formal town garden of the 18th century remains at the *Dr. Alexander Hamilton Bayly House* (Figs. 19 & 114), Cambridge, where there were at least twelve square box parterres. On the main axis of the garden evidently once stood another homestead, before the present *Bayly House* was brought over from Annapolis in the late 18th century and eventually set up on one half of the garden. Note the site of the wine house, from which extends a brick wine drain. In Dr. Bayly's time the grass formed a carpet of velvet sheen, and there were a smoke bush, tamarisk tree, hollyhocks, magnolias, sunflowers, roses, and a strawberry bed (*see* Addenda).

Fig. 17. (Top) The knot-garden forecourt showing balancing dependencies at *Holly Hill,* Anne Arundel County, as well as plat of the property, on oil painting which hangs in the house. (Bottom) Paintings in *Holly Hill* passage showing round tower, and in Dining Room overmantel showing harbor, boats, and residence. Oil-on-wood panels like these often decorated old Maryland rooms. Leet Bros. Courtesy, LeClair.

There appears to be a garden of Federal style still existing at the *Rose Croft,* St. Mary's City: the design comprises two boxwood stars inside a rectangle (Fig. 167). *St. Giles* on the Eastern Shore (Fig. 126) has an early 19th-century garden of semiformal nature, where the small box parterre at the rear may have resembled a roughly-designed knot. An asymmetrical garden of naturalistic design of the 1840s existed at *Clairmont* (Fig. 250, top) in Baltimore and was the location of the Clairmont Nurseries. Another naturalistic garden is at *Burley Manor* (1832-33), Worcester County, of which a gate is here illustrated (Fig. 18).

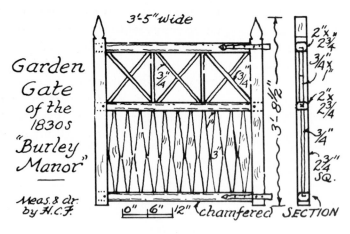

Figure 18

As the reader is reminded in a later chapter, a garden is one of the most perishable evidences of a culture. There must have been many noted and extensive gardens in the Free State before the Civil War, but few or no traces remain, either in the ground or in the records.

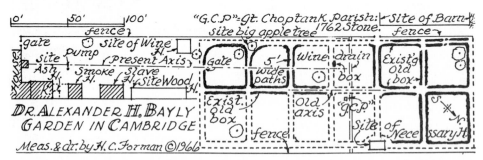

Figure 19

The word "folly," as used about a Maryland property, like "Folly Quarter," or "Bladen's Folly," is widely believed to refer to an uncomfortable owner who made a foolish mistake and regretted it. On the contrary, the word derives from the Latin, *folium,* through the French. We have almost the same word in English: foliage. "Folly" referred to land shaded by trees, and not to a foolish act.

How They Furnished Their Rooms—
For Better or For Worse

This is not intended to be a definitive article on the subject, but one to present the reader with a picture of a bygone era. The chapter may sound like a lot of lists; nevertheless it forms the first attempt, it is believed, to describe to some degree how the early Marylander lived during the 17th and 18th centuries in the types of buildings described in this book.

Life in the Free State a century and a half ago was different from today. In those days a common suspicion of events which forebode no one any good accentuates this difference. On record is a case in Talbot County in 1810 when an eagle perched on the roof of a plantation-house called *Wakefield* for a considerable time one day, during the severe illness of an occupant of the house, Joseph Leonard's wife. According to William E. Bartlett, of Baltimore, who sketched (Fig. 20) that particular event years later, "she died a few days thereafter."

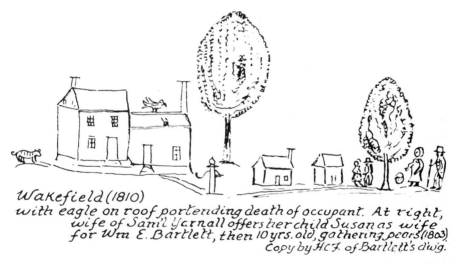

Wakefield (1810)
with eagle on roof portending death of occupant. At right,
wife of Sam'l Yarnall offers her child Susan as wife
for Wm E. Bartlett, then 10 yrs. old, gathering pears (1803).
Copy by HCF. of Bartlett's dwg.

Figure 20

In the same drawing Mr. Bartlett represented himself in 1803 as a boy of ten, a little girl called Susan, and her parents, Samuel and Sarah Yarnall. That was an even earlier time at *Wakefield*. "I went up the pear tree," he wrote, "and gathered them some good fruit; when handed them, Sarah Yarnall told me she would give me their daughter Susan for my wife. Dr. Kemp married her." This event suggests that in those times it was the custom to betroth a little girl.

In Maryland the early inventories list the belongings and goods of the deceased carefully and accurately. Sometimes the tabulation was made at the auctioning of the effects, as in 1640, when Andrew Chappell's goods were "sold at outcry on the pin[n]ace called the francis." For the most part the belongings of the decedent were appraised. For example, in 1658 William Eltonhead's inventory showed that there were "two shoates which were in the woods when the Appraysers were here, & not yet appraysed."

A DANIEL BOONE KIND OF LIFE

Most early settlers lived with so few worldly goods that today we would call the life "camping out." Consider the scant furnishings in Richard Heevens' 1673 shanty in Talbot County: one small bed, one little bed—obviously for a child,—two old chests, two small iron pots, a pair of pothooks, and a frying pan. Perhaps the seating, if there was any, was so crude and boxlike that it was not worth an appraiser's listing. Note the lack of cutlery: the Heevens family and guests may have eaten with their fingers, as is customary today in India.

Bench on East Gallery
Brick Meetinghouse
Cecil Co.

Figure 21

Early colonist Richard Bradley died in 1638 leaving no furniture at all—simply a Bible, a suit of clothes, some linen, working tools, a fowling piece, and shot baggage. He was a poor man and probably made no complaints about it.

Another Marylander who went through life without much to bear him down was Thomas Payne, who filled up his tenement room, wherever it was located in the Province, with a chest, a leather cassock, a grey suit, two shirts, a couple of pairs of old stockings, a hat, a pair of old shoes, a piece of a comb and case, a gun, and a shot bag. The original Daniel Boone, indeed.

In 1711 the meager possessions of lowly John Clark of Baltimore County comprised two old books, an old Bible, about two bushels of beans, three and a half bushels of Indian corn, and some young hogs and pigs. No apparel, no furniture, no refrigerator, no house nor plantation—nothing but the good earth, his own initiative, and God.

One John Dernall, or Darnall, owned a wee bit more than the above Clark. In addition to a wife and daughters, he had a bed tick or covering made of canvas; a poor rug which formed a coarse, woolen coverlet for a bed; a pair of blankets; and a bolster ticking—a cover for a long, stuffed pillow.

Regarding that rug for a bed, Pepys wrote of "only a rugg and a Sheet upon me." It is evident that in those days a rug was not a carpet. It was said that "December must be . . . clad in Irish rugge, or coorse freeze."

Dernall also had some books; a small chest, which formed the wardrobe closet of that era; some old pewter; two wooden dishes, mark of a poor household; some beads; a tub, perhaps for washing and taking baths; and a canoe for going places. Clothing comprised an old coat, two waistcoats, drawers, an old gown and petticoat, a hat, linen, and "some other rags." Finally there were an anchor and small runlet or cask. Those were Dernall's worldly goods.

THE APPOINTMENTS OF THE GREAT HALL, EVEN IF A CUDDY

Rather than list the ordinary contents of the average Maryland home, or those of the wealthy, we will cite the objects that were used in the most important rooms and emphasize some unusual or little-known pieces. It goes without saying that the comparatively few who were rich in early Maryland did not have to camp out, but could live among elegant surroundings—though perhaps not as fine as those to which they had been accustomed in the Old Country. In America before 1800 there were no Blenheim Palaces or Hampton Courts.

The Great Hall or Great Room formed the living and eating space of the early settler and contained a variety of furnishings. It was ordinarily the place for eating before the "Dining Room" came into general use. There might be a "joynd" table, as in Gov. Leonard Calvert's large framed house, *East St. Mary's* (1647), in St. Mary's City, the first capital of Maryland. This particular table was one having its parts joined together with mortises, tenons, and pegs: a framed table. Included also in this room were two chairs; a "form" or long seat without a back; a gold reliquary case; and a picture of "Paules"— probably St. Paul's Cathedral in London.

In the Hall of Wenlock Christison's Talbot homestead, *The Ending of Controversie* (*c.* 1670) there were a large standing table and a round table; and in the Great Room (1711) of Arthur Young of Calvert County stood one large and one small old Dutch table.

Philemon Lloyd's *Wye House* (Fig. 36B) in Talbot County in 1685 had a square table with a carpet under it. The cuddy-sized Great Hall of *Slicer-Shiplap* or *Edward Smith House* (*c.* 1723) in Annapolis contained only a square table and three old flag-bottom chairs. Flags are long, sword-shaped leaves or blades, or coarse grass or reeds.

Besides flag chairs there might be cane, "matted," wooden, leather, or turkey-work chairs—that is, those having a weave of richly-colored wools and a deep pile and cut in a manner to resemble velvet (Fig. 22). Such chairs frequently had turkey-work cushions. In Dorchester County one house had (1764) a cushioned-bottom armchair in the Hall. In 1727 Richard Tubman's Great Room had six "rush leather chairs," as well as a "French" table. Tubman's couch bed held six coverlids.

Russia leather chairs were popular. The durable leather was made of skins impregnated with oil distilled from birch bark. At *Cedar Park* (Fig. 151A) in 1736 in Anne Arundel County, the Great Hall held a dozen of those sturdy chairs, an elbow chair, and an easy chair with cushion. That important room also contained two glass sconces, a large and a small oval table, a bookcase, a tea table and an escritoire or a scrutoire. The Maryland scribe or clerk had difficulty with this last item: he wrote it as "scrulose" (screwloose).

Besides all these pieces in the Hall there might be a couch—even a leather couch, as at Samuel Layfield's (1709) in Somerset County,—a clock and clock bag, framed pictures, a looking glass, screen, chests with and without bottles, stands, stools, and a "leaf" of a table. This was a way of listing a drop-leaf table with one leaf. For instance, in Capt. William Lewis' homestead of 1658, presumably *Lewis Neck* in St. Mary's City, there was a "Leafe of a smale table" and a "forme made by a Scurvy carpenter." Two leaves would be a table with two drop-leaves.

English Turkey-Work Chair

Oak frame, 17ᵗʰ C.

Figure 22

Various items were set on the tables. There might be a knot of sheepshead line, a tobacco box, and a snuffbox. In Leonard Calvert's dwelling (1647) were a white box without lock or key and a red-leather letter case. Additional articles could be a spice box, a glass case, and an ink horn—a small bottle made of horn to hold ink.

In the Great Room the fireplace usually contained iron or brass andirons—sometimes called "dogs," as at *Quinn* or *Sweet Air* (1774), Baltimore County, where the Back Room had a pair of cast dogs. In 16th-century England such articles were rests for the fire-irons. Completing the set would be fire tongs, fire forks, fire shovels, and bellows. Topping off the fireplace would be a chimney bar with curtain and rods, presumably to cover the opening when there was no fire burning. In 1778 the pair of polished steel andirons in the Talbot home of John Goldsborough must have been unusual.

Candlesticks were of tin, iron, pewter, or brass—rarely silver (Fig. 23). The Great Hall could also be lighted by an iron or brass lamp like a Betty lamp, a rush light and candle holder, or, as mentioned, by sconces.

Rarer objects in the Hall would include books, such as a psalter, Testament, "English" books, a "small book of presidents," small books "in French," prayer books, manuals, a Table book and Discipline, and Pulton's book of Statutes. The largest of these might be set on a book rest, as was the case in John Cockshutt's 1642 habitation.

Candle Holder of Early 1800s from Dorchester Co., now in Md. Hist. Soc.

Figure 23

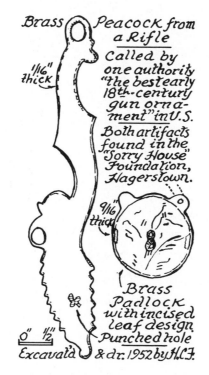

Brass Peacock from a Rifle

Called by one authority "the best early 18th-century gun ornament" in U.S.

Both artifacts found in the "Sorry House" Foundation, Hagerstown.

1/16" thick

9/16" thick

Brass Padlock with incised leaf design

Punched hole

0" 1/2"

Excavated & dr. 1952 by H.C.F.

Figure 24

Then, too, the Hall sometimes contained the paraphernalia of music, like the cithern, which Marylanders apparently pronounced "gitterne," a kind of guitar played with a plectrum of ivory, quill, or metal; a Viol glass; or a box of lutestrings. A Viol is an instrument having five, six, or seven strings and played by a bow.

Scattered around the Great Hall usually would be found the accoutrements of weapons for hunting and protection: rapiers, swords, cutlasses, scabbards, pistols and holsters, muskets, fowling pieces, guns such as the "Long Gun," blunderbusses, and the like (Fig. 24). Gov. Leonard Calvert at *East St. Mary's*

Fig. 25A. The Great Room or Hall at *West St. Mary's Manor* (1700–30) has closets on one

owned one harquebus or arquebus—an early type of portable gun having a tripod or trestle support when used in the field; also three small guns, one with a lock, the others without. John Stringer, early settler who worked as a carpenter, protected his hearthside by a wheel-lock carbine—a form of gun in which the powder was fired by a wheel against iron pyrite.

As for rapiers, at *Slicer-Shiplap* or *Edward Smith House* (*c.* 1723) in Annapolis, there were stored two very old brass-mounted swords. Some households had daggers, dagger-blades, and similar items.

Often ammunition would be strewn about the Hall; for example, the roundlets of drop-shot and small shot at Mr. Thomas Egerton's in 1639, and of goose shot, at William Smith's (1711) of Dorchester County. In 1648 at

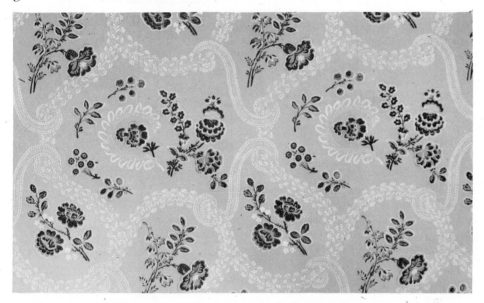

Fig. 25B. Detail of Hall wallpaper at *West St. Mary's Manor*, copied from old fragments found on wall of the room.

Thomas Allen's were a pair of shot molds; and in some homes there was probably "sweet head powder" in a powder box, used for filling guns. There were large and small powder horns. A dog formed part of the hunting equipment, as the hound and hunting piece owned in 1638 by Richard Loe; William Wassell owned a water dog or retriever.

In the Great Room might be found a "universal" sundial, a brass theodolite—a portable surveying instrument,—a pair of brass compasses for drawing, and a pair of "stilliards." A steelyard is a level with unequal arms that moves on a fulcrum—like the old Roman balance. Finally, there might be a pair of dividers and a scale, a pocket glass for magnifying, and an ivory rule in a "Shagareen" case—that is, of Chagrin, a rough-skinned Oriental leather.

For the little lady of the bower there might be a sidesaddle, and a "honester" saddle along with some bridles. On the wall one might catch a glimpse of a pillion, a woman's light saddle or pad or cushion attached to the back portion of an ordinary saddle. And there could be a pair of spur leathers, and a couple of "heckles" or hackles, which were feather-flies for angling.

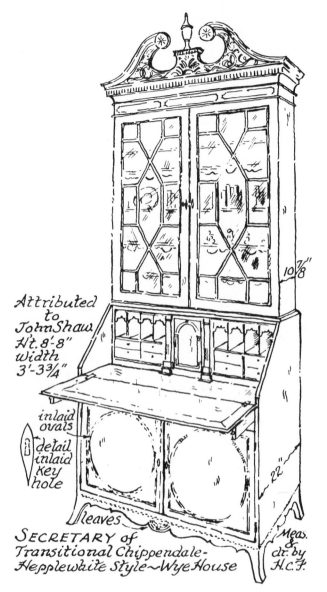

Figure 26

Of course, if the Great Room were used for cooking, as was frequently done in early, small habitations, there would be many of the furnishings as listed below for the Kitchen.

Generally speaking, we have noted that the Great Hall in the 18th century, especially after 1730, reached a point of more elegance than previously, but was still far from its prototype in Great Britain. Maryland was still the frontier, though mahogany and walnut pieces instead of pine were becoming more in evidence there. In 1774 at *Quinn* or *Sweet Air,* the room contained two square mahogany tables, two card tables, a tea table, desk, and bookcase with glass doors. There were also two looking glasses, a floor carpet, two arm chairs, and ten small chairs with mahogany frames and hair bottoms. Besides the usual fire-tools there was a brass fender. On the other hand, in the room known as the "Old Hall" there were two linen wheels for spinning, a five-fork bread toaster, and three tin candlesticks, and eleven brass ones. In his home Samuel Layfield had a "silk shagged" carpet.

A woolen wheel for spinning wool decorated the Great Room of William Smith (1711) in Dorchester County. There were also a nutmeg grater, cork-ing irons, spoon molds, a walking cane, and a currying knife and steel for leather. But the parcel of flowerpots found in the Hall of the dwelling (1711) of Col. Walter Smith of Calvert County was rare.

Returning to Dorchester, we find in Joseph Cox Gray's 1764 Great Room a corner cupboard, large and small corner tables, and a small case of drawers— all of walnut. There were other elegant furnishings in the room: a tea chest and teaboard, both of mahogany, and a waiter, or tray for dishes. That his Great Hall was used as a dining room is shown by the large number of eating and drinking utensils there, such as the 107 wine glasses, the large flowered glass tumbler, large china punch bowl, two blue-and-white china bowls, five blue-and-white china teacups and saucers, and a small Delft punch bowl.

Following the middle of the 18th century one could expect to find in the Hall a riding chair, a silver punch saddle, and a "teackle fall with two blocks" —probably referring to a tackle or hoisting rope.

At *Phillip's Purchase,* Col. James Rigbie's Harford County residence, in 1790 there were a walnut oval table, a walnut desk, stand, square table, and mahogany rocking chair in the best room in the house, presumably the Great Hall.

The "gands Vafixt" at *Wye House* (1685) in the Great Hall is any reader's guess.

"WILL YOU SLEEP IN MY PARLOR?"

The next or second room of the early Maryland house was usually the Parlor and might contain some of the same things found in the Hall or Great Room. The Parlor sometimes doubled as a bedchamber, as at *Cedar Park* in 1736, where there were two beds, a chest of drawers, and a large looking glass. Further, William Smith's 1711 Parlor in Dorchester County held a very ordinary standing bedstead as well as a "Truck"—that is, a truckle or trundle bed.

Philemon Lloyd called his parlor at *Wye House* (1685) the "New Room," meaning, no doubt, that it formed an addition to the Great Hall. There he had eighteen Shalloon chairs—Shalloon, named for Chalons, France, was made of a closely-knit woolen material chiefly used for linings. There were also a couch, two old tables, two chests of drawers, the usual window and door hangings and carpets, some wearing apparel, including a pair of new silk stockings, and a sword and belt.

In the Parlor there could be a pine square table, a chest of glassware, a bed with all its appurtenances, and a parcel of iron, as in the Little Parlor

(1639) of Justinian Snow in St. Mary's County. Sometimes small lumber was piled in a parlor.

In St. Mary's City a well-to-do gentleman, Robert Ridgely, had in his Parlor (1682) a chimney cloth—as was in the Great Hall,—a clock, three hooks for hanging clothes, a brush, a gun, a glass case with six glasses, six leather chairs, two ordinary chairs with cushions, and six other chairs. Also there were a stuffing dish, meaning a dish for forcemeat or other seasoned mixture used to stuff meat before cooking, and snuffers and extinguishers for

PINE
CORNER
CUPBOARD

from
Port
Jobacco
Md.
Now in
Chicago
Art Inst.

Figure 27

lamps and candles. In the Parlor closet were a quart decanter, a tin box of sugar, an old bedstead, a small chest of drawers, and several cases of bottles.

Stored in the closet in the "Room," which corresponded to the Parlor, in Joseph Cox Gray's home of 1764, were a small parcel of books and other trifles: "old acts of Assembly," "Bisseth abridgment," "small dictionary," "Conductor General," and "the Countiss of Kent's Choice Marvell's," which may have been exciting to some readers.

In the rare 17th-century dining room there might be a canvas tablecloth and some Lockram napkins and towels, as in Robert Parre's 1658 home. Lockram, it seems, was a linen fabric made in the Brittany village of the same name. The *Wye House* dining room (1685) kept three old-fashioned Spanish "laced" cupboard cloths.

Those families fortunate enough to have a separate room for dining during the 18th century, as at the *Edward Smith* or *Slicer-Shiplap House* in Annapolis (*c.* 1723), might have in it a dozen leather chairs, a large and small oval table, as well as a small painted oval table. A "parcel" of pictures would hang on the walls. In one corner might be a pair of old gaming tables— for, after all, Edward Smith was an innkeeper. There could be a small "joynt" stool, made of parts fitted or joined carefully together; a large looking glass; and even two short boards for a table, but no legs. Perhaps the boards were supported by trestles. Often the dining room had silver plate and other kinds of dinnerware and appurtenances. The corner cupboard was common, as in Col. James Rigbie's home, *Phillip's Purchase* (1790), in Harford County.

CHAMBERS WERE FOR BEDS AND BED PACKAGES

In studying the furnishings of the bedrooms or chambers, as they were usually called in earlier days, one finds the varieties of beds and coverings a little short of amazing. What we call the bed was usually considered part of a larger package having bedstead, bed ticking—the mattress,—rug, blankets, quilt, coverlet, pillows, bolsters, curtains, and valances. The coverlet was also called the counterpane. All these items formed "bed and furniture," or "bed and furniture belonging to it," or "bed and its appurtenances." At the *Edward Smith* or *Slicer-Shiplap House* were beds with "old furniture"—meaning the ancient, appropriate trappings. When the appraiser wrote (1685) at *Wye House* "two beds onely," the equipage around the bedsteads was not included. At *Cedar Park* in 1736 the Hall Chamber, or bedroom over the Great Hall, held a couch with a bed—the bed being the ticking. In the Parlor Chamber there was a parcel of "Bed Cloathes" covering the ticking. In 1790 Col. James Rigbie's mansion contained one bedstead and—believe it or not—a "sacking bottom."

To repeat, the bed generally was not the bedstead, as in Robert Ridgely's home in St. Mary's City where the Nursery Loft contained a quilted bed, two bolsters, two pillows, and a bedstead. Consequently the first-named object was a ticking covered by a quilt. At William Smith's (1711) in Dorchester County was a very ordinary *standing* bedstead. Evidently some bedsteads in Maryland did not stand, but were set on the floor—a situation which we today have forgotten.

Two of the most primitive kinds were the old straw bed—without bedstead—and bolster at Capt. William Lewis' in 1658 and the old "Cattayle" bed, bedstead, "suite" of green curtains, and green carpet, at William Eltonhead's in the same year. Even Daniel Curtis' home (1680) in Somerset County had cattail beds.

Servants' beds were probably the most primeval of all, and no doubt in many cases comprised simply a ticking stretched out on the mud, plank, or brick flooring. In Jane Paine's Kitchen Loft (1675), where the servant slept, there was a wall bed with canvas ticking—possibly meaning that the bed was hinged to the wall as a space-saving device, the predecessor of the modern Murphy bed. You could scarcely say that Mistress Paine lived in elegance when her whole house contained but one sheet.

In the Quarter at Col. Walter Smith's (1711) in Calvert County there was merely an old canvas bed or ticking. At *Wye House* (1685) the four servants' beds must have been rugged—perhaps containing corn husks. At Arthur Young's (1711) in Calvert County there was a chaff bed, meaning that the ticking was filled with wheat husks. *Wye House* also contained a hammock, and it is surmised that many a Marylander used to sleep in one.

Young children were put to sleep in trundle beds, like the one in the Parlor Chamber at *Cedar Park*. There were cradles, too, such as the "cradle and quilt" in the Lodging Chamber at Samuel Layfield's in Somerset County.

More primitive beds, in the Garret of the *Slicer-Shiplap* or *Edward Smith House,* were the eight bed cots with old canvas bottoms. The word "cot" is Anglo-Indian and means a light bedstead. Canvas cots probably had X-legs, like the 18th-century cot which stands in the *Jethro Coffin House* on Nantucket Island. Sometimes a feather ticking was put over the cot for comfort, as in the small chamber at *Slicer-Shiplap,* which had a feather bed in a cot, but lacked curtains.

The rope bed must have been common in the Free State, where a rope was stretched through the bedstead frame. As late as 1774 at *Quinn* or *Sweet Air* the Back Room had some "Bedstead Cord." The same situation obtained in Queen Anne's County where Robert Ashly's home (1764) had a bedstead cord, a "brown [canvas] tick," a bolster, blanket, sheet, green rug, and hide. The rug and hide were not for the floor, but coverings for warmth upon the ticking.

John Goldsborough of "Four Square," Talbot County, in 1778 had, besides a bedstead and some cord, "some old deposted bedsteads." This evidently means that bedsteads without posts were on the floor.

Many beds had flock tickings and bolsters: flock is a material of coarse tuft and refuse of wool or cotton. Thus, Philemon Lloyd owned two flock beds and four bolsters of the same stuff in the Black Chamber at *Wye House* (1685). Flock beds and flock pillows were in the dwelling of Christopher Martin and Joseph Edlo (1640); and Richard Loe had a flock quilt. Bob Parre had two "slight" flock beds. A most unusual item was the "sea flock bed" of John Glantham in 1640; perhaps he was an ancient mariner.

Feather or down beds were common in the early days, and bags of feathers to fill such tickings were kept in closets. In the Parlor at *Slicer-Shiplap,* for example, were two feather beds, and furniture including curtains; and in the room facing Capt. Gordon's property were the same items, the curtains being blue. In 1642 John Cockshott owned a feather bed, bolster, two pillows, a couple of blankets, and a large red rug. The Upper Chamber at *Wye House* in 1685 had a "downe" bed.

On the other hand, Thomas Allen (1648) had a slightly more primitive kind of feather bed because the ticking was of rough canvas. Nevertheless, there were a feather pillow, a white rug as coverlet, and even the luxury of a handsome deerskin with feathers in it. Samuel Layfield's Parlor Chamber had a feather bed, "one furnished, the other not." The curtains of a bed were described as a "suite," as in Col. Walter Smith's Hall Chamber (1711), where three "suits" of Cheney and two of Ansey curtains belonged to three old beds. At Rigbie's (1790) in Harford County there was a feather bed with suite of blue curtains—the bedding or ticking weighing forty-five pounds and the coverlet one pound.

The equipment of some beds comprised a "pair of pillow beres" or "pillowbers," as at *William Smith's House* (1638), St. Mary's City. Another man of the same name, who lived in Dorchester County, had (1711) in his Parlor Chamber "five pillowbeers very much worn"; and Robert Ridgely's Chamber in his St. Mary's City town house contained "two fine holland pillowbrs"— meaning they were made of fine linen or cotton. *Wye House* (1685) had also thirteen "holland pillowbears." By 1790, it seems, they were called "pillowcases," as at Rigbie's. However, in 1678 Wenlock Christison had two pillows with "cases" in his *Ending of Controversie* home.

Along with these early Maryland bedsteads went flaxen sheets and flaxen "pillowbers," Holland sheets and Holland "pillowbers," hempen sheets and hempen "pillowbers," Locram or Douglas sheets and "pillowbers," canvas and "ornabrigg" (Ozembrigs) sheets and "pillowbers"—and coverlets or counterpanes. Many of these items were undoubtedly kept in the "Bedding Chest," like the one at Justinian Snow's (1639) in St. Mary's County.

It is hoped that the foregoing information has given some idea of how chambers were furnished with beds. Then there were the necessary warming pans and hot bricks for beds; the early colonists really needed them in their heatless rooms, because if the bedchamber had a fireplace, a fire was only lit when the occupant was sick or on very special occasions. Even in the year of this writing, we experienced midwinter living in a heatless chamber in an English country house in Essex. Both day and night the temperature in the room was about 42° Fahrenheit. It was a blessing that hot water bottles were customarily placed between the sheets. Surely the early Marylander needed such things in his frigid bedrooms in winter. But Capt. William Lewis had only one warming pan in his St. Mary's County home in 1658; and Wenlocke Christison had (1678) in his two-chambered Talbot home only one warming pan, of brass, to heat the beds.

Chamber pots were important items at night or in bad weather, especially when the necessary house was a long way from the bedchamber, as we found by measurements at *Cedar Park* (Figs. 146–149) in Anne Arundel County. Shakespeare in at least one instance made humorous reference to using the fireplace in an old English cottage.

In the bedchamber Henry Crawlie in 1640 had "1 chamber pott & 4 spoones," and William Eltonhead kept two chamber pots along with salt cellar and candlestick. *Slicer-Shiplap House* contained nine old earthen chamber pots, but, of course, that was an inn.

Akin to the above necessary utensil was the "close-stool." For example, Robert Ridgely kept in his bedchamber in St. Mary's City a close stool and a pan to go inside it. In the Back Chamber of *Slicer-Shiplap* was an "old broken Close Stool pan and frame."

The usual Chamber would have curtained windows for privacy, as at *Cedar Park,* where the Hall Chamber had two pairs of window curtains with iron rods.

Other articles of Chamber furniture might be chests, both large and small—like the "great old square chest" in Leonard Calvert's home, *East St. Mary's*; the "great trunk" in William Smith's house in St. Mary's City, or even a great hair trunk, like the one at *Wye House* (1685); a large wainscot chest, and one with personal initials on it like "MC," for Mary Christison (1678), in Wenlock Christison's dwelling, *The Ending of Controversie*; boxes, like a box of drawers; a desk, or small cupboard; leather chairs or chairs that were cane-bottom, wood-bottom, cushion-bottom, flag-bottom, rush-bottom, turkey-work, calfskin, or green "chearge."

Mr. Robert Ridgely's own Chamber in St. Mary's City had a "great" chair and cushion, as well as a "haire and foot"—probably a hair-covered footstool. There might be large or small oval tables, or a small painted tea table, as at

Early Maryland Smokers' Names on Clay Pipes: Rubbings of Stems Excavated at Palace of St. John's (1638) by Author.

Figure 28

Slicer-Shiplap, or round or square tables. A couch and stools would also be appropriate.

On a table or chest of drawers might be found a "seale-ring" and other articles of jewelry, or a lustrous silk purse of taffeta containing a parcel of silken threads and buttons. There might be a sideboard and sideboard cloth, as in the Parlor Chamber of Robert Ridgely. Looking glasses were necessary in the bedchamber, like the case of drawers and looking glass in 1790 at Col. James Rigbie's. Madam Lloyd's Chamber at *Wye House* (1685) contained a rare olivewood table stand and a looking glass. A dressing table and looking glass, nine cane chairs, and an elbow chair were some of the pieces decorating the Hall Chamber at *Cedar Park*.

The fire tools would be similar to those in the Great Hall, but smaller in size to fit a narrower opening. The Parlor Chamber at *Slicer-Shiplap* had a pair of brass tongs, fire shovels, and small hand-bellows. Along with the bellows would be some snuffers and a snuffing dish. Not all andirons in the chamber would be wholly brass: Jane Paine, of St. Jerome in St. Mary's

County, owned a pair of andirons with "brass heads." A "Chamber'd chimney," by the way, was a fireplace in a bedroom.

By the late 18th century Oriental influences were evident in some home furnishings, and Col. Rigbie used a "screen," Japanned sugar box and Japanned salvers in his Harford home.

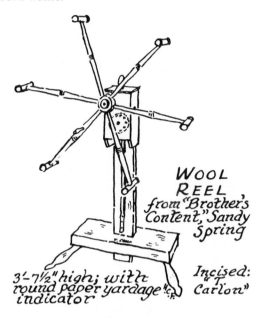

WOOL REEL from "Brother's Content," Sandy Spring

3'-7½" high; with round paper "yardage" indicator

Incised: "T. Carton"

Figure 29

Other items in the Chamber were tea canisters or cases or boxes for holding tea, coffee, shot, and the like, Cheaney saucers, pewter teapots, Dutchware cups and saucers and other dishes, silver, linen, towels, a snuffbox and steel tobacco box, bottles, a spotted jug and spotted drinking cup—as in Jane Paine's own Chamber. She also had an "iron pound case."

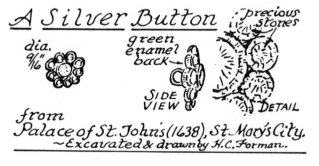

A Silver Button

dia. 9/16"

green enamel back

SIDE VIEW

precious stones

DETAIL

from Palace of St. John's (1638), St. Mary's City.
~Excavated & drawn by H.C. Forman.

Figure 30

There was almost no end to the list of small objects found in a chamber: a powder box, a pair of shears, the necessary razor case with strap and hone, and scissors. In addition to carbines, fowling pieces, muskets, swords, and the like, you might have a bundle of deerskins put away—Mr. Philemon Lloyd had fifty-five stored in the Blue Chamber at *Wye House* (1685). In his own Chamber, Robert Ridgely had a "Raffune" case and four "Rafurs," along with a watch. A "Raffune" case may be made of *Raffia,* a soft fibre from a palm used for weaving baskets and the like. There could be flax spinning wheels, called "wheels," in bedchambers, reels for winding wool (Fig. 29), and quilting frames.

The Children's Chamber in the homestead (1711) of Col. Walter Smith of Calvert County contained only a bed quilt and blankets—suggesting that the little ones slept on the floor,—two calico carpets, a large chair, and warming pan.

The chamber closet held a variety of things, some unusual. You might find a fifty-pound bag of feathers, umbrellas, a chimney-piece or mantel, parcels of old books and of parchment, a box trunk, a gross of corks, some round bottles, some lumber, a buff belt, a box and scales, paper boxes, whalebone, casks, tools, a Dutch case, a box of medicinal pots and bottles, and a "furring lanthorne"—evidently one with wood panels to make it dark when needed. A buff belt is one made of stout buffalo- or ox-hide. Stored in the closet might be a trumpet, colors, and staff; dust shovels for cleaning out the fireplaces; and a safe for valuables.

Far back in Col. Walter Smith's closet in 1711 were a walnut desk, trunk, box, and several volumes: two old folios, six books of small folio, and ten quarters in octavo—this description suggests that perhaps appraisers were confused about book sizes.

Soon after the beginning of the 18th century, some of the chamber furnishings had more ornamentation and elegance; for example, the "inlaid" chest of drawers in the Porch Chamber and the spice box and glass case in the tiny "Peake Room" at *Cedar Park* in 1736. Col. Rigbie had an escritoire and a "beauroe." The "Dressing Box" at Samuel Layfield's plantation-house of 1709 in Somerset County gives an idea of the elegance spreading over parts of Maryland in that era: among other items it contained three silver watches and a gold one, a silver quill, snuffbox, twenty gold rings, and a gold locket, besides cash and silver plate.

The Lodging Chamber of Arthur Young's retreat of 1711 in Calvert County held silver plate and lots of money. There were seven-and-a-half ounces of *New York* plate, some twenty-eight dollars valued at three shillings sixpence, some new "mill'd" money, seventeen Arabian pieces, three Spanish pistoles, three and a half guineas, a Portuguese piece, a parcel of Peru pieces, three pairs of gold buttons (Fig. 30), and "weighd" or weighted money of several sorts. One wonders if anyone in the neighborhood was aware of that little gold and silver hoard hidden away at Young's.

WHEN COOKING IN THE KITCHEN WAS AN ART

The furnishings of early Maryland kitchens are too many to enumerate in a chapter of this size; nevertheless, we will list some of the most common and the most unusual ones. The kitchen was often capacious enough to store old lumber, as at *Wye House* (1685), and ladders long enough to be used to extinguish fires on the roof. There were corner cupboards (Fig. 27), tables, chairs of all kinds, stools, and "forms" or benches. At Capt. William Lewis' dwelling in St. Mary's City, the Kitchen had a "forme of a split plank."

The pièce de résistance of the kitchen was, of course, the cooking fireplace; sometimes it was large enough to accommodate a twelve-foot log. The fireplace was the center for all sorts of paraphernalia: fire irons; cranes; pot-hooks; heaters—like the one at *Cedar Park*; tinder box and steel, for lighting the fire; spits and spit racks; iron chains; grates, and gridirons. There were pot trammels—a trammel was a series of rings or links to hold up a crook at different heights over a fire. The trammel-bar was usually a wood sapling built across the flue of a fireplace to support the trammel; it was sometimes called the "chimney bar."

The fireplace spit, sometimes an iron basket, was usually turned in a slow manner by a jack mechanism of pulleys and heavy weights. The meat on the spit could then be "cooked to a turn." Occasionally a smoke jack turned the spit by means of the strong draught of the fire. The "Jack Infixt" described in Jane Paine's Kitchen (1675) at St. Jerome was probably a fireplace jack.

In front of the roaring blaze stood a "copper plate Warmer"—a metal cabinet with shelves, open on the side of the fire, with a door on the opposite side. A copper "sampan" often accompanied the warmer, and sometimes Dutch ovens were used.

The cooking utensils were legion. For preparing certain foods, the pestle and mortar were invaluable and were a part of every kitchen. A mortar is a hollow-shaped vessel of stone or other hard material in which ingredients, such as corn, are ground and pounded by a pestle, usually club- or cylinder-shaped. An iron mortar and pestle were in Henry Crawlie's cottage (1640). They could also be of wood, glass, brass, or bell metal; *Slicer-Shiplap* Kitchen had an old bell metal pot and a mortar and pestle of the same material—an alloy of about four parts of copper and one of tin. Among its kitchen utensils *Quinn* or *Sweet Air* (1774) had a tiny spice mortar and pestle.

Cooking pots and potlids were of iron, brass, copper, and pewter. Ridgely in St. Mary's City had a brass potlid, four copper pots, and one large copper—evidently a brewing copper. Also he had a brass "coale iron" or cauldron. *Cedar Park* Store held a copper coffee pot and a copper chocolate pot. At *Wye House* (1685) there were five posnets—small metal pots or vessels for boiling, each having a handle and three feet. Still, one of the most interesting was the "latin" pot on John Bryant's hearth in 1638; it was of latten, a mixed metal of yellow color, either identified with or quite similar to brass.

Many earthen pots were used in Maryland homes, but not over the fire. A portion of one (Fig. 160) was found some years ago in St. Mary's City and is marked by shallow rings on the exterior. It must have been either a pot or a bowl used by the early colonists.

Among other utensils in the kitchen may be listed kettles of iron, copper, brass, and tin, like the "Tin fish kettle" or the old copper teakettle and frame at *Cedar Park*; baking kettles; brass chafing dishes, which are portable grates or vessels to hold burning fuel for cooking something; brass, copper, or iron skillets; frying pans and trivets (Fig. 32), copper saucepans, tin or wood cul-

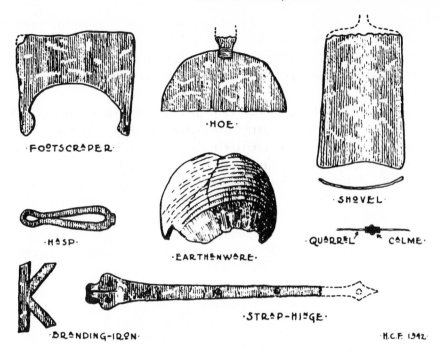

Fig. 31. Artifacts used by early colonists found in a refuse pit near the site of *Leonard Calvert House* in St. Mary's City.

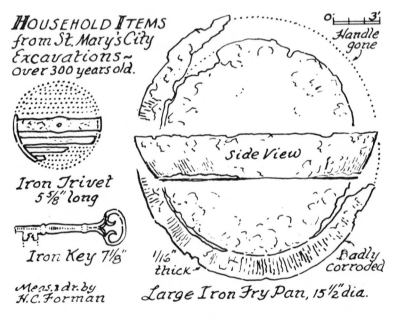

Figure 32

lenders, dripping pans with lids, hominy pans, brass stewing pans and their lids, and pudding pans; brass skimmers; copper gridirons and spit gridirons. The skillet is a utensil used for boiling liquids or stewing meat, usually having three or four feet and a long handle.

There were water dishes and water plates; brass ladles, pot racks, basins of all kinds and shapes; water buckets and others, such as "girth" buckets with leather or cloth bands; milking pails, such as "ironbound payles"; milk trays, sifting trays, sifters, like wire wheat sifters, and sifters' irons, rolling pins, and smoothing irons for laundry work.

In 1645 the kitchen at *St. Inigoe's Manor,* St. Mary's County, had a box of a dozen cheese trenchers—evidently small round or oblong boards on which cheeses were served.

Pipkins—small earthenware pots or pans—were in common use in England in the 16th century. There were also powdering tubs, washing tubs, meal tubs, and others of the same sort; pint pots, pottle pots, where the "pottle" is a measure of one-half gallon, and quart pots; stone jugs, pickle cases, cases with bottles, and piggins—meaning small pails, especially wooden ones with a stave longer than the others to serve as a handle; and chopping blocks.

Yes, cooking was an art in early Maryland, judging from the varied and numerous implements and vessels swarming around the great fireplace before the age of cooking ranges, T-V dinners, and pie-and-ice-cream-for-dessert fare.

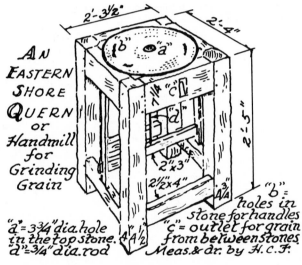

Figure 33

Brass scales and steelyards were useful for weighing foods. Roundlets or small casks were common; for example, the two-gallon roundlet at William Smith's homestead (1638) in St. Mary's City.

Because kitchen floor space was precious, many objects were hung from walls or ceilings, like the basket of tinware and clay pipes in the 1658 domicile of one John Stringer, carpenter. Also hanging were old saddles, bridles, warming pans, jacks, working tools, foods like hams, salt boxes, bags containing salt, pepper boxes, tin sugar-pots, and bill and can hooks, iron chains, hides, hide-tanned leather, guns, and the like. In the 1642 kitchen of Leonard Leonardson there were fifteen arms' length of roanoke, probably on the wall. This was the Indian "rawranoke" or "rarenawock"—a kind of wampum made of white and colored shell beads. The cart, collar, and saddle in Jane Paine's kitchen probably required a large floor space.

The kitchen was usually lit by candlesticks of tin, iron, brass, copper, or pewter; sometimes there was a brass lamp and a candle box, as at Robert Ridgely's in St. Mary's City; "lanthornes," candle molds, and candle snuffers and stands, such as the ones in the *Cedar Park* Kitchen; and glass sconces, such as those at *Slicer-Shiplap*.

Rushlights in Maryland held rushes which had been peeled, leaving only one rib to support the pith, bleached in the sun, and dipped in scalding fat. In remote cottages in Yorkshire, England, rushlights were still being used in the 20th century for lighting the kitchen.

John Stringer had "four pounds of Candles" put away for his kitchen. Wenlock Christison in his *Ending of Controversie* house (*c.* 1670) had a brass "twined" candlestick that may have been used in the kitchen.

In Justinian Snow's kitchen in 1639 were two pounds of match, which is a fuse of cotton wicking prepared to burn either quickly or slowly.

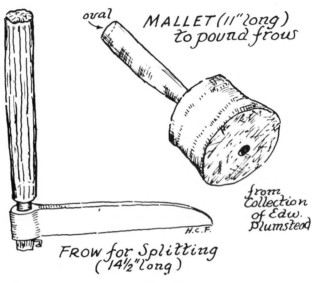

oval MALLET (11" long) to pound frows

from Collection of Edw. Plumsted

FROW for Splitting (14½" long)

Figure 34

Many of the tools for the plantation were set or hung in the kitchen (Fig. 31): all kinds of saws, like the crosscut saw, "tenant" saw, or whipsaw—one with a narrow blade used especially for curved work; hammers, like the "lathing" hammer; augers, gimlets, drawing knives, digging and "Dutch" spades; felling, narrow, and broad axes; "hilling" and weeding hoes, watering pots, pitchforks, sedge hooks, garden rakes, garden spades, and garden shears; grindstones, ploughshares, ploughs and harrows, cheese presses, handmills, and hangers.

In 1644 there was a ploughshare belonging to Lord Baltimore at "West St. Mary's" that had been "sent to Engl: 1 plow, 1 harrow."

Sedge hooks and picks must have been used in Maryland for both fuel and thatching. It is said that in Old England bedmakers in the Cambridge colleges were given sedge gloves to protect their hands when laying fires of sedge for the undergraduates.

Among the hundreds of joiner's tools kept in the Maryland kitchen may be included chisels, planes and plane irons, bits, wedges, pincers, hatchets, and and even "spokeshaves"—a kind of drawing knife or shave used for shaping and finishing the spokes of a wheel. Sometimes there were scythes with rings and a "ring for a beetle," meaning a mallet or maul.

The "frow" or froe (Fig. 34) was in common use in the early days and was a wedge-shaped tool for cleaning and riving staves or shingles. Sometimes there were "marking irons"—branding irons (Fig. 31) for animals— and "pikes" or pickaxes.

At Leonard Calvert's home in St. Mary's City was a small smith's vise; at *St. John's* in the same town were (1644) certain carpenter's tools of Lord Baltimore which remained in the custody of one John Kent.

The well-appointed kitchen also contained a clothes basket, a waiter or tray, toasting forks, toasting irons, a pair of tormentors—evidently riding spurs,—an alemic or distilling apparatus, a cold still, toddy irons, apple roasters, fish plates, shredding knives, cleavers, funnels, boxes of long clay tobacco pipes, and a wired bird cage—as in Joseph Cox Gray's 1764 Kitchen in Dorchester County.

Also there would be spinning wheels and cards of wool, cotton wheels and gins (1764), fishing lines, and "jackallot sticks"—probably a game. At Samuel Layfield's (1709) in Somerset County was a silver tobacco box and "taylors goose"—a tailor's smoothing iron. However, in 1800 a tailor's goose was a game played with counters on a board featuring a picture of a goose. A little glue kettle used for fastening the "joynt" stools and other articles of household furniture was in Jack Cockshutt's Kitchen.

Among the other items in the *Slicer-Shiplap* or *Edward Smith* Kitchen (1723) were "15 old Iron Skivers"—knives for leather-splitting in bookbinding work; two wine "Coolers"; tin funnels, old patty pans, an old brass egg slicer; boxes of pepper, sugar, and mustard; and a "Sillibub cup." This was a dish for making a drink of milk or cream containing liquor.

While it is literally impossible to list all the objects in the early Maryland kitchen, some items might prove surprising to us today. In Capt. William Lewis' house at St. Mary's City was an old "dryfatt made of boards"; a dry-fat was a large vessel used in the 17th century to hold dry things as opposed to liquid. For cuts or burns or sores you would delve into a box of "salves" and medicinal "in struments," like the one on a shelf in the *Wye House* Kitchen (1685), or a glass balsom—a vessel with a medicinal preparation for healing wounds.

Because of lack of space we shall have to wait for another time to describe the eating utensils and dinnerware in the Maryland kitchen.

In the Weaving Room, or House, off the kitchen end of the plantation-house, like the one at William Smith's home of 1709 in Dorchester County, would be a loom; a slay—the reed guiding the warp threads in a loom; a shuttle quill and wheel quills; a "sacking" with some flock and feathers in it; some wool on the loom "with nothing to fill it with"; and a package of ordinary shoemaker's tools and lasts. In Robert Ashly's lodging of 1764 in Queen Anne's County the women must have worked on the lint wheel, woolen wheel with its pair of cards, and small hair sifter.

GOOD PLACES FOR OTHER PARAPHERNALIA

Other interesting articles used to furnish the early Maryland home were ink-ing "boddines"—having to do with making printing type; horse- and hand-bells; spyglasses; jagging irons—ones with sharp barbs or projections, often used in milk houses; gallipots—small, earthen pots used by apothecaries; cruets—small bottles or vials; deal boxes, made to a certain size from slices sawn from a log or timber.

Luxury items that have not yet gone out of style were the five cakes of Castile soap in the *Palace of St. John's* in St. Mary's City in 1658.

Nowadays if you were told that your own dwelling contained "double-tens," would you think that you had a gaming device? On the contrary, a double-ten was a nail double the cost of the tenpenny nail.

A speaking trumpet, used to call the farm hands, was kept in the enclosed front porch at *Cedar Park*.

Cellars, like the one at *Slicer-Shiplap* in Annapolis, contained small casks of rum, claret, white wine, and the like; sour bottles "good for nothing"; Murkavdo sugar; a pair of old money weights and scales; a flock bed and blankets "for the Negroes"; linen, Huckaback and flax tablecloths, sheets, napkins, pillowcases; "twells," meaning twilled cloth; a "piece of Cherry Derry," silk crape, and a gold ring; cash, silver plate, a watch, black walnut lumber, garden pails, and an old sawhorse. The cellar evidently was the place to store old unwanted things. But Robert Ridgely's Cellar in St. Mary's City appears to have held only two dozen bottles and three empty casks.

In the "Stair Case" at *Wye House* (1685) stood an old red clock, probably in a tall case.

Stuck out in the Quarter and Quarter Loft would be a handmill and its frame (Fig. 33), half anchors, and a "grapnail"—a small anchor with three or more flukes.

Can the reader guess the identity of the two "faucheons" in Thomas Eger-ton's habitation in St. Mary's City or the "tearce" in Henry Crawlie's home-stead of 1640?

The two old "Limbecks" in the Kitchen at *Cedar Park* were obviously stills; but the reader may guess what were a brass plate rail, a "Barber's Pot," and an "Iron Crow" there. In the Parlor of William Smith's (1711) in Dor-chester County was a hackle, an implement for cleaning flax and hemp, con-sisting of a set of teeth fastened on a board. What was the "old Drum line" in Arthur Young's Great Hall of 1711 in Calvert County?

What were the "ozenbriggs" or "oznabourg" wallets at Col. Walter Smith's (1711) in Calvert County? Coarse linen was manufactured in Osnabrück, a town in Prussia. One can understand Smith's tenement holding two pottle pickle bottles, eight deerskins, and an old cart with small wheels and axle tree, but the wallets of distinctive make are a puzzle.

Today cartwheels are frequently placed at the entrance to a driveway, yet Samuel Layfield had a pair of old cartwheels in his Great Hall.

II.

The Upper Eastern Shore

II.

The Upper Eastern Shore

The *Wye House,* Its Garden and Village

"**O**UTSTANDING among the old estates of Maryland . . ." is "Wye House"—thus commenced a 1953 magazine article[1] which would be difficult to surpass in breadth of description and technical accuracy. For example, the *Captain's House* (Fig. 36B) on the "Wye House" property was correctly named a dependency of the original homestead (*c.* 1660). Likewise, the *Corn House* (Fig. 49B) was not called a dependency, because it was only an outhouse and nothing more. That account will long remain the scholarly study on the subject.

This present writing is to reveal further discoveries about the plantation called "Wye House" since the above-mentioned article appeared; to illustrate by plot plans and drawings what a large going farm of the 18th century was like; and to preserve on paper a description of what we believe to be the greatest 17th-century garden extant in the United States.

It should be emphasized that a garden is one of the most perishable evidences of a culture, and the "Wye House" garden has been no exception.

THE 17TH-CENTURY PLANTATION

The "Wye House" story began in 1658 when Edward Lloyd, the first of his name in Maryland, purchased 600 acres, called "Linton," on Wye River, and an adjoining tract, "The Grange," containing 150 acres, to the west of "Linton." Although the present-day, extensive estate, "Wye House," straddles both of these properties, the *Wye House* (1784; Fig. 40A)—hereinafter called the "mansion"—lies on "The Grange" portion, according to two 17th-century plats or surveys hanging on a wall in the mansion.

51

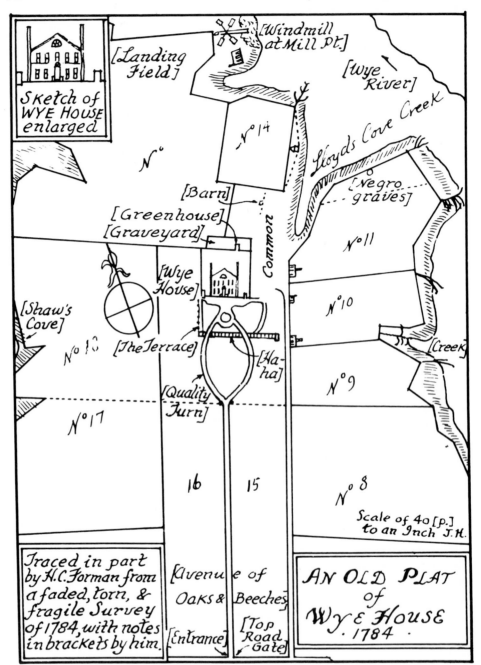

Figure 35

The first Edward Lloyd could have lived at "Wye House" as early as 1660. Consequently, it is the custom to consider that date for the first *Wye House,* of which today only the *Captain's House* dependency remains above ground.

In 1668 Edward Lloyd went back to Britain, leaving his newly-established estate under the management of his young son, Philemon Lloyd, who married Henrietta Maria, in 1668 or 1669. She was the daughter of Capt. James Neale and his wife, Anne Gill, and widow of Richard Bennett. Along with many other Eastern Shoremen, the writer belongs to the group claiming descent from Henrietta Maria Lloyd's parents. Named for her godmother, the wife of Charles I to whom her mother was lady-in-waiting, Henrietta Maria Lloyd is known as the "ancestress of the Eastern Shore" and is buried in the second oldest tomb (1697) in the graveyard at "Wye House."

When Philemon Lloyd died in 1685, he left a careful inventory of every piece of the furnishings and goods in the original *Wye House* (*c.* 1660), as has been shown in the preceding chapter.

From that time onward a succession of Edward Lloyds owned "Wye House." There was one who married Sarah Covington in 1703, one who wed Anne Rousby in 1739, and another who built *Wye House* mansion (1784) and in 1767 married Elizabeth Tayloe, of *Mt. Airy,* Richmond County, Virginia. One became the husband of Sally Scott Murray and was Governor of Maryland (1809-11), and another married Mary Key Howard and died in 1907.

All in all, this 17th-century plantation was a great one in more than one respect. The list of contents in the "Store House" there in 1685 is crammed with four and a half pages of items, covering about 265 kinds of goods and merchandise, like "4 girles pretty coates [petticoats]," 151 pairs of Irish hose, and 83 falling axes. In fact that particular store—its exact location is still unknown—must have served as trading post and supply depot for much of the middle Eastern Shore.

The 17th-century estate was laid out along the length of a rural lane, known as the "Long Green" or "Common," which led down to a landing or wharf on Lloyd's Cove Creek on Wye River from the main road or path leading from the central part of Talbot County—because in those days Easton, the present county seat, did not exist. The lane is shown on both "An Old Plat of Wye House (1784)"[2]—hereinafter referred to as the "Old Plat" (Fig. 35)—and the "Detail of Long Green" in the writer's garden plan (End Papers). Those outhouses which are definitely known have been entered in the latter diagram; in themselves they formed a little village, as follows:

First, the existing *Quarters House,* a red frame cottage (Fig. 38C), is located back from the Long Green lane and on a subsidiary branch road on the east side; then two outhouses of unknown use, marked "p," on each side of the Long Green road; next, on the right hand of that lane, in order, the half-underground *Ice House,* a *Brick Quarters* of two storeys, a *Carpenter's Shop,* a *Blacksmith's Shop,* a *Corn House* (Fig. 49B), and a brick *Horse Stable,* located directly above the great wharf or "Landing" on Lloyd's Cove Creek. Except for the first of these, all have gone along with Father Time, and most of them in date were probably 17th-century or replacements thereof.

Beyond the red wooden *Quarters House* there stood along the subsidiary road and close to the creek a brick *row Quarters,* containing three servants' apartments or houses contiguous to each other; and in a field behind them was the negro graveyard.

On the left-hand, or west, side of the Long Green stands the *Captain's House,* which, as has been noted, was part of the original *Wye House* (*c.*

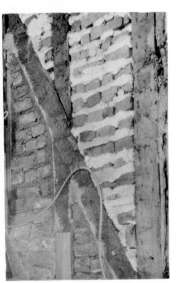

Fig. 36. A(top). In the *Wye House* boxwood garden. Author, 1964. B(bottom left). Brick *Captain's House,* part of the original *Wye House* (*c.* 1660), is noted for its chimney with "withe." Author, 1966. C(bottom right). Brick nogging in the walls of the *Wye House* mansion (1784). Author, 1955.

1660). It used to be a dependency because it formed an integral part, it is believed, of a composition of which the central section and the opposite dependency have disappeared. The *Captain's House,* by the way, was named for the master of the plantation sailboat during the latter portion of the 19th century. It is a medieval hall-and-parlor dwelling with most of its outside openings now changed and with a small north addition of about 1810 vintage. The Tudor chimney stack with offset base and vertical "withe" (Figs. 36B & 38B) is rare in Maryland, but common in Old and New England.[3]

It is unfortunate that all the interior woodwork of the little brick cottage is of the last part of the 18th century and later. At the owner's request the writer designed the present chimney on the later north wing, exactly replacing an earlier one destroyed. In a correct restoration the whole wing would be removed, and the openings, woodwork, and other details replaced to the style of 1660 in rural Maryland.

Beyond the *Captain's House,* at a distance, was an ancient *Cow Barn,* marked "p," which had a couple of auxiliary buildings near it, such as the *Chicken House.*

There are records of a Store, Overseer's Houses, Cooper Shop, Weaver's House, Smoke House, and Dairy, mostly belonging to the older *Wye House* (*c.* 1660). For decades carts and wagons were driven up and down the muddy or dusty Long Green lane on the active business of shipping to and from the Landing. The noise and confusion at times must have been deafening and annoying to the residents of the old dwelling situated squarely in front of that thoroughfare.

The 17th-century boxwood garden (End Papers) was laid out on the axis of the original homestead (*c.* 1660) as far as can now be determined, and was both symmetrical and balanced. The central walkway between the box was some eight feet wide and about 435 feet long, presumably ending in an open field, where Shaw's Cove and Wye River could be seen in the distance. On either flank of this axial promenade there were, conjecturally, nine elongated rectangles of box—panels, as it were—filled with grass, vegetables, flowers, and fruit trees. The right-hand, or northern, box rectangles were each approximately 150 feet long and varied from 38' to 60' in width. On the other side, to the South, the rectangles were probably at first about 150 feet long, like their counterparts across the axis, but were cut down to about 120 feet when the mansion (1784) was constructed. Still, for the time being, that probability remains in the realm of theory.

Originally a cross-axis walk must have centered on the original *Orangerie* or *Greenhouse* (Fig. 45), which from the evidence of the brickwork may have been coeval with the original *Wye House* (*c.* 1660). Possibly there was still another edifice at the south end of the cross-axis to balance the original *Orangerie* structure, thereby making dependencies to the early domicile, because they would have been part of the formal composition of the dwelling complex. The fact that traces of foundation walls were discovered a few years ago north of the western wing of the mansion (1784) might tend to substan-

Fig. 37. The *Wye House* garden from the air, in winter (top), and in summer (bottom). The Ha-ha wall, boxwood parterres, Orangerie, Captain's House, dairy, and loom house are discernible. Hollyday.

tiate the theory of a 17th-century dependency in that location—but that, too, remains an hypothesis.

Probably four box rectangles were removed when the Bowling Green was put in about the time of the mansion (1784). Interestingly enough, there is evidence of a wide horseshoe-shaped walk or driveway laid out through the 17th-century box rectangles in front of the original *Wye House* (*c.* 1660). To facilitate good drainage the ground was raised four or six inches, not only for that thoroughfare but also for some boxwood paths which have now disappeared, shown dotted on the garden plan (End Papers).

Furthermore there is one portion of the 17th-century garden upon which we have not yet touched: we have named it the "crooked knot garden," lying to the east of the *Orangerie,* where the long, slender rectangles of box were abandoned for more squarish forms in order to fill a particular area. The knot parterres had vegetables and flowers; and one section—that having a terminal boxwood scroll or curl—contained an herb garden.

To give the reader some idea of the task of measuring an old garden as large as the one at "Wye House," in the "crooked knot garden" the writer had to crawl on all fours with a steel tape down the long boxwood walks which had grown together after decades of disuse. But neither snakes nor black widows were found.

At the rear of the *Orangerie* is the 17th-century graveyard plot (Fig. 40B), known as one of the oldest and possibly one of the best preserved family cemeteries in this country. Capt. James Strong's tomb, the oldest, is dated January 8, 1684. Upon or among these graves—of Henrietta Maria Lloyd, Admiral Franklin Buchanan, General Charles Winder, Gov. Edward Lloyd, and others—many children of the Lloyd family have seated themselves while they were having their school lessons.

Bearing some relationship to the original *Wye House* (*c.* 1660) is the boxwood walk, eight feet wide, starting almost in front of the site of that domicile and running parallel to it a goodly distance southward; then turning at right-angles, as may be traced out on the garden plan. In the 17th century this walk may have continued on southward to reach as far as the now-vanished *Men's Necessary House,* the age of which is unknown.

One of the old boundary stones preserved at "Wye House" stands in the garden and reads: "The 1st of Roberts -nfancy, & 4th of Tanners Help." Those were evidently properties on the great plantation.

In the future more aspects of the 17th-century garden may come to light; meanwhile we know already a great deal about what may be considered America's greatest garden of that century.

THE LATE 18TH-CENTURY GARDEN

At "Wye House" a later landscape design was superimposed upon its predecessor of the 17th century. The two air views (Fig. 37) give some idea of how the grounds look today in winter and summer. The Edward Lloyd married to the Tayloe girl from Virginia was the one who by 1784 had completed the basis of the existing mansion. Fortunately the "Old Plat" (Fig. 35) shows several more features of interest. To begin with, it is a moot question whether the present principal driveway leading in from the Top Road Gate to the mansion was there in the 17th century. This drive is lined with oak and beech trees, replacing earlier ancient lindens, and was probably made when the mansion was built.

In an earlier day it was a country custom to have your fields numbered. Therefore, when you pass through the Top Road Gate, you drive between fields numbers "15" and "16." Then you reach the site of another gateway, no longer existing, to enter an almond-shaped or oval road to a forecourt directly in front of the mansion. The left-hand side of the almond was called the "Quality Turn," because that was the side habitually used by the family and their guests; the other side had a service branch road extending down to the Long Green.

The great wrought-iron gates of the "Wye House" were made in 1929 in Italy, and probably replaced early wooden gates. We find that a Ha-ha—meaning a sunken wall, similar to the one in front of George Washington's *Mt. Vernon*—and two of the great iron gates intersect the oval driveway and mark the outer edge of the forecourt (End Papers). On the mansion side of the Ha-ha there was once a "Horse Gravel Path," and, in turn, it connected with a curved boxwood footway,[4] already described, leading past the brick *Men's Necessary* to the site of the original *Wye House* (*c.* 1660).

Directly in front of the great house was a small, formal circle around a sundial, and also mounting blocks and hitching posts, as the garden plan shows. Of these features only the sundial remains.

The approach to this mansion is a sophisticated 18th-century scheme, the result of centuries of English landscape designing.

Bounding the forecourt on the west side is a raised walk, the "Terrace," running beside a ditch, where members of the family used to walk on summer evenings to take the air and, perhaps on a moonlight night, to watch Wye River and Bennett's Point in the distance. There is a little grassy ramp used to ascend the "Terrace" by those coming from the mansion.

On the "Old Plat" the dots may indicate that originally there was an arbor on the "Terrace." At any rate the elevated walkway must have served in the capacity of a mount, a feature of many extensive 18th-century gardens.

Especially interesting in the "Old Plat" is the sketch of the mansion in three separate parts: main block and two flanking dependencies—with no colonnades or curtains. It therefore seems patent that, when first built, the great house had separate balancing pavilions; in fact the bonding and divisions in the brickwork of the foundations prove the correctness of that statement.

The most unusual feature of the late 18th-century garden layout is that the axis of the mansion is not at right angles to the axis of the 17th-century garden, but is askew by several degrees. To put the matter another way, if you stand inside the front doorway of the great house and look down the center of the building, through the verandah or back porch door, and along the

Bowling Green, your eyes follow a line intersecting not the middle of the *Orangerie* but the right-hand brick window pier of the west wing.

Likewise, the "Old Plat," although pretty crudely drawn, shows the *Orangerie* definitely off the center of the axis of the mansion. In that drawing the reader may also note the graveyard enclosure behind the *Orangerie* and the fence in back of that area which separated the Common, with its ancient barn, from what purports to be field number 19. At a further distance was what was called "The Landing Field," which extended all the way westward to Shaw's Cove.[5]

At Mill Point, beyond field number 14, there once whirled around the sails of a "post" windmill—one sitting on a giant wooden column. Beside it stood a miller's house. Both structures are the victims of Old Man Time.

The raised "Terrace"—and the continuation of it, called the "Lovers' Walk," along the ditch which bounds the garden on the west—was laid out roughly parallel to the axis of the great house and obviously was contemporary with it. That ditch probably cut off portions of the two western boxwood rectangles, which have been shown dotted on the garden plan.

At the end of the "Lovers' Walk" the arbor and the brick wall between the box garden and the graveyard were constructed in the first half of the 19th century. That graveyard wall, although charmingly copied in the garden of the Talbot Historical building in Easton, comes pretty close to 1850—if the brickwork in the wall is any indication of its true age. At the same time, the very small boxwood parterres which once had a rose arbor belonging to them, located near the end of the west wing of the mansion, are of 19th-century date.

Curiously enough, the Bowling Green, made as an allée for the mansion, was found by our measurements to be three feet wider at the great house end than at the *Orangerie*. This causes an optical illusion making the *Greenhouse* seem further away than it actually is. But if the Bowling Green had 17th-century box parterres in it which had been taken up, then the tapering was an accident, not planned.

The periodical, *Landscape Architecture*,[6] illustrated a plan of the "Wye House" garden showing the mansion (1784) laid out at right angles to the 17th-century garden axis, when actually it is definitely askew. Moreover, Mr. Alden Hopkins, a landscape architect of Williamsburg, Virginia, sketchily drew a garden scheme of "Wye House" which was published in *Old Gardens of Talbot County, Maryland*,[7] showing the off-axis arrangement of the late 18th-century garden, but not the present boxwood rectangles in their correct shape and number, nor the western boundary ditch in its slanted position and other features.

A row of outhouses (Fig. 39), presumably all of the late 18th century, stands along a brick-paved courtyard off the east end of the mansion. They are the *Dairy* (Fig. 38A) with its portico on two sides supported by stubby, square posts; the *Loom House* (Fig. 39), now a garage; the *Wood Shed,* which has been slightly moved and changed into a dog kennel; and the *Smoke House* (Fig. 49A) with its tower. Two of the outbuildings repeat the

Fig. 38. A(top). The brick-paved service court on the east end of *Wye House* mansion is lined with a porticoed dairy (right) and loom house. Author, 1955. B(bottom right). The *Captain's House* (HABS, Peterson, *c.* 1936). C(bottom left). The old Quarters. Author, 1963.

classic gable motif of the great house. Mr. Charles E. Peterson, of Philadelphia, has described the *Smoke House* as "a remarkable frame building with an architectural false front fitting into the monumental layout of the grounds."

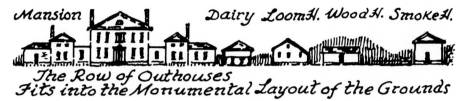

Figure 39

Behind the *Loom House* once stood the wooden *Ladies' Necessary House,* with its three seats and two little window apertures, located high up on the walls for privacy.

THE BIG HOUSE—A TALE OF CHANGES

As has been shown, the mansion of 1784 (Fig. 40A) was completed at first with separate balancing pavilions by the Edward Lloyd (1744-96) who married Elizabeth Tayloe of Virginia. A fine portrait[8] (Fig. 5A) done in 1771 by Charles Willson Peale, hanging in the Henry Francis du Pont Winterthur Museum, near Wilmington, Delaware, represents that Edward Lloyd, his wife Elizabeth, and their daughter Anne. In the upper left-hand corner of the portrait (Fig. 5B) was not the original *Wye House* (*c.* 1660) as the Museum claimed in the *Baltimore Sun* account of 1964. Others have attempted to identify the edifice in the painting with the rear of the *Chase-Lloyd House* (1769-1774) in Annapolis, which the Edward Lloyd who married Elizabeth Tayloe had purchased in 1771 from Samuel Chase, a Signer of the Declaration of Independence, and upon which the architect, William Buckland, had worked, beginning the same year.

The house in the painting illustrates an upper Palladian window with keystone and balustrade—features which show on the back of the *Chase-Lloyd House;* but what about the roof balustrade with urns, the colonnades, and the flanking pavilions with quoins or blocks at the corners? That Annapolis house has none of them.

Under the limitation of the data so far discovered, the writer has held the theory that Peale may have painted the rear of the *Chase-Lloyd House* according to the way it was planned, but not built. The third storey of the Annapolis pile does not show in the painting.

No one today knows exactly when the *Wye House* mansion was commenced; nevertheless there is a record that a home of the Lloyd family at "Wye" was ransacked on March 13, 1781—possibly indicating that the above great house had then been completed. Future research will probably disclose the years of construction. It seems that "1782-84" would be the probable dates of building, because it would take at least two years to construct such a large

Fig. 40. A(top). By 1784 *Wye House* mansion had been constructed in the Late Georgian Style with central block and separate pavilion dependencies. Author, 1964. B(bottom). Graveyard and Orangerie. Author, 1963.

edifice; the American Revolutionary War had ended in 1781; and it would be natural for an owner to have a plat, like the "Old Plat" of 1784, drawn up within a reasonable time after the completion of the mansion and laying out of the grounds.

The general design of the mansion is, as we have seen, a central block, two storeys and loft high, with a fairly steep pediment, plus identical pavilions with squashed second floors and equally steep pediments. The style is Late Georgian in transition to Early Federal. The outside walls are brick nogged (Fig. 36C). The corners of the main block have broad unfluted colossal pilasters—flat columns rising more than one storey,—and the corners of the pavilions, narrow colossal pilasters, in order to suggest subsidiarity. The central pediment has been criticized as being too steep; on the other hand, the large lunette window helps to fill the space. Small modillions embellish the main cornices as well as the pediments of the central block. It has been thought that Architect Robert Key may have been the designer of the mansion; at least, it is on record that he made some alterations to the building.[9]

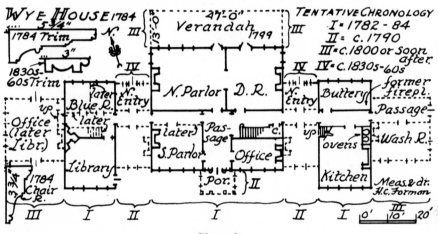

Figure 41

The great house conforms to a custom, often followed after the Revolutionary War, of placing the gables to face the street, the square, or the approach driveway, like the *Semple House* (c. 1781) in Williamsburg, Virginia; and *Indian Purchase* (c. 1790), *Finlay Farm* or *Kennersley* (c. 1800), and the *Teackle Mansion* (1801), on the Eastern Shore of Maryland. At that time men were becoming "temple" conscious and gradually came to consider their buildings in terms of Greek or Roman pedimented temple fronts.

The plan of the first floor (Fig. 41) of the *Wye House* mansion shows the evolving and changing conditions of the place, as far as present research has disclosed. The second stage of development, Phase II, evidently soon after 1784, illustrated the construction of connecting curtains to the pavilions. Each curtain contained a small room and a narrow passageway and had a pent roof—a roof of one slope, as at *Mt. Vernon* in Virginia—which could not be seen from the front of the great house. The front porch (Fig. 42A) in the Palladian manner is probably contemporary with the curtains.

Fig. 42. A(top). At *Wye House* mansion the porches were additions: the front porch was built in good Palladian style soon after 1784. B(bottom). The rear is Federal, with capitals resembling palm leaves. Author, 1955.

The third stage, Phase III, evidently included the end additions—a spacious plantation office on the west, and a wash room and brick passage on the east. It is significant that the adding of plantation office and the corresponding opposite wing made the mansion of seven-part composition—a rare example in the United States. The only Georgian residence of more parts in its design known to the writer is *White Hall,* near Annapolis, which was planned for nine parts. The total length of *Wye House* mansion is 151 feet; the width of its central block, including porches and stone steps, is half that dimension.

The long piazza or verandah (Fig. 42B) on the north or garden side, facing the *Orangerie,* has jalousies on the sides, fluted columns, delicate palm-leaf capitals, and slender balustrade on the roof. It dates from 1799, is in the Early Federal or Republican style of architecture, and may be represented in the third stage of the great house.

Still another step, Phase IV, is illustrated by the little north entries to the curtains which have door trims of Greek Revival style, with a date around 1830-60. The roofs of the curtains were extended out to cover these entries, but pitched at a lower angle, thereby giving the effect of a flattened half-gambrel.

In 1914 the two pavilions had their roofs raised about a foot and a half[10] to give more bedchamber space and to lift the lie-on-your-stomach windows above the floor level. There have been other changes in the mansion; still, the five Phases which have been outlined give a fair idea of development.

Arriving before the mansion, the discerning visitor may note the front doorway with its classical features, now entirely shaded by the front porch addition. The door itself has a fan transom window under a broken pediment—a feature shown on the "Old Plat" of 1784 (Fig. 35)—and side windows. Also flanking the door are engaged Doric columns, and on the outside of the windows, Doric pilasters. The same main entrance motif, but in the Ionic Order, obtains at the *Chase-Lloyd House.* The trained eye, moreover, may notice that the front porch repeats in a general way the columnar and pilastered front doorway, although the arch was placed not on the front of the porch, but on the sides.

Upon entering, the visitor finds himself in a passageway with a handsome stair (Fig. 44A) beyond an elliptical arch, in an "ell." The bottoms of the steps have S-shaped undercuts or soffits, like those of *Myrtle Grove* in Talbot County, *Shirley* in Virginia, and several other Georgian homes. On either side of the passage are two doorways: the one on the right leads to a small room with mural painting in the over-mantel which was used as an office, but now serves as a writing-room; the other on the left leads to the South Parlor, which does duty as a reception room and den for the family. The South Parlor was larger before a narrow corridor running to the western portion of the abode was taken from it.

At the end of the passage lies the great room of the mansion—known as the North Parlor (Fig. 43, bottom)—the real pièce de résistance of the place. Some of the furnishings, like the tall gilded mirrors, the French chairs, and

Fig. 43. Late Georgian rooms at *Wye House* (1784) include the Dining Room (top) with paneled and dog-eared overmantel, and (bottom) the North Parlor with four large windows with blue damask curtains. Hollyday.

the crystal girandoles, were ordered in 1780 and have always been in that room. The London bills of lading for them are extant.

Both the North Parlor and the adjoining Dining Room (Fig. 43, top) have some "jib" windows, meaning that their lower parts comprise double-doors—a feature enhancing the *Hammond-Harwood House* in Annapolis, and other buildings.

From the North Parlor the Dining Room, hung with elegant portraits, is entered by means of an elliptical-arched opening with doors which slide back into the wall—a later construction, because marks of a division in the floor boards of the Dining Room show that the North Parlor took up part of that room.

In the "ell" of the front passage is a doorway which used to give upon an outdoor space opposite the Kitchen pavilion. At this mansion, as in many early English homesteads, the food prepared in the kitchen was carried out-of-doors to the place where it was eaten. In the Kitchen were two Dutch ovens and a large fireplace—now all filled up to make room for modern requirements. It is interesting that the north end of the Kitchen pavilion appears at first to have had a porch with an outside fireplace in the location of the present Storage or Locker Pantry—actually a buttery. The Pantry still preserves a sloping wood floor from the old "Porch" days. At one time a brick hearth was discovered under the southeast corner of that floor.

The opposite pavilion, the one on the west, held the old Library with outside door and cater-cornered fireplace, and the old Blue Room,[11] situated to the north—also with diagonal fireplace. It is possible that in the early days there was a small porch off the old Blue Room to balance that one off the Kitchen, already described. Probably in the alterations of 1914, the old Blue Room was carved up into a small chamber, bath, and corridor with staircase. Upstairs in both pavilions are small "knock-head" bedchambers.

The large plantation office built onto the western pavilion formerly had no access to that pavilion, and the way up to the space above the office and the pavilion was by winding staircase—no longer existing—located next to the office fireplace.

The interior of the mansion has several similarities to the *Chase-Lloyd House*, notably the door escutcheons, drop handles, and flat friezes with curved ends over some inner doors on the first floor. Some of the drop handles are of silver.

In the front passage there is a desk bearing the label and date (1796) of John Shaw of Annapolis. In the little writing-room is a secretary (Fig. 26) made by him but lacking his label. This article of furniture is believed to have been made for the house because the wall behind it was found to have had only one coat of paint.

A windowpane has been preserved revealing the scratched signatures of Edward Lloyd and his wife, Elizabeth (Tayloe) Lloyd, under the date of 1792.

Actually *Wye House* mansion forms an unusual kind of museum. It is not a building with rooms spruced up and painted to the nth degree and artificially

Fig. 44. A(top). The stairway at *Wye House* (1784) is in an ell off the main passage and has S-shaped undercut steps. Hollyday. B(bottom). Sheep graze in front of the Ha-ha wall on a summer day. Author, 1964.

Fig. 45. The *Wye House* Orangerie was called the Greenhouse in the 18th century, and has within it the nucleus of an earlier structure. In spring the orange tree tubs are moved out of doors (bottom). Note rustic wood keystones and limestone quoins. Author, 1963.

filled with furnishings collected from all over the country—a condition prevailing in our present museums—but a unique museum, *in use* over the centuries, showing how one Eastern Shore family lived through several generations. The charm of the great house is its naturalness and its authenticity, preserved after many changes.

DISCOVERIES AT THE *ORANGERIE*

Most monumental of the outbuildings at "Wye House" is what was called the *Greenhouse* in the 18th century, but which today we term the *Orangery* or *Orangerie* (Fig. 45), a brick edifice mostly covered with stucco. It is still used to house a few orange trees. There is in existence a Lloyd letter from the early 1800s praising the medicinal benefits of one lemon from this *Orangerie* carried some eighteen miles by horseback. We who can easily procure oranges or lemons from the nearest supermarket or corner grocery store find it difficult to imagine that just one lemon would be worth an eighteen-mile horseback ride and a long letter about that fruit's healing properties.[12]

The drawings (Fig. 46) of 1963 made for the Historic American Buildings Survey in the Library of Congress illustrate the south front of the *Orangerie,* eighty-five and a half feet long, with a central portion flanked by lower wings. In the middle are four large windows 12'-8" tall—more than twice the height of a man—and square-headed. The flanking windows are lower and round-headed. Nonetheless, all the openings on the downstairs front are real 18th-century picture windows and let in a tremendous amount of southern sun.

The flooring of the main part of the *Orangerie* is of bricks, eight inches square, two inches thick and laid on sand—although much of the paving has disappeared. Behind the central room is what may be called the North Shed room, with an earth floor and a fireplace—perhaps to keep a gardener warm.

Upstairs in the central section is the Billiard Room. There was an 18th-century billiard table of inlaid woodwork in this room until about 1960. An antiques dealer was shown that table, with the end result that it is now handsomely situated in the Winterthur Museum in Delaware, where lots of people see it. It could be argued that it would have been more appropriate to have repaired the billiard table and kept it at "Wye House," the natural and becoming setting for one of the two known early American tables of that kind. In this case Maryland has lost another of her great treasures—along with the *Genesar* mansion and paneling.

The drawings made for the aforementioned Survey correct some mistakes made in 1930 by the delineator, Kenneth Clark, in *The Monograph Series.*[13] On the side, Marylanders may be surprised by Mr. Clark's statement that "Edward Lloyd the first came to the Colony of Virginia from Wales in 1623 and was burgess in the Virginia Assembly which met at 'Preston-on-Patuxent.' " In describing the *Orangerie,* he revealed that "One will receive a great surprise to discover that what seems to be four flat arches with wedge-shaped voussoirs [blocks] over the four large [central] windows are nothing more than wood lintels [beams], hewn and carved to carry out the treatment of the stone rustication [deep joints] below." On the contrary the wedge-shaped voussoirs are not lintels, but only carved and painted boards to imitate ashlar stonework. The boards have been applied against, and cover up, the actual stone beams of the windows. The trick of carving boards to imitate stones was used elsewhere in Talbot County and in this country.

The present 18th-century *Orangerie* has within it an earlier, "T"-shaped structure, which may be of the period of the original *Wye House* (*c.* 1660). It was found that the bricks and brick courses in the *Captain's House,* a part of the early homestead, are similar in size to those in the rear wall of the original portion of the *Orangerie*.[14] Of course that discovery is only an indication, not a proof, of being contemporary.

In short, the first *Greenhouse* was the same shape as the present one, except that the wings were each only six-and-a-quarter feet long instead of the present twenty-six, and there was no East Shed room (Plan, Fig. 48). In the little west wing the early staircase, now gone, rose up to the Billiard Room, and the access to that room was by a tiny doorway, 5'-2" high, which has been securely bricked in and plastered.

It is probable that the rustication or deep grooving of the blocks on the front of the *Orangerie* was done in the Palladian fashion when the building was remodelled and enlarged, presumably at the time of the mansion (1784) and the late-18th-century garden. The early *Greenhouse* may have been plain brick, without stucco, and with downstairs sash of smaller size—to match somewhat the width of the Billiard Room sash above. One of the two chimney flues appears to have always been connected with the North Shed room fire-place, and the other with the heating-duct system.

On a cold day in December, 1962, the writer discovered the remnants of a wood-burning furnace (Fig. 63, top right) under a dirt floor and debris in a dark corner of the East Shed room. After digging through loose brickbats and a 1½-foot-deep bed of packed ashes containing five live snakes, we learned that the furnace was built up of brick without mortar, and is about 7'-6" long and 16" wide. From the iron grate, made of closely-set wrought-iron bars, to the crude, triangular-shaped vault, the inside height is about three feet—although most of the vaulting had collapsed long ago. Beneath the grate was found the ash pit—the grey ashes of the consistency of soft cement and the home of a vigorous six-foot black snake.

The wrought-iron furnace door, of which a detail has been presented, had permanently rusted in an open position after the last fire went out decades ago.

The wall ducts were found by accident while the writer was examining a small, dark hole at the back of the North Shed room fireplace. There was barely space to poke hands and arms into the black recess in order to use a flashlight and hold a mirror at the proper angle to see down a tunnel, which was found to be some 10" wide and 17" high, extending in murky darkness probably the whole length of the edifice. That moment was probably the first time in over 100 years that anyone had looked down that wall duct; it was an eerie experience.

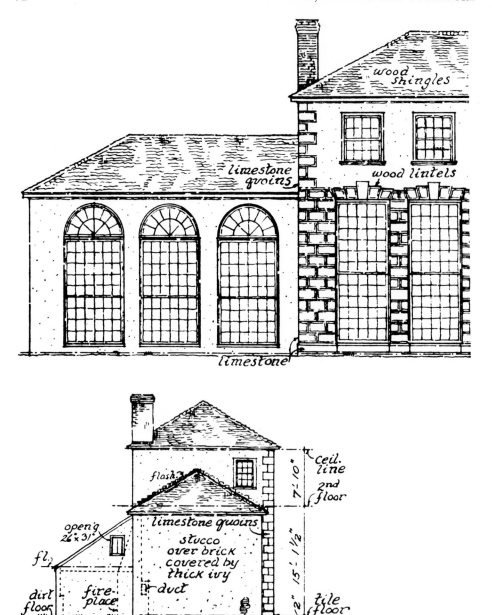

Fig. 46. *Wye House* Orangerie, South Elevation. (Bottom left) West Side; (Bottom right) East Side.

The isometric drawing of the heating arrangement (Fig. 47) shows the *Orangerie* by dotted lines. The hot air rose up an incline at the rear of the sunken furnace, then passed along a floor duct[15] in two sides of the building, and finally in wall benches in the remaining two sides. As the ducts extend outward from the furnace, they become larger in order to create suction for the hot air. The wall duct apparently rises from the floor four times to higher levels by means of ramps, one of which was identified upon the occasion of first looking through the hole at the back of the fireplace.

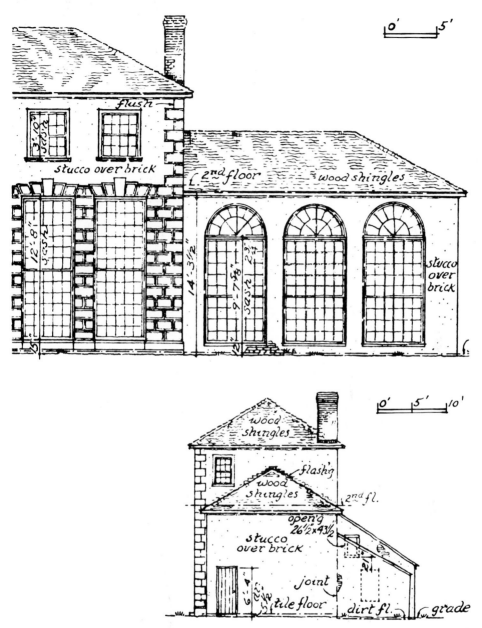

These drawings are a part of the HABS measured drawings of the Orangerie by Forman, 1962.

Inasmuch as the heating duct runs through the early section of the *Orangerie,* as well as through the long wing additions, the edifice was evidently used as a greenhouse for fruit trees long before the mansion (1784) was built; consequently Elizabeth (Tayloe) Lloyd, wife of the builder of that great house, was not responsible for the idea of the *Orangerie* at "Wye House," even though her girlhood home, *Mt. Airy* in Virginia, had one.

According to our present theory, what has been labelled the "pass-through" (Fig. 48), a capacious hole 29″ wide and 3′ high through the thick back wall

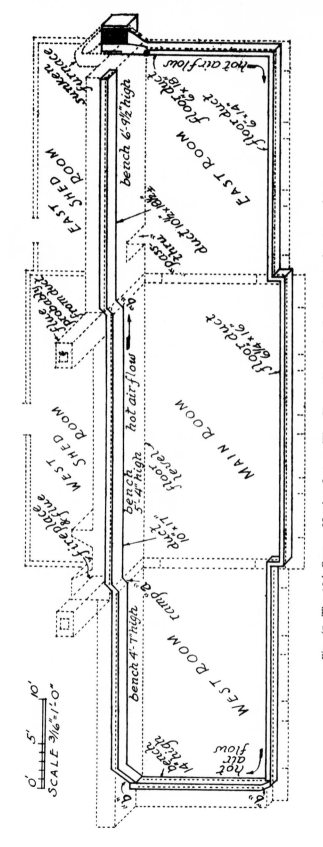

Fig. 47. The 18th-Century Heating System, *Wye House* Orangerie. An isometric drawing, subject to further discoveries, made for HABS by Forman after excavations in 1962. Existing wood-burning furnace and hot air ducts are shown by solid lines; "a": known brick ramp seen from inside duct; "b": probably brick ramps.

and under the duct of the eastern stubby wing of the early *Orangerie,* may well have been an access tunnel from outside for supplying wood logs and kindling for the early furnace, hitherto undiscovered. There is an old wooden door still in place on the outer face of this tunnel. The later furnace, already described, was placed outside the wall, and partly under it, in the long wing addition on the East. At a later time the East Shed room was erected over the later furnace.

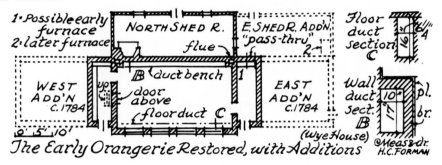

Figure 48

In December, 1962, the mystery, then perhaps a century old, about how the fruit trees were heated in cold weather was solved and the method exactly traced out on paper.

The plaster basecoat (Fig. 249, center right) of the original *Orangerie,* upstairs and down, was discovered to consist of a thick coat of hard clay, roughly scratched in lozenge patterns in order to receive the white plaster finish. That kind of undercoat is rare in this country, but was used in Guilford, Connecticut, and elsewhere.

Remains of early orangeries exist at *Eyre Hall,* Virginia, and *Hampton,* Baltimore County, Maryland, in addition to those at *Mt. Airy,* the Tayloe home.

SMOKE HOUSE OR MARIONETTE THEATRE?

The most intriguing outbuilding on "Wye House" is the *Smoke House.* Its tower with pedimented gables makes it a unique smoke house in this nation. There is no other like it.

The restoration drawings of it (Fig. 50) are based largely on our sheets of 1962 for the Historic American Buildings Survey which show the structure as it then existed—even to the felt on the roofs and the tin on the walls. The interior is mostly blackened from smoke, and remains of a meat rack are in the tower. The thirty-five hours we spent inside that outhouse studying construction details were necessary to make a careful record of a building which had been turned into a meat house after having served some other purpose. One does not discover everything the first hour. Several visits are necessary to record and interpret the details.

Fig. 49. The outbuildings at *Wye House* help to give a picture of how a large 18th-century plantation in Maryland was operated. A(top). The Smoke House has a tower with pediment. Author, 1963. B(center). The old Corn House before destruction. HABS. C(bottom). The grass allée to west of Orangerie. HABS.

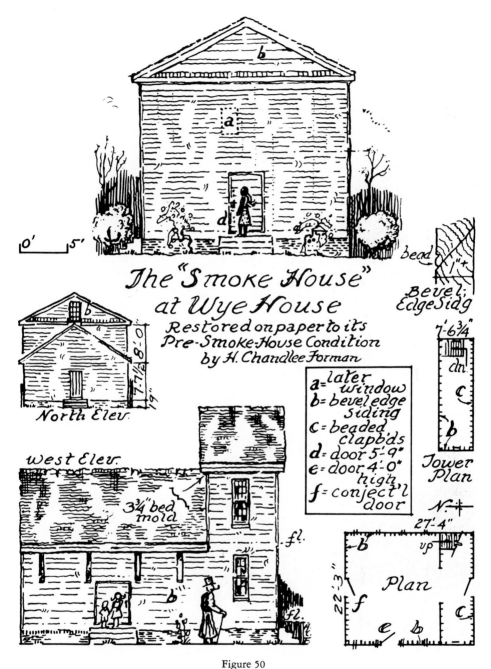

The "Smoke House" at Wye House

Restored on paper to its Pre-Smoke-House Condition by H. Chandlee Forman

bead 1"

Bevel; Edge Sidg

a = later window
b = bevel edge siding
c = beaded clapb'ds
d = door 5'-9"
e = door 4'-0" high
f = conject'l door

North Elev.

West Elev.

3¾" bed mold

Tower Plan

Plan

Figure 50

There used to be a stepladder or very steep stairs leading up to the tower floor, but unfortunately the ladder and the floor planking have totally vanished. Not only that, the upstairs is pitch black because all the windows have been boarded solidly across, so that one has to be a kind of blind acrobat to move about in the tower, a flashlight in one hand, notebook, pencil, and ruler in the other. A dark second floor with no floor boards is exciting to negotiate.

Fig. 51(top). *Oak Lawn* was erected in 1783 in the Late Georgian Style by Benjamin Sylvester
    with a brick, round-arched arcade leading to the Kitchen House. Johnston, 1930s.
Fig. 52(bottom). The *Old Wilson House* (*c.* 1800). Author, 1965.

Perhaps the most important single discovery was downstairs, where seven feet back from the front wall of the *Smoke House* there was once a partition, proven by mortise holes in a cross-beam overhead; the partition did not extend the full width of the outhouse, but was open for seven feet immeditaely opposite the front door. Why was there a gap in that wall except for a seven-foot-wide proscenium for a stage? Why is the front door itself only five feet, nine inches tall and the blocked-up former door on the west side only *four* feet high, except that the building was intended to be used by children? Was not the tower built to roll up stage flats? Perhaps this uniquely shaped smoke house was at first a children's marionette theatre.

One of the puzzling things about the construction is that the studding is set close together, as in antique gaols. In a theatre there would have been no need for studs of that kind. The small four-and-a-quarter-inch-wide louvres on the long sides of the outhouse may have held inside shutters or casements, because the rebates or grooves for them are still there. The iron bar down the middle of each louvre may have been set in later to protect the hanging hams.

When this meat house was remodelled, evidently the wood flooring upstairs and down was removed and a brick floor laid on the ground. Tiny auger holes for ventilation were punched in the lower gable of the north façade. Also at some later date all the windows except the louvres were boarded over with bevel-edge siding (See detail, Fig. 50) to match the existing boards. At one time some of the framework apparently became unsteady, because inside the north wall of the tower there are two areas between studs which have been strengthened with brick nogging; the same situation obtains around the inside of all the louvres.

Another curious feature about the *Smoke House* is that on the west side of the tower the sash, now gone, were of different widths and heights—the upper being three inches wider and four inches taller than the lower. The window on the east side of the tower, also boarded up, matches that opposite; and the one on the north—actually inside the rear pediment—was even wider than any of the others. There may have been a garret floor in the tower; nevertheless traces of it have gone. The pediments, with their original bevel-edge siding boards, have their bottom members capped with shingles to throw off rainwater.

The front door, sagging on long T-hinges, is battened with horizontal beaded boards outside and vertical within. There are two pairs of keyholes, yet the two great rim locks have already disappeared.

It has been related how the great 17th-century garden at "Wye House" had a late-18th-century garden superimposed upon it; how that going plantation included a village of outbuildings; how the unusual seven-part mansion of 1784 is the result of a chronicle of changes; and how the *Orangerie* and *Smoke House* have some unique features recently discovered.

Fig. 53. A rustic Chinese-Chippendale stair railing and carved elliptical arch in the front passageway of *Oak Lawn*, an Eastern Shore plantation. Johnston, 1930s.

One little-known event in which the owner of "Wye House" participated was the uniting of the shipbuilders and the planters of Talbot County in defense of St. Michaels in August, 1813. Most people think that only the shipbuilders with their naval batteries and their log boom across St. Michaels harbor figured in the first British surprise attack. On the contrary, the naval engagement formed but a part of the affair. Major Edward Lloyd, of *Wye House*, commanded five troops of cavalry in the force of General Perry Benson: a troop each from St. Michaels, Easton, Trappe, Centreville, and Preston, which were present in the battle. Those cavalries kept vedettes—mounted sentinels stationed well ahead—on many points of land to watch British ship movements and continued outflanking threats to the strong body of enemy marines who marched from Claiborne in the second attack.

Those horsemen, led by the master of "Wye House," along with two regiments of local infantry and the Easton Artillery Company, stopped the advancing marines a mile northwest of the town of St. Michaels.

In conclusion, the reader is reminded that in *Tidewater Maryland Architecture and Gardens* it was told how "Uncle Ned" as a child was won at cards at *Wye House* by the owner of *Perry Hall*; and how the Edward Lloyd who married Elizabeth Tayloe owned a large deer park close by his mansion at "Wye Town" or "Doncaster."

Catalpa-Hidden *Spencer Hall*—Detective's Paradise

Obscured by great trees and dense thickets, *Spencer Hall* stands forlorn in the middle of farm lands on the western side of Eastern Neck Island, a part of Kent County. The house is located near the coastal bench mark called "Spencer" on the maps.

The farm was owned by Alexander Harris and Spencer Harris, supposedly from 1860 to 1890. The Martenet Map of Kent County shows the dwelling as belonging to Alexander Harris. From *Spencer Hall* Spencer Harris was believed to have departed in 1890 to find gold in Alaska.[16]

A look at the existing cottage, gone to seed, suggests that later owners and tenants have likewise left to look for their kinds of gold. The thicket of poplar and catalpa, from which the gambrel roof is slightly visible (Fig. 55A), is slowly taking over the premises; the next stage will be trees growing up through the floors.

The mural painting on a wood panel depicting New Yarmouth shipping on Grey's Inn Creek, Kent County, now owned by the Maryland Historical Society, is said to have originally been in an over-mantel in *Spencer Hall* before having been removed to *Wickcliffe,* a neighboring homestead on Eastern Neck Island which has been destroyed.

The early portion of *Spencer Hall* is roughly 24' by 20'-6" (Fig. 54), with a gambrel roof and one brick gable-end punched by four small windows in the Eastern Shore manner. Although the Great Hall has a medieval flavor in its exposed post-and-beam construction, the architecture of that section of the

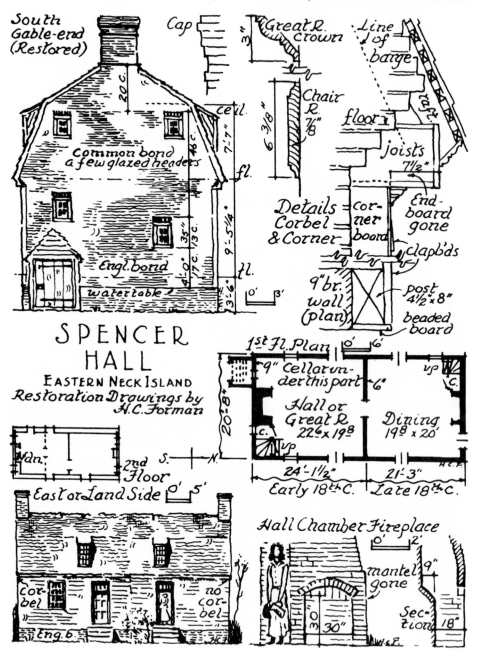

Figure 54

domicile indicates a date in the first half of the 18th century—probably 1725–1730. While the lower portion of the gable-end is laid in English bond, the upper relapses into common bond.[17] The cornices with classical profiles are terminated by brick corbels, in this case a hangover-medieval style feature.

It is unusual to find the brick gable-end to be only one brick thick; much of its strength comes from the great chimney acting as a buttress. There is a watertable of one step. The end-boards to the cornices are flush with the brick gable wall and therefore snugly cut to fit around the brick corbelling.

Fig. 55. A(top). Reputed to have been owned in 1860 by Alexander and Spencer Harris, *Spencer Hall* slowly gives up the ghost. B(bottom left). Remains of Great Hall staircase (A,B) and mantel (C). Author, 1958. C(bottom right). View taken from northeast showing later additions. Author, 1957.

Fig. 56(top). The boxwood garden at *Ratcliffe Manor* (1749) appears to have an allée with loops at the upper end. Hollyday.

Fig. 57(bottom left). "No one cares for me. I am the *Luke Parsons* or *George Cottingham House* and a 'goner.'" Author, 1954.

Fig. 58(bottom right). Detail of Chinese-Chippendale rail in *Daffin House*. Johnston, 1930s.

But they were probably not always that way, because the first floor joists projecting seven and a half inches were exposed to view; thus, there was no box cornice originally, nor was there a double-cyma bed molding as at present (details, Fig. 54).

The later gambrel wing, probably commenced in the second half of the 18th century, about doubled the length of the original cottage, but omitted the brick corbels. Next, a Victorian one-storey appendage was stuck on to the end of the wing, and its board-and-batten construction shows in various photographs of the ancient bower.

The Great Room, now a shambles, has a broken-down winding staircase (Fig. 55B) beside the great fireplace and remains of a pilastered mantel (C), which appears to have fallen or have been removed from the room. Beneath the Great Room is a cellar with arched fireplace-foundation span measuring nearly six feet—indicating that the present Great Room fireplace used to be much larger. Details of the crown molding and chair rail are shown in the drawing. It is obvious that such millwork was put over the exposed post construction, the pegs of which are still visible. The plaster with hair in it for a binder is attached to hand-riven oak laths.

The Dining Room is in the gambrel addition and has a fireplace of five-foot span, as well as a tiny and steep "break-your-neck" staircase with closet under it. It is interesting that in the woodwork area over the closet door there are two wood panels which disappear into the plaster ceiling, the moldings having been cut off by the plaster line.

On the right of the Dining Room fireplace is a door through the north brick gable-end which led to the original kitchen or kitchen outhouse, now gone.

Upstairs the Hall Chamber, or room over the Great Room, has a transverse partition down its center. This was a divider of vertical boards, which may or may not have been original. Even so, we have shown it dotted on the second floor plan. The small bedchamber fireplace, its arch fallen and mantel stripped, is also illustrated.

Altogether, there is enough remaining preserved at old *Spencer Hall* to make it an archaeological detective's paradise.

The Ashby Plat—What a Slice of History

One of the important topographical surveys of Maryland is now so faded and torn that it is almost illegible, but by careful scrutiny with a large magnifying glass, the writer has made a fairly complete copy (Fig. 59), with other landmarks added to make the plat more complete. This is the ancient Ashby Plat, some twenty-three inches in length, with its lines done in dark ink except for the red and green lines used for the compass diagram. On the Plat the surveyor wrote: "Plotted by a Scale of 50 p[erches] in an Inch." In recent years there has also been inscribed: "Content: 800 acres. The 23 June 1687–8."

This last notation referred to the grant known as "Ashby," a tract of 800

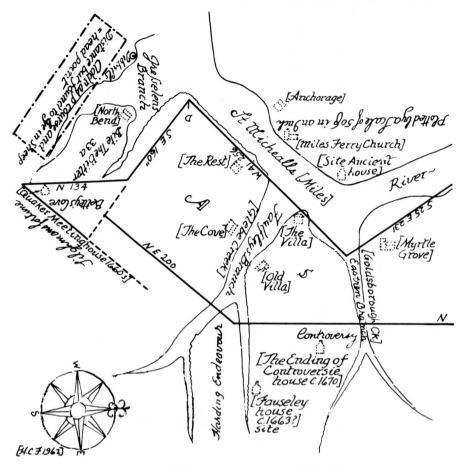

Fig. 59. Left side of copy of ancient Ashby Plat.

acres surveyed for Roger Grosse on July 20, 1663, and laid out on the east side of the upper St. Michaels—later the Michaels or Miles—River in Talbot County. "Ashby" extended from a point on Miles River above the existing *Ashby* mansion (1854) three and a quarter miles down the river, past the present Miles River Bridge, to the site of the *Betty's Cove Friends' Meeting-house* on the south side of the *North Bend* house. In the 17th century that whole area was "Ashby."[18]

As the "Ashby Plat" is traced out in further detail, we find that many persons who lived within or near its boundaries made together a sizeable slice of the early history of the Free State. Further, those individuals had their share in making the United States come to world power.

Let us begin at the south or downriver end of the "Ashby" survey. *Betty's Cove Meetinghouse*, called *Michael's River Meetinghouse*, is considered the first church or building of public worship erected in Talbot County—although it is possible that two Quaker meetinghouses near Wittman and Bozman may have been earlier.[19] *Betty's Cove* was constructed about 1665—about the time the "Ashby" grant was made to Roger Grosse—and was abandoned in 1693.[20]

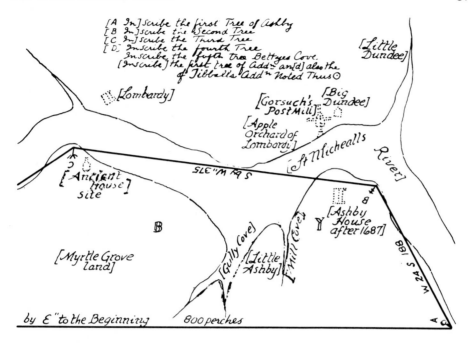

Right side of copy of Ashby Plat.

It was located beside a small creek of the Miles River called Gresselen's Branch which bounds the "North Bend" property on the northwest. On our drawing this meetinghouse has been dotted, at a point where old brickbats are strewn across a field.

George Fox, the founder of the Religious Society of Friends in England and one of the world's great men, attended a series of meetings held at *Betty's Cove* in 1672 and 1673. At the time he wrote home to Britain that the meetinghouse was not large enough to hold the attenders, even though it had been enlarged shortly before then, and that there were many people present who had received the "truth" with gladness.

In 1676, one hundred years before the American Revolution, *Betty's Cove Meetinghouse* contained a library of books called the first public library in Talbot County and perhaps in the State.[21] As a subscription for buying books, a group of wealthy Talbot Quakers, including John Dickinson, John Edmondson, Howell Powell, and Ralph Fishbourne, raised 4,750 pounds of tobacco. These volumes were later added to by George Fox before his death in 1690. Also there was a schoolhouse connected with *Betty's Cove* and a teacher employed by the Friends—one of the earliest schools in the South. No one today knows how the old meetinghouse appeared, but there were clapboards on the gable-ends and loft, the customary sliding "windows" in the center partition, and pales around the burial plot.

To the west of the "Betty's Cove" land, which, as has been shown, was a part of the "Ashby" tract, bounded in part by the "fifth tree," was a parcel of thirty-three acres with the curious name of "Bite the Biter," marking the location on Miles River of *North Bend*, a mid-19th century mansion, with a small wing, believed 18th-century in date.[22] *North Bend* has mistakenly been known first, as the birthplace of William Henry Harrison, who was born at *Berkeley* in Virginia, and second, as being on part of "Tilghman's Fortune" or the "Manor of Tilghman's Fortune." The Ashby Plat plainly shows that the "Ashby" tract stood between "Bite the Biter"—the estate surrounding the *North Bend* house—and "Tilghman's Fortune."

While the writer was in the process of making drawn records of the picturesque 18th-century *North Bend* barn (Fig. 60), a building contractor came along and junked it. The high roof on the front of that outhouse made a four-foot overhang, and there was a little door on the second floor at the rear for taking in hay. A wood rim-lock of 18th-century type adorned a downstairs batten door, and it probably was thrown on the scrap heap. The entire framework of the barn was oak, pegged together. The drawing shows board-and-batten siding, but the original covering could have been clapboards, ship-lap, or bevel-edge boards.

Delving a little further into the "Bite the Biter" parcel, we find that it contained thirty-three acres granted in 1743 to one Elizabeth Davis, and that in 1802 it was resurveyed, along with some adjoining pieces of land, for a gentleman with the strange name of Abednego Botfield, under the new name of "Botfield's Addition."[23] Then, in 1847, James Dixon (1810-90) purchased the whole tract, containing 119¼ acres, except for one acre for a school; and that plantation, under the name of "North Bend," remained in the Dixon family for over 100 years, until the 1950s, when it was subdivided into building lots.

In 1833 James Dixon married Mary Ann Bartlett,[24] both of whom are pictured in the Dixon Silhouette of 1841 (Fig. 61). Their son, Robert Bartlett Dixon (1834–1921), was State Senator and president of the Easton National Bank. When married, Robert and his bride, Sarah Amanda (Amos) Dixon, came in 1861 to *North Bend* to live, and their son, the second James Dixon (b. 1873), later became president of that same bank.

Since about 1680 that line of Dixons has been identified with their county. They descend from a brother of the William Dixon, glover (d. 1708), who married Elizabeth, widow of the distinguished Wenlocke Christison.

Immediately to the east of "Betty's Cove" was the back part of "Tilghman's Fortune," which fronted upon the Tred Avon River. On that rear part a building, evidently not an old house, still stands and is known as *Shipshead Farm*, formerly belonging to members of the Price and Hayward families. There was once in the area of that farm the "Free School for Poor Children," established

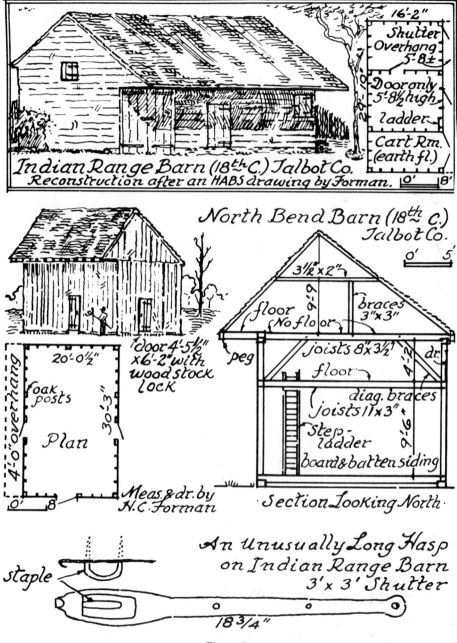

Indian Range Barn (18th C.) Talbot Co.
Reconstruction after an HABS drawing by Forman.

16'-2"
Shutter Overhang 5'-8±
Door only 5'-8½ high
ladder
Cart Rm. (earth fl.)
0'   8'

North Bend Barn (18th C.) Talbot Co.
0'   5'

Plan
20'-0½"
4'-0 overhang
oak posts
30'-3"
0'   8'
door 4'-5½" x6'-2" with wood stock lock

3½"x2"
floor (No floor)
9'-0"
braces 3"x3"
joists 8"x3½"
floor
peg
4'-2"
dr.
diag. braces
joists 11"x3"
Step-ladder
board & batten siding
9'-6"

Section Looking North.

Meas. & dr. by N.C. Forman

staple

An unusually Long Hasp on Indian Range Barn 3'x 3' Shutter
18 3/4"

Figure 60

in 1723 to give instruction "in the knowledge and practises of the Christian religion as professed and taught in the Church of England." Organizer of the school was Thomas Bacon, rector of St. Peter's Parish in Talbot County.[25]

Across the little creek, Gresselen's Branch, from "Bite the Biter" and "Betty's Cove" lay "Tiball's Addition" to the "Ashby" tract; but according to the writing on the Ashby Plat was "found to lye in Sheephead point," and consequently, like "Tilghman's Fortune," was not part of that great tract. "Shipshead Point," by the way, must lie on the present Doncaster neck of land.

Fig. 61(top). The Dixon Silhouette, made in 1841 by Augst. Edouard, was owned by James Dixon (I). After his death in 1890 it remained hanging for 70 years at *North Bend*, Talbot County. Left to right: James Dixon (1810–90), Robert Bartlett Dixon (1834–1921), Elizabeth Shannahan Bartlett (1783–1852), Elizabeth Dixon (1836–43), James Dixon, Jr. (1839–69), Mary Ann Bartlett Dixon (1809–55), wife of James Dixon (I). Courtesy, Robert Dixon Bartlett.

Fig. 62(bottom). *Boxley,* a Blackiston brick cottage. Author, 1957.

Next upriver from "Betty's Cove" and *North Bend* stood a pile called *The Rest*, burned in 1863, then rebuilt, and torn down in the 1960s. This was the home of Admiral Frank Buchanan (1800–74), commander of the *Virginia* in the first Civil War encounter of naval ironclads in 1862. In 1835 he married the third daughter of Governor Edward Lloyd, and in 1847 purchased *The Rest*. In 1853 he accompanied Commodore O. H. Perry on his famous visit to Japan, and in 1855 became the first superintendent of the U.S. Naval Academy.

Across the Miles River from *The Rest*, and therefore not on the "Ashby" tract, is *The Anchorage*, the central portion of which is reputed to have been built as early as 1720 and the flanking wings before 1894. The plantation at one time had a windmill, of which there is a drawing extant. Among the owners were Edward Lloyd, Governor of Maryland, his daughter Sarah, and son-in-law Commander Charles Lowndes, who served in the Federal Navy during the Civil War. But the prize story about *The Anchorage* is that in the 1760s the Rev. John Gordon, a minister of the Episcopal Church, lived there and used it as a rectory. Immediately after holy services were held in his nearby church, the congregations enjoyed horseraces on a track located behind it.

The Miles River Ferry, which dated almost from the beginning of Talbot County, stood between *The Anchorage* and the place where the *Miles River Ferry Church* is situated. This last fane was not the Rev. Gordon's, which was burned, but is a Gothic Revival stone church of 1835–38, now quaintly crumbling. It also served as the Maryland Nautical Academy Chapel. As for the Ferry, now replaced by a bridge, it is recorded that in 1677 one Daniel Walker, original owner of "The Anchorage" tract, kept "ferriage over [Miles] river with [dugout] canoine." The point now called "Ferrybridge" is reputed to be the site of an old house, but nothing is known of its appearance.

Above *The Rest*, on the same side of the river, is what the Ashby Plat called the "Fauseley Branch," now Glebe Creek, on the upper left bank of which stood, possibly as early as 1663, *Fauseley*, the birthplace of Col. Tench Tilghman (1744–86), Maryland's "Paul Revere," and his brother, the Hon. William Tilghman. Their homestead was on a property of the same name comprising 250 acres granted in 1663 to Roger Grosse, who also owned the "Ashby" tract.

Tench Tilghman was Aid-de-Camp to George Washington. His fame rests largely on his safely bearing a letter from General Washington to the president of the Continental Congress in Philadelphia with news of Lord Cornwallis' surrender on October 19, 1781, at Yorktown, Virginia. By horseback and ferry, Tilghman travelled to Philadelphia in four days, arriving on October 23—an astounding rate of speed for those days. The trip was so rough that on the way he caught a fever, and his sailboat went aground on Tangier Island in Chesapeake Bay, causing him to lose a whole night. For lack of wind it took him a full day to sail from Annapolis to Rock Hall in Kent County, where there still remained a 100-mile horseback ride to the Quaker City. The last night he had to ride up to various farmhouses, beat his sword on the doors,

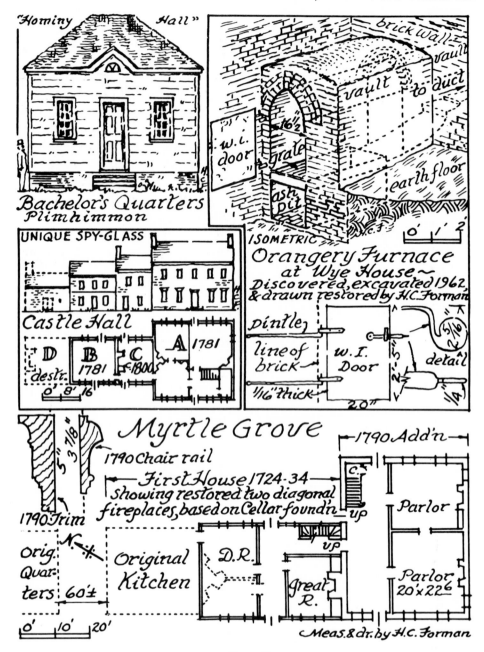

Figure 63

and shout that Cornwallis was taken and he needed a fresh steed for the Congress.

The father of Tench and William was James Tilghman, who had been Attorney General of Pennsylvania and held a Master of Arts degree from the University of Pennsylvania. He became Chief Justice of the Pennsylvania Supreme Court and was known for his pure life.

Down Glebe Creek from *Fauseley* and well within the limits of the "Ashby" tract stands a "neo-telescope" building called the *Old Villa* to distinguish it from the new *Villa,* which once stood next door. The *Old Villa* has been dubbed erroneously "The Ending of Controversie," which was another, distinct property, as the Ashby Plat shows.

At the confluence of Miles River and Glebe Creek stood *The Villa,* a wooden Italianate pleasure palace constructed in 1853–54 by "Lottery-King" Richard France and razed in the 1950s. Its gardens were laid out by James McFarlane Spence, a noted landscapist of the Edinburgh Botanical Gardens. In 1875 *The Villa* was purchased by Simon Brady 3rd, who incidentally never did hide there the notorious Tammany Hall "Boss," William Tweed. In 1879 the place became the Maryland Nautical Academy cadet training school.

The Villa had a coal generating plant with two furnaces for making illuminating gas; a tank-room with lead-lined tanks for water storage connected with rain gutters from the eaves; a marble fountain in the front hallway; and the summerhouse was graced by a dome forty feet high.

Adjacent to the "Ashby" tract and situated back from the "Eastern Branch," now Goldsborough Creek, was the cottage, *The Ending of Controversie,* built about 1670 by Wenlocke Christison (d. 1679), but not named for him, as the Maryland Tercentenary Commission in their bulletin and some other persons and authorities would have us believe. "The Ending of Controversie" had been granted in 1667 to Francis Armstrong, a planter, and owner of the "Betty's Cove" parcel. In 1670 Dr. Peter Sharp, a physician, and his wife, of the "Clifts," Calvert County, gave "The Ending of Controversie," 150 acres, as a present to Wenlocke Christison, who by that time, no doubt, had had enough of being buffeted around in Old and New England on account of his religion.[26]

Christison, according to Oswald Tilghman in his *History of Talbot County,* was a "notable personage." In *Tidewater Maryland Architecture and Gardens*[27] this writer noted that "Wenlocke Christison . . . was no less a pioneer of religious freedom in this country than John Bowne of New York, or Samuel Gorton of Rhode Island," and he was Maryland's foremost pioneer of religious freedom. The early Lords Baltimore, who based their policies on religious toleration, were not actually Marylanders, but gentlemen of England, and did not have to undergo the persecution and sufferings which Christison endured in Boston and other parts of New England. Among his punishments for being a Quaker were twenty-seven cruel stripes applied to his bare body during a Plymouth winter, banishment from Boston on pain of death should he return, and a long whipping while tied to a wagon pulled through Roxbury, Dedham, and Boston.

Christison's home, *The Ending of Controversie,* destroyed in the 1940s in spite of the writer's efforts to have it saved, was a hall-and-parlor combination, with brick gable-ends and long sides of "palisaded" board-and-batten siding.

After Christison's death his widow Elizabeth, *née* Elizabeth Gary, married William Dixon, the glover, who then lived in *The Ending of Controversie* homestead. Dixon, owner of other plantations including "Dixon's Lott" and "Cumwhitton," is remembered as the first person in Talbot County to free his

Fig. 64. (Top) *Myrtle Grove,* the brick portion of which was completed in 1790, was once the home of the "Chesterfield" of Maryland. Author, 1959. (Bottom) The Early Georgian paneling in the Parlor of the frame wing. Hollyday.

Fig. 65. A(top). The modern, left portion of *Myrtle Grove* replaces the ancient kitchen. Author, 1955. B(bottom). A "neo-telescope," *Myrtle Grove* has a frame middle section built 1724-34 by Robert Goldsborough. Note the ten-panel front door. Author, 1934.

slaves—long before other Quakers did the same thing. What is believed to be the first Friends' meeting recorded in that county was held January 24, 1676, at Wenlocke Christison's home—one hundred years before the American Revolutionary War.

In later years Christison's property became known as "Woodstock," with an early 19th-century brick house, used from the early 1870s as the home of Dr. Samuel Alexander Harrison.

On the north side of Goldsborough Creek and within the "Ashby" tract stands venerable *Myrtle Grove* (Fig. 64), a neo-telescope mansion where the kitchen wing has been approximately replaced on its original site. Still standing, the middle part (Fig. 65) was erected between 1724 and 1734 in the

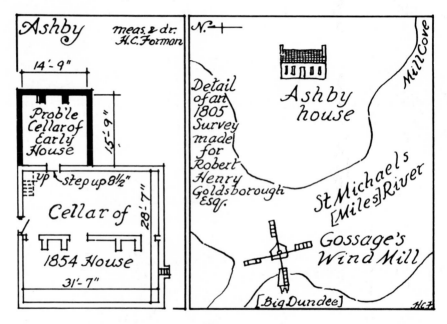

Figure 66

Early Georgian style by Robert Goldsborough 2nd; the large brick addition, in the shape of a narrow city house of Late Georgian style, was completed in 1790 by his son, Robert Goldsborough, third of the name, according to a diary of the painter, Charles Willson Peale.

The great house is enriched by a stairway (Fig. 68A) undercut with "S"-curves and by two reception rooms (Fig. 67A) with plaster friezes of rinceaux and cornucopias. On the left-hand side of an "ell" passageway in the middle section of the house there were originally two small rooms which had back-to-back catercornered fireplaces, in place of the present large dining room (Fig. 63, bottom). Remnants of the foundations of those fireplaces may still be seen in the cellar. Near the mansion stands one of the oldest law offices in the country (Fig. 67B). On the river side is a box garden (Fig. 68B), much of which has now disappeared.

Fig. 67. A(top).   The East Parlor in the 1790 part of *Myrtle Grove,* Talbot County, has a broad plaster frieze with cornucopias in circles. Hollyday. B(bottom). The law office at *Myrtle Grove.* Author, 1965.

Fig. 68. A(top). The *Myrtle Grove* stairway of 1790 is undercut with S-curves, like that at *Wye House* (1784). Author, 1934. B(bottom). In the box garden at *Myrtle Grove,* the late Mr. and Mrs. Robert Goldsborough Henry; and the late Mrs. James Dixon of *North Bend,* which stands next to the old "Ashby" tract. Author, 1955.

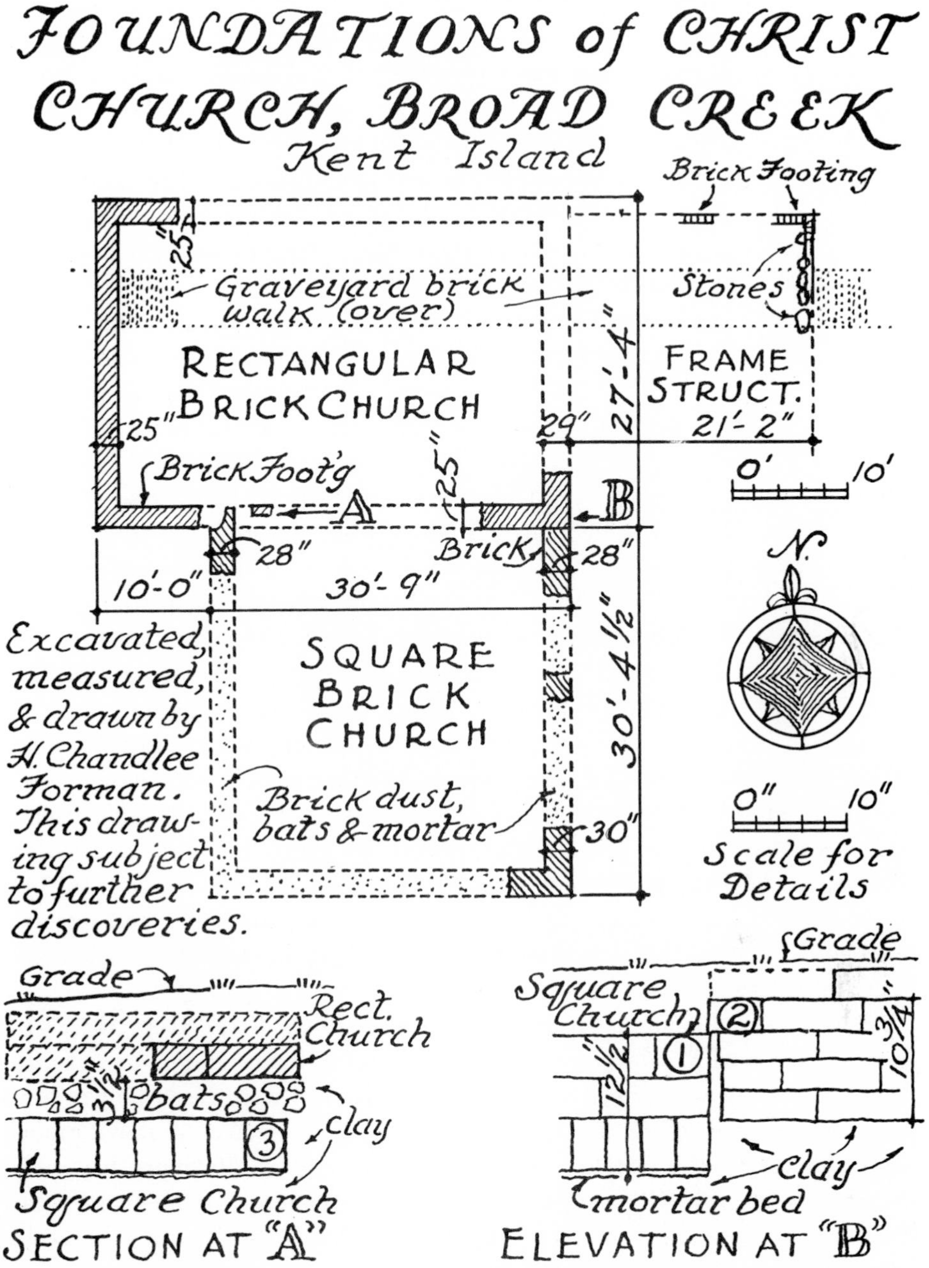

FOUNDATIONS of CHRIST CHURCH, BROAD CREEK
Kent Island

Brick Footing

Graveyard brick walk (over)

Stones

RECTANGULAR BRICK CHURCH

FRAME STRUCT. 21'-2"

25"

25"

29"

27'-4"

Brick Foot'g

A

B

28"

Brick

28"

10'-0"

30'-9"

30'-4½"

Excavated, measured, & drawn by H. Chandlee Forman. This drawing subject to further discoveries.

SQUARE BRICK CHURCH

Brick dust, bats & mortar

30"

0'   10'

N.

0"   10"

Scale for Details

Grade

Rect. Church

bats

clay

3

Square Church

SECTION AT "A"

Grade

Square Church

2

1

12½

10¾

clay

mortar bed

ELEVATION AT "B"

Fig. 69. Excavation plan and details of the *Broad Creek Church* site in 1959. What the writer calls the "Square Brick Church" was probably in existence as early as 1692. Because of its dimensions the "Rectangular Brick Church" was probably the 1712 church on the site, and the "Frame Structure," the latest of all. Footing details show brick no. 2 of "Rectangular Brick Church" overlaps no. 1 of earlier "Square Brick Church." No. 3 is N.W. corner of "Square Brick Church."

The family at *Myrtle Grove* was long a leader in both county and province. Robert Goldsborough 2nd (1704–77), "a high-minded gentleman, esteemed for probity and intelligence," was Burgess in the General Assembly, a Justice, Deputy Commissary General for his county, and Register of Wills. He had five brothers, of whom Nicholas was Deputy Collector of the Port of Oxford in 1731; Charles was a distinguished attorney and known as "The Councillor"; William was Judge of the Admiralty, Judge of the Provincial Court, and member of the Governor's Council; John was a Burgess in the General Assembly; and Howes served as Clerk of Dorchester County.

At the beginning of the 19th century "the Chesterfield of Maryland," a man widely known for his courtly manners, lived at *Myrtle Grove*. The original Chesterfield was an 18th-century English earl, distinguished for his polite deportment and his "Letters" to his son depicting correct conduct. The Free State "Chesterfield" was Robert Henry Goldsborough (1779–1836), who became in 1817 U. S. Senator from Maryland. In 1805 he had a resurvey made of the "Ashby" tract with his house, *Myrtle Grove*, pictured in a crude fashion by a surveyor. Of interest is that the resurvey presents in red and green ink what purports to be the original *Ashby House* (1690 or soon after), which once stood where the existing *Ashby* mansion of 1854 (Fig. 66) is now located. The older homestead was a typical storey-and-loft cottage with flush chimney at each end and a front door flanked by pairs of windows. A careful check of the basement of the 1854 mansion indicates that the east wing was earlier and probably contains the cellar of the original *Ashby House*.

This original dwelling was built by the first Robert Goldsborough after he had received a deed for "Ashby" on October 16, 1690. He is reputed to have lived there fifty-six years, during which time he brought home (1697) a bride, Elizabeth Greenberry. After his death in 1746, the homestead remained untenanted, because his son Robert, 2nd, to whom he willed it, had already built the frame portions of *Myrtle Grove*.[28]

On the "Big Dundee" property, across the Miles River from the *Ashby House*, there used to stand a post mill which was called *Gossage's* or *Gorsuch's Wind Mill* (Fig. 66, right). Such timbered structures were easily blown down, and that one has been no exception, since there is no trace of it above ground. "Big Dundee," not a part of the "Ashby" tract, was a Stichbury place—but the old habitation has likewise gone. Further, opposite to *Myrtle Grove* across the same river, stands *Lombardy*, also outside the "Ashby" tract; the largest part of the mansion was destroyed by fire, leaving a brick wing, still extant and now part of a fine, large modern home. In 1776 *Lombardy* is believed to have been erected and named by a Frenchman, and in more recent years has belonged to members of the Cowgill and Bartlett families.[29]

The people of the "Ashby" lands, and of the surrounding tracts, helped form the history of Maryland, and in a small way, the history of the nation.

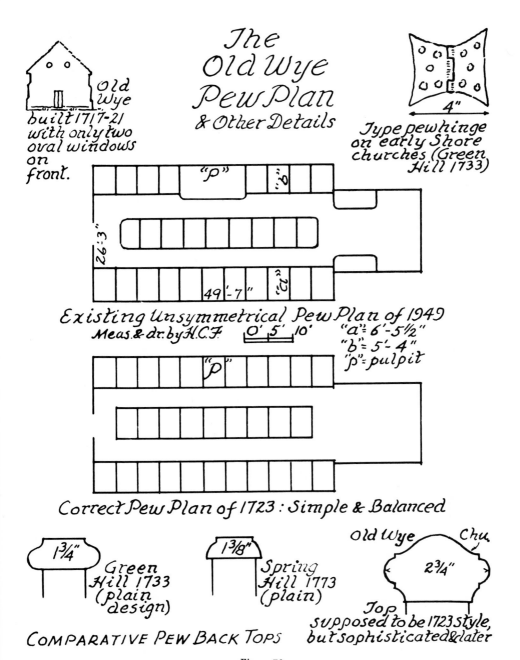

The Old Wye Pew Plan & Other Details

Old Wye built 1717-21 with only two oval windows on front.

Type pew hinge on early Shore churches (Green Hill 1733)

4"

26:3"

"P"

"b"

"a"

49'-7"

Existing Unsymmetrical Pew Plan of 1949
Meas. & dr. by H.C.F.   0' 5' 10'

"a"= 6'-5½"
"b"= 5'- 4"
"p"= pulpit

"P"

Correct Pew Plan of 1723: Simple & Balanced

1¾"
Green Hill 1733 (plain design)

1⅜"
Spring Hill 1773 (plain)

Old Wye Chu.
2¾"
Top supposed to be 1723 style, but sophisticated & later

COMPARATIVE PEW BACK TOPS

Figure 70

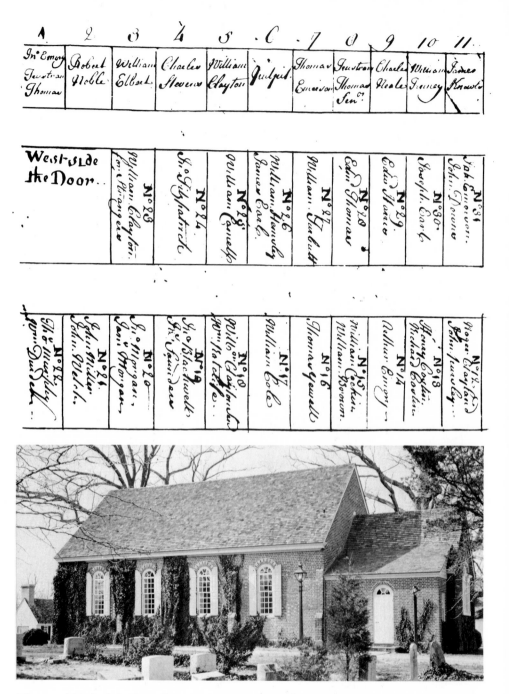

Fig. 71. A(top). A Register of the Pews of *Old Wye Church* (*St. Luke's Chapel*) ordered to be recorded by the Vestry, September 17, 1723. Courtesy, St. Paul's Church, Centreville. B(bottom). *Old Wye Church* was renovated and partially restored in 1949. Author, 1958. See page 145.

A Buffer-Zone Lot, "Randall's Prospect"

When William Penn seized a generous slice of Maryland below the 40th parallel, he set up a small settlement or "principality" against Marylanders which was called the Nottingham Lots. These lots were laid out in May, 1702, and covered 18,000 acres. The thirty-seven divisions each averaged less than 500 acres.

In that year, 1702, one Randall Janney took up 1,000 acres, comprising two lots, numbers 15 and 34, of the Nottingham Lots. The former lot appears to have been named "Randall's Prospect" and was close to the *Brick Meetinghouse*, sometimes spoken of as the *East Nottingham Meetinghouse*.

In 1706 Randall Janney sold to Abel Cottey (d. 1711), a well-to-do citizen of Philadelphia, and *first* of the "six Quaker clockmakers,"[30] the above-mentioned Lot number 15, then named "Randall's Prospect," which became the first Chandlee plantation-house in Maryland. Cottey also acquired from Janney the other Lot, number 34.

It was Sarah Cottey, daughter of Abel Cottey and his wife, Mary, who married on second month [Feb.] 28th, 1710, Benjamin Chandlee, of Philadelphia, son of William Chandlee, of Kilmore, in the County of Kildare, Ireland, who in turn was the son of William Chandlee the Elder, born in 1591 in England. Abel Cottey's widow, Mary, willed in 1713 to her son-in-law Benjamin Chandlee "Randall's Prospect—the Lot whereon we now Live" and "my south Lot of land," which was number 34.

This first Benjamin Chandlee (1685–c. 1745) became the second of the six Quaker clockmakers and established a clockmaking industry at Nottingham which was carried on by his descendants for over 130 years.

On a plat of the Township of Nottingham, according to a survey made of it in the 3rd month, 1702, and copied from the original in 1777, made by Mordecai Churchman, a very crude drawing (Fig. 74, top) of the first Chandlee homestead is portrayed on Lot number 15. Shown is a 2½-storey building with two gable-ends drawn in the same plane, whereas in reality they must have been opposite to each other. That was a surveyor's convention found in other plats and even elsewhere on this one by Churchman.

Moreover, Benjamin Chandlee was one of four Quakers who were granted by the Penns of Pennsylvania forty acres of the Nottingham Lots around the *Brick Meetinghouse* for use of Friends in that area.

The traditional site of the Chandlee clock factory is on "Randall's Prospect," ⅞ mile north of Calvert and a little to the west of Maryland Route 272. Furniture, clocks, and surveying and mathematical instruments were manufactured there. Clocks made at the Chandlee factory sell today for $3,000 or more. One important item fabricated in Winchester, Virginia, was a surveyor's compass made for Lawrence Washington, nephew of George Washington, by Goldsmith Chandlee, fourth of the Quaker clockmakers.

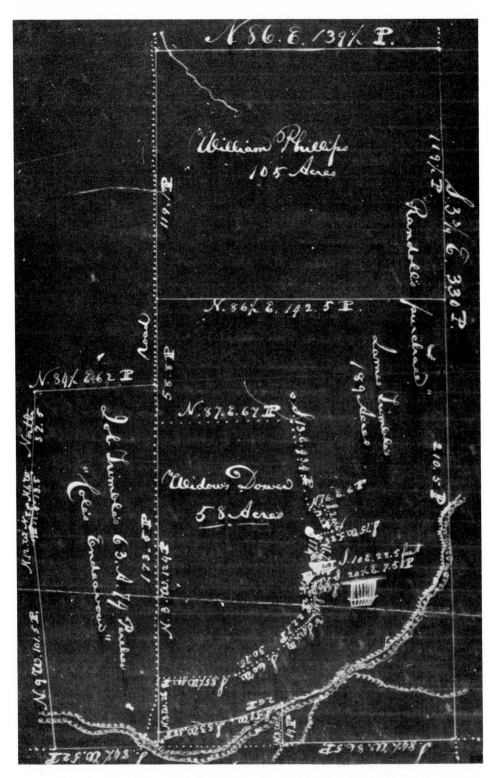

Fig. 72. Plat of 1832 showing *Randall's Prospect,* the Chandlee-Trimble dwelling and two out-houses, upside down, with unusual line of "Widow's Dower" going through house. Hall of Records, Annapolis, Md.

In 1741 Benjamin Chandlee and his wife Sarah sold "Randall's Prospect" to James Trimble and moved to Wilmington, Delaware. Their son, Benjamin Chandlee, Jr. (b. 1723), then moved to the forty-nine-acre commons which Abel Cottey had purchased in 1703—probably adjacent to the *Brick Meeting-house*,—and continued the clockmaking industry, in 1770 forming the firm of Chandlee and Sons. Another brother of Benjamin, Jr., was William Chandlee (b. 1721), of Cecil County, whose son George Chandlee married Deborah Brooke and founded the Sandy Spring, Maryland, branch of the family.

When the Mason and Dixon's line was finally set in 1767, Benjamin Chandlee, Jr., awoke one morning to find himself living in Maryland. The same happened to James Trimble, who had purchased the old Chandlee homestead, *Randall's Prospect*.

Fig. 73. *The Parson Thomas Bane House*, of the Singletons, falls on evil days. Author, 1934.

For some reason Lot number 15 of the Nottingham Lots had its name changed from "Randall's Prospect" to "Randall's Purchase"—at least by the year 1796, when the property was conveyed by William Trimble to another James Trimble and contained 289½ acres.[31] In 1832 when the land was surveyed by Joseph Wilson, "Randall's Purchase" comprised a large tract in three parts: William Phillips had the north end, 105 acres; James Trimble had the south end, 189 acres, except for the 58 acres of the "Widow's Dower"—an irregular slice, laid off for Elizabeth G. Trimble, widow of James Trimble, Sr. (d. 1832), and apparently containing the "western division" of the Trimble dwelling-house. This plat of 1832 is reproduced (Fig. 72) and shows upside down the old stone house, which is still standing—although only a shell of its former self—and illustrates, too, an outhouse and barn or carriage house.

In 1833, when Elizabeth G. Trimble was given the dower right during her lifetime to 58 acres of the "Randall's Prospect" tract, she was allowed, besides the west portion of the dwelling, the use of the corn crib, the "southern division" of the carriage house next to the corn crib, free use of the well for water, and the right to pass and repass through the cellar stairway. In dividing the old residence, she had her property line of the "Widow's Dower" pass through the "Eastern wall of the Western Division" of the house.

The existing stone dwelling on the property was built in two sections (Fig. 77), the smaller being to the East. It is presumed, because of the 1832 plat,

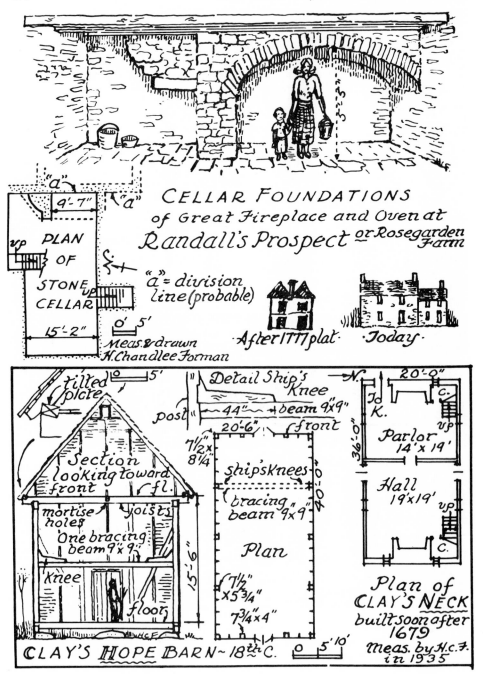

Figure 74

that she lived in the western or larger section of the building. Inasmuch as the Trimble home has been generally stripped of its early details on first and second floors, a cellar diagram (Fig. 74, top) has been made showing at "a" the probable property line.

Randall's Purchase, later *Randall's Prospect*, is now called *Rosegarden Farm*. In the western section there is a stone cellar with foundations for a huge first-storey fireplace and a bake oven, both now gone. Evidently the fire-

Fig. 75(top). *Beaver Neck* is one of the little Eastern Shore brick abodes sometimes encountered far back from the country roads. This house has fine checkerboard bond. Almost all the old paneling has been stripped, but the Parlor fireplace spans six feet. Author, 1932.
Fig. 76(bottom). Gate at *Old Wilson House* is said to be a careful replacement of an earlier one. Author, 1965.

Fig. 77(top). *Randall's Prospect,* now *Rosegarden Farm* and greatly changed, was the Chandlee-Trimble home. The line of the "Widow's Dower" went between the two sections. Author, 1964.
Fig. 78(bottom). *The Great House,* on the plantation of that name, was constructed by the Labadists. The wing may be 17th-century. Author, 1963.

place had formerly a span of almost ten feet and a depth of five feet—one of the largest fireplaces built in the Free State.

The oven was supported by a rounded, corbelled, stone bracket set about three feet above the cellar floor, which was probably paved with flagstones.

The outside cellar stair, four feet wide, where the widow Elizabeth Trimble went up and down freely, still exists. The bottom step of the interior cellar stairway is made of stone, while the other steps are of recent wood construction. But the underside of the first riser of the first floor steps is evidently early in date because the riser board has been bowed in for headroom space.

The Great House of Brothers and Sisters in Christ

For "making the Mapp of this Province," Augustine Herman, of Prague, received on May 11, 1676, the 6,000 acres of "Bohemia," a feudal manor situated on both sides of the Elk River, Cecil County.[32] In 1679 this immigrant welcomed to Maryland two members of the communal type of religious body known as Labadists, Petrus Sluyter and Jasper Dankers, and gave them in 1684 the 3,750-acre "Labadie Tract." The Labadists owned all things in common, ate their meals in silence, and dressed simply.

One of their buildings was called *The Great House*, situated upon the "Great House Plantation," in the grant given by Herman, according to old deeds. Petrus Sluyter was buried in 1722 "after our humble way in the garden of the so-called Great House, where several of my brethren and sisters in Christ repose." His kinsman, Hendrick Sluyter, since 1722 ancestor of all the Bohemia Manor Sluyters, about 1717 constructed a dwelling, which was decayed in 1938. It was situated at the confluence of Bohemia River and Labadie Mill Creek. The Sluyter graveyard stood there until it disappeared through neglect. Likewise the old *Labadie Mill* and the early Episcopal *Church of St. Augustine* on Bohemia Manor both failed to withstand the ravages of time and pilferage. In fact the pews of the church were cut up for kindling wood.

Another founder of the "Labadie Tract" was Petrus, or Peter, Bayard, a Deacon of the old Dutch church in New York. For purposes of meditation and prayer Bayard was at one time a grantee of, and hermit on, Bombay Hook Island, in Delaware. His son, Samuel Bayard, born in 1675, married Elizabeth Sluyter and owned "The Great House Plantation." Samuel's second wife was Susanna Bouchelle, friend of the Reverend George Whitefield.

The Great House (Fig. 78) originally was a small one-storey-and-loft stone dwelling, 29' by 22' in size. Probably a little before 1721 a large two-storey-and-double-loft brick addition, with cellar, was constructed; certainly it was before 1740 when the Reverend Whitefield visited the plantation and gave the name to "Whitefield's Room," the northwest bedchamber.

An iron fire-plate stood in the Parlor at one time. It was three feet wide and four feet high, ornamented with the figures of Jesus and the woman at the well, with the disciples in the background. On it were the words: "C. D.

Fig. 79. (Top) The portion of *White Hall,* a Hopper, Denny, and Brinsfield homestead, having brick gable-end laid up in English bond, appears to have been built in the last quarter of the 17th century. (Bottom) The rear door, some five feet high, is barely tall enough for yesteryear's children. Author.

Anno 1667." Possibly this fire-plate came from the first house, and if so, might have shed some light on the Labadists' date of original construction.

In appearance the larger part of *The Great House* follows the general pattern of Kent County buildings, like *Ringgold's Fortune* or *Bungay Hill*, with chimneys T-shaped in plan and ornamented with brick caps—also with segmental arches over the first floor windows. Curiously enough, the north façade was built of English bond. *Occuli* or bull's-eyes, which light the "peake" room or "supra-attic," occupy the crown of the gables.

In this habitation there is some fine woodwork. The Great Room mantel is an eminent classical example—having a large bolection molding around the opening, with overmantel and shelf above—the whole flanked by fluted Doric pilasters of good proportion and crowned with seven triglyphs. Both stair passage and dining room have corner cupboards of extremely delicate carving.

The upstairs apartments are reached by a broad stairway, and the room at the top of the stairs has a fireplace and thin panelled partition, placed against the stair rail presumably to keep out cold draughts. "Whitefield's Room" has a spacious catercornered fireplace and round-headed glass closet door beside it. The mansion has not only a double attic, but also a double cellar—the lower one for wine.

The elaborate front porch with dentil moldings is one this writer admits having designed in the early 1930s at the request of the owners, who in no sense wanted to restore this old seat. Prior to that time a one-storey porch extended the length of both the front and rear of the main part of the residence. Sawed-off wooden rafters are still visible in the brick walls and show how the original brick bonding had been broken to insert the wood into the walls. The writer calls this type of porch a "farmer's porch," of the 19th century.

The Great House was inherited by James Bayard, son of the above James Bayard, and was sold in 1788 by the second James' son, John Bayard, to Edward Foard. John Bayard (d. 1807) served as mayor of New Brunswick, New Jersey. Bayard Lane in Princeton was named for this family.

Another Pigmy Back Door, at *White Hall*

Anderton and *White Hall*, both located on the Upper Eastern Shore, were obviously designed by the same person. The English-bonded gable-end (Fig. 79) was the earliest portion of *White Hall*, probably dating from the last quarter of the 17th century. Like *Anderton*, the earliest part has the same high front eaves, the catslide roof low to the ground, and the low back door—in this case only 5'-2½" high. As may be seen in the floor plan (Fig. 80), the brick wall, which faces east, has a later wooden dining-room addition against it. At right angles to the dining room is a large kitchen, still preserving its ladder to the loft and connected by a curtain.[33]

The Great Room or Hall is 17' by 23' in size, and a little winding staircase is diagonally opposite the fireplace. A crude box cornice—actually a beaded wall plate and summer beam with a cyma molding at the ceiling level—extends along the two long sides of the room but not on the remaining two sides. Under the catslide roof are two "cells" or "aisles"—a bedroom about nine feet square, with sloping ceiling, and a tiny dining room with miniature, catercornered fireplace, scarcely large enough for a two-foot log.

Originally *White Hall* belonged to members of the Denny family. Richard Denny left by will the property, "Denny's Purchase," bought of Daniel Cox Hopper and Philemon Blake Hopper. In March, 1853, Solomon Brinsfield, who owned a number of slaves, received the conveyance of the 130 acres of "White Hall" from Richard A. Denny, his wife, and his mother.[34] The Hoppers were from Queen Anne's County.

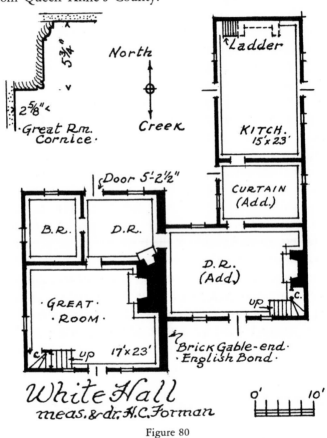

Figure 80

The Spyglass House on the Eastern Shore[35]

One kind of housing which the early settler in the Free State was fond of and developed was the "telescopic" dwelling. For a little over two centuries— from the 1630s through the mid-1800s—he built hundreds of such buildings on both sides of the Chesapeake Bay and over in the Maryland mountains as well. While most of these "telescopes" have disappeared for one reason or another, there is a sufficient number remaining to illustrate the type. It does appear that fate has kindly preserved more of them on the Eastern Shore than in other sections of the State.

This type of building received its name because its external appearance resembled a small telescope, or spyglass, of which the parts could slide one within the other, to be folded up compactly. Of course a structure erected in that fashion was collapsible only in a figurative sense. Still, there must have been times when the owners of such places—their ten or twelve children grown, married, and living elsewhere—wished that they could literally fold up their homes to avoid the care and liability of empty rooms.

The theory of collapsibility brings us to the reason for "telescopes" in the first place: a need for expansion. They were primarily the result of the necessity for larger living quarters for growing families; although it is conceivable that there were some owners who merely wanted a larger house for social éclat and easier entertaining.

Now what exactly was the early settler, living in his space-saving rectangular cottage, to do about room when faced with the birth of his tenth or twelfth child? He could dip heavily into his piggy-bank and his labor pool, and construct a new and larger habitation; nevertheless, that was the most expensive way. He might double the size of his existing home, thereby forming a central passageway running from front to rear, as was done in many early Maryland dwellings. Or the choice could be a wing off one side, thus making his quarters into an "ell" or a "T." At the same time he could follow the simplest method of all: add a large or small wing to his gable-end. Then the telescopic form naturally came into being with the addition of a *second* wing— both sections being placed in line with the original house and rhythmically increasing or decreasing in size.

A true telescopic building is almost invariably a work of art. It did not "just grow" like Topsy. As each part came into being, it was carefully thought out by the owner. An evolutionary expansion in construction cannot be accomplished successfully without a degree of skilful planning and design, and in Maryland "spyglasses," proportion and rhythm count heavily.

You might say that your home is a true or legitimate "telescope" if the roof lines are all approximately the same slope, the outside walls make somewhat regular setbacks, and the sections figuratively could collapse neatly into one another. If your home does not meet these requirements, you have a "neo-telescope."

On the Eastern Shore are several which may be classified as the best and most interesting of the Maryland examples. *King Hayes House* or *Indian Hill*,[36] one of this writer's "discoveries" in the early 1930s, has ten windows in the gable-end facing Wye River and possibly takes the prize for interest because the story of its development as recorded in brick and wood has been puzzling and intriguing.

Various theories as to which part was first, and so on, have been advanced. All in all, it does seem that the smallest section, of the 1720s or '30s, was erected first as an "early-settler" brick cottage of a storey and a half and with handsome Flemish bonding on front and back. Possibly as early as the 1770s a new owner became affluent enough to erect simultaneously the other two brick portions as a unit. Then in Civil War days or thereabouts, someone raised

Fig. 81(top). The *Gibson Wright's Mill House* is a post-Revolutionary brick seat. Author, 1961.
Fig. 82(center). *Tarbutton's Mill House*. Author, 1956.
Fig. 83(bottom left). *Old House on Bats Neck*. Author, 1932.
Fig. 84(bottom right). *Old House on Quaker Neck*. Author, 1932.

the roof of the smallest section, at the same time fortunately retaining some-what the same roof pitch. The omission of one of the wall setbacks makes *King Hayes House* a "neo-telescope" and not a true "spyglass."

An old photograph taken before 1898 shows that the original wood kitchen wing of *Myrtle Grove* (Fig. 65A) was very much like the present kitchen, except that on the approach front the setback in the wall to the middle portion no longer exists. This frame central or "dining room" segment of the mansion was constructed between 1724 and 1734 by Robert Goldsborough, son of a gentleman of the same name who lived at nearby *Ashby* (Fig. 66). Then, in the final stage, a tall, brick structure of the town type, with bull's-eye windows in pedimented gables, was completed by 1790 by Judge Robert Goldsborough. Perhaps *Myrtle Grove* is Maryland's handsomest "neo-telescope."

When Miss Frances B. Johnston was travelling about the South in the early 1930s taking her superb photographic portraits of early buildings, she once complained to this writer that she had never been able to find *Claylands*. Even though this small, frame, telescopic snuggery in Talbot is still hidden away, it deserves to be included among the quaintest examples on the Shore. Its clapboarded walls once had a soft mellow tint of yellow, and a tamarack tree grew beside the miniature kitchen end of the house.

In Caroline County, brick *Castle Hall* (Fig. 63, center left), the two earliest divisions of which were built in 1781 by Thomas H. Hardcastle, used to be the most interesting of the known Eastern Shore "spyglasses" because it had a quadripartite design, of which the four sections diminished regularly in size. Swepson Earle in his *Chesapeake Bay Country* presented a fine picture of *Castle Hall*, taken before an owner got the alteration fever about 1917 and tore down the fourth or latest part, containing the old kitchen, and replaced it with a higher roof and "novelty" wood siding.

The astonishing thing about *Castle Hall* is that about 1800 the owners, re-placing a curtain or colonnade, squeezed a brick house complete in itself be-tween the first and third sections, of 1781 date, as the diagram shows. That was a feat in creating a true, four-part "telescope."

Gibson Wright's Mill and Seat, and Wye Mill

From 1956 through 1962 this writer made studies of the old mill building once belonging to Gibson Wright. Termites had eaten away the wall plates, studs, and rafters. By 1962 the structure had passed the halfway mark to total destruction (Fig. 85). More interesting than the earlier *Wye Mill*, this particular fabric was probably built in the 1780s or '90s, and several changes were made to it in the first part of the 1800s.

Gibson Wright's Mill is a square, one-and-a-half-storey frame building on a brick basement set on the bank of a stream. The cellar door is made up of two leaves, and formerly had a crude sliding bolt on the inside of each leaf. Also there were strap hinges with heart-shaped terminations. On the side toward the modern water wheel, the bond is English; the other sides have common or

Fig. 85. Four views of *Wright's Mill* (1780s or 90s), going, going, . . . gone. Author.
Fig. 86(bottom right). Old cellar shutter of *Wye Mill*. Author, 1964.

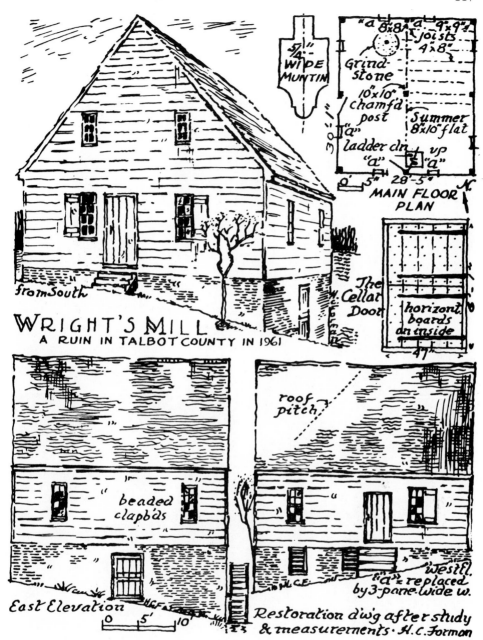

Figure 87

American brickwork. Lighting the cellar are two small windows with horizontal iron bars set on the diagonal, which may or may not be original.

Access from cellar to main floor, and then to upper storey, was by ladders. The interior framework is exposed; there were no laths and plaster. The huge grinding stone of the mill lies on the north end of the main room, along with its chutes for meal and other machinery. The great king post in the center of this room has chamfers and lamb's tongues, and the summer beam is laid flat. On the north the two windows lighting the room were placed up next to the ceiling—possibly to be out of way of the mill wheel.[37]

Fig. 88(top). The *Wye Mill* probably dates back as early as 1760 and was built on or near the site of a 17th-century mill. Author, 1964.

Fig. 89 (bottom). *The Cecil Friends' Meetinghouse* (believed as early as 1694), Kent County, from a print taken from an old glass plate in the writer's family, one of whose members, James Coursey, was in bygone days a founder of the Meeting.

It was not possible to explore the upper storey because of the missing ladder and the state of collapse of the two floors. In fact, as early as 1956, it was extremely dangerous to even walk inside the building, considering the rotten floor and angry bumblebees.

The exterior siding was originally all beaded clapboards, held by rose-headed, wrought-iron nails, which may still be seen on the south gable-end. At a later date, a very early type of siding—bevel-edged boards, exactly one inch thick, with the square pressed nail of the early 19th century—was to replace those clapboards which had deteriorated. Five main floor windows, marked "a" on the floor plan (Fig. 87), were widened from two to three panes. There were probably always board shutters on the windows which could be reached from the ground. The door in the south gable-end was off-center because of the middle post supporting the end of the huge summer beam.

While much of the woodwork of the south side had been modernized, it was possible to trace out from the remaining beaded clapboards and interior framework that there were two small, lie-on-your-stomach windows, in line with the windows below. Some may criticize the fenestrated design of the south gable-end in the reconstruction drawings (Fig. 87), but a mill was not designed in the same way as, for instance, was the *Petit Trianon*, Versailles. A milling structure was strictly functional.

A small detail of *Wright's Mill*—the muntin from the two-pane-wide sash—is unusual; consequently the profile of this muntin has been drawn next to the floor plan.

The brick *Mill House* (Fig. 81), near which Gibson Wright was buried,[38] stands across a small stream from the mill itself, and forms a two-storey-and-attic dwelling with a lower kitchen wing—all of a date around 1790 if the style of house and brickwork is any indication.

In the general area of *Wright's Mill,* where you might come upon it only by chance, stands *Tarbutton's Mill House* (Fig. 82), owned in the first quarter of the 19th century by Robert Bartlett of *Old Bloomfield.* The story of the development of the Tarbutton structure is one of erratic and picturesque additions. The main cornice has been Victorianized. On the place is an old plank-log corn house and a barn with a tilted plate and beaded clapboards. Across the road stood *Tarbutton's Mill,* of which there are few signs remaining.

The grist-operated *Wye Mill* (Fig. 88) is older than, but not as interesting as, *Wright's Mill.* The former is of course not the original "Old Mill" on the tract of that name patented in 1664 by James Scott, nor is it the mill of record about 1680. Those little 17th-century wooden structures, located in low, damp places, with water running past them, were usually short-lived and had to be replaced from time to time. The present *Wye Mill* is probably not over 200 years old and supplied flour for the Continental armies in the Revolutionary War.[39]

In 1959 *Wye Mill* was renovated and repaired by a building contractor without professional direction. As a result it is not surprising to find in the mill a concrete block wall exposed next to the mill wheel; windows with narrow,

Fig. 90(top). The small wing of the mansion, *Cedar Point,* may be the 17th-century home of the noted Quaker, John Edmondson. In 1672 George Fox was a guest there. The chimney is an improvisation. Author, 1937.

Fig. 91(bottom). Historic *Plimhimmon,* the brick part of which is Late Georgian of *c.* 1790–1800, was the home of Col. Tench Tilghman's family after his death. Johnston.

Fig. 92 (top). *West Martingham*, now known simply as *Martingham*, was built on a tract surveyed in 1659 for William Hambleton of Scotland; the Transitional Style of dwelling indicates a date of erection perhaps between 1680 and 1730, although tradition has it built in the 17th century. Johnston, 1930s.

Fig. 93 (bottom). *Clay's Hope* is the birthplace of Samuel Alexander Harrison. Author, 1964.

Fig. 94(top). Never dependencies, these quaint outhouses—milk house, smoke house, and little stable—are good examples of useful ornaments to an Eastern Shore plantation, in this case *West Martingham*. Johnston, 1930s.
Fig. 95(bottom) *East Martingham* nears its end. Author, 1934.

one-inch-wide frames of modern style; contemporary sash and glass; and outside cellar doors with small beaded boards of modern "Victorian" type and
concrete sills.

The visitor there may also note the modern-style, thin, small wood shingles
on the roof; the "builder's" cornices, done without refinement; and the corner
chimney with slanted brick hood on the top—a chimney which does not belong
to the early mill. The bevel-edge siding was replaced, and was put on not
with roseheaded nails, but with cut nails. It was left unpainted. How long
do the owners expect the siding to last without a single coat of paint?

Of particular interest are the old cellar board-shutter (Fig. 86) and the
Dutch-type front door with two leaves, which may pre-date 1800.

All in all the *Wye Mill* is not as old as claimed and in no sense has had a
restoration. While the writer has taken the liberty of criticising the repair
work, it may be stated that architectural criticism is as free as air and is a
healthy thing; anyone can criticize the *Taj Mahal.*

Once Upon a Time, Two *Martinghams*

"Martingham" one of the earliest tracts in Talbot County, contained 200
acres, surveyed July 28, 1659, for William Hambleton, of Scotland. In 1663
he was High Sheriff of Talbot County.

For 200 years this property remained in the possession of members of the
Hambleton family. Born there in 1777, Purser Samuel Hambleton formed a
close friendship with the renowned Commandant, Oliver Hazard Perry, and for
his services in the Battle of Lake Erie (1813) received a Congressional medal.

Within the memory of contemporary man two very old homes stood on this
domain; one still exists, *West Martingham* (Fig. 92), today known simply as
Martingham. The other, *East Martingham* (Fig. 95), was a derelict in 1934
and has been completely swept from the earth.

The *West Martingham* house is believed to have been constructed about
1670, although its *Transitional* floor plan of two rooms deep (Fig. 99, bottom) indicates that it could have been built any time between 1680 and 1730.
The rear, or waterside, view of the dwelling resembles the back façade of the
Third Haven Meetinghouse (1682–84), Easton.

One enters the house by a little square porch with concave plaster ceiling
and octagonal columns, such as were built around 1800. Through the front
door is a narrow passageway only 6'-4" wide. On the left is the Great Room
or Hall; on the right is a dining room, which may have been the Parlor in
the old days. Both rooms reveal heavy, corner-post construction in the outside
walls.

Inasmuch as the passage does not run all the way through to the back, the
little rear "cell" or "aisle" rooms are entered through the Great Room and the
dining room; but it appears that the Great Room orginally included the narrow
passageway as well—the partition between the two areas having been a later
addition.

Fig. 96(top). A Hall-and-Parlor dwelling of 1795 and Victorian vintages, *Locust Grove* on Goldsborough Creek encased a smaller and earlier building. Author, 1955.

Fig. 97(bottom left). House with Jetty, *Cecilton,* owned by William Brown. HABS.

Fig. 98(bottom right). *Willow Grove* or *Turkey Farm,* Kent County, a Jarvis and Hepburn farm. Author, 1934.

Actually, as the floor plan shows, *West Martingham* is of the hall-and-parlor classification, with back "cells" and a curtain-kitchen wing. Moreover, the larger of the two "cells" was probably not part of the original house but attached at an early period.

The curtain area, another addition, was probably a milk room or pantry. In the late 17th century or early 18th — whenever the edifice was constructed— there may have been an actual colonnade over to the kitchen outhouse; or the kitchen may have been entirely a separate structure.

Forty years or so ago, *East Martingham* was a one-and-a-half storey, narrow habitation—gaunt, grey, and desolate. It formed an original block with additions strung out from each end in a row, like a string of sausages. Although the building was plain, there was an unusually-designed front door of six panels. Who knows—the place could have been older than its western counterpart? With due grains of allowance, no one had the time or interest to make a thorough scientific study of it before its destruction. It unfortunately slipped through this writer's fingers, like the *Samuel Adams House* and some others.

The Goldsborough Creek *Locust Grove*

In 1810 William Dixon—whose family had owned *The Ending of Controversie* dwelling most of the time since Christison's widow, Elizabeth Harwood Christison, had married in 1681 a previous William Dixon, called "the Glover"—sold to Isaac Atkinson the following lands on Miles River, Talbot County: "All that part of the tract of land called 'Ashby,' also all that part of the tract called 'Ending of Controversy' and, a tract of land called 'Ending of Controversy Addition'—all adjoining each other, beginning at 'Fausley' on Fausley [Glebe] Creek."

Then in 1853, Isaac Atkinson[40] conveyed to Richard France land "commonly known by the name of 'Locust Grove' "—being the above-mentioned three properties, amounting to 189 acres.

The name "Locust Grove" brings to mind the little, old dilapidated wooden cottage *Locust Grove* (Fig. 96) at the east end of that tract, and situated on the edge of Goldsborough Creek—an ancient Atkinson homestead, now entirely abandoned.

The empty habitation is a 1795-type storey-and-a-half structure with full cellar. It has the typical "hall-and-parlor" plan, with nothing appearing very unusual about it but that the heart of the building comprises an earlier structure (Fig. 99, top). As is often the case in Maryland domestic architecture, this home has been Victorianized—woodwork of narrow clapboards, dormers, sash, and all doorways but two. Under some of the later siding are original shiplap boards (*see* detail). On the river front and east gable-end are some bevel-edged siding boards. A Victorian kitchen was added to the Dining Room end of the house.

While the present *Locust Grove* is 37'-3" long, the earlier building (Phase

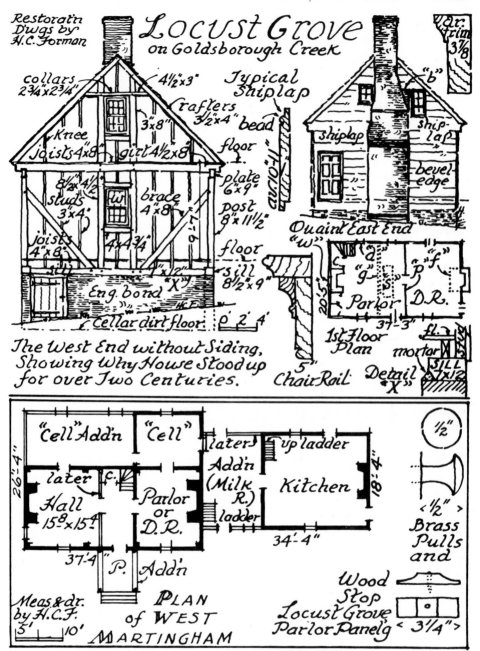

Figure 99

I) was thirteen feet shorter, and may have been a room, loft, and cellar. The original gable-end stood at "g" as seen on the floor plan, and the chimney "f" was flush with the wall. With Phase II the domicile was lengthened, and there were two windows, at "w," one above the other, in the west gable-end. At that time the "hall-and-parlor" plan probably came into existence—the division being the wall "g."

Next, in Phase III, about 1795, the last step before Victorianizing, a chimney, staircase, and closets were inserted inside the west gable-end. Also the partition "g" was removed, and a vertical board wall "p" was erected.[41] New millwork was put all through the house.

Although the sash of the two windows at "w" were removed, the chimney was built directly against the window frames and the plaster wall. An earlier doorway, "d," with space for a 3'-6" wide door was found by this writer inside the wall of the extension to the dwelling. All these matters sound a bit complicated; they did take a long time to figure out, and the floor plan is the key to understanding them.

To suggest how a place like *Locust Grove* could stand up for over two centuries, we have made a restoration diagram of how the west gable-end was put up before the chimney of about 1795 was constructed. The main timbers were framed together—Roman numerals incised on them were the guide to the prefabrication. Joints were mortised and tenoned with big pegs, and the members could hardly have been pulled apart in a hurricane. Instead of 4" by 6" main sills, which are commonly employed for ranch-type houses today, those in *Locust Grove* are 7" by 12" and 8½" by 9". In place of thin 4" square corner posts without diagonal braces, now in current use, we meet with much larger ones—8" by 11½", braced by 4" by 8" diagonals, both sides. The other frame members of this early cottage are also proportionately large.

We close with a brief note concerning some of the interesting smaller features of *Locust Grove*. First, the cellar door on the west gable-end was restored on paper by the only evidence then available: marks of the door frame, which had disappeared, upon the underside of the main sill of the house. Second, we found in the cellar in the 7" by 8½" sill of the original gable-end wall, "g," some triangular holes in which small joists around the former stair well, "s," rested. Third, the later staircase, next to "d," is very steep—there are twelve risers in 180° of turning—a true "break-necker." Fourth, there are two original 1795-period doors remaining in the abode—one showing in the east elevation, the other in the second floor cross-partition. Finally, the picturesque east gable-end, mostly covered up by the ungainly Victorian kitchen, has a four-inch projecting brick course, "b," of the bedchamber fireplace. The right-hand six-pane sash may have been four-pane, like the one on the other side of the east chimney.

Our drawings are largely based on two Historic American Buildings Survey sheets of *Locust Grove* which this writer made for the Library of Congress in 1962; it will be noted that the chair rail has been corrected.

Many a Metamorphosis at Old *William's Venture*

This early hearthside has seen many changes and has been mistaken for *Liberty Hall*, Kent County, which long ago succumbed to erosion and now rests under Hunting Creek to the South of Rock Hall. "William's Venture" comprised 114 acres on Swan Creek in that county, and was patented in 1725 by William Bradshaw. By a will of 1753 he left part of the "William's Venture" estate to his daughter, Frances Bradshaw, who had married William

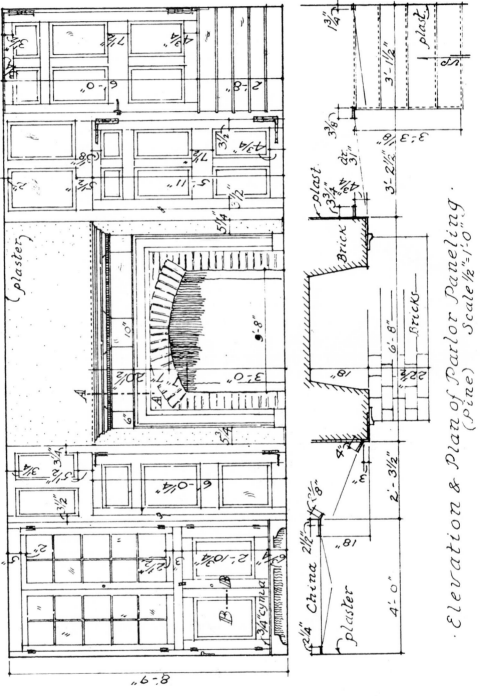

Fig. 100. *Locust Grove* on Goldsborough Creek: Woodwork of *c.* 1795 in Parlor or Great Room. HABS Forman 1962

Fig. 101(top). *Clay's Neck* was probably built soon after 1679 for Henry Clay of Talbot County and resembled on its exterior *The Ending of Controversie* (*c.* 1670). Author, 1932.
Fig. 102(bottom). *William's Venture* or *Humphrey's Point,* Kent County. Wilfong, 1953.

Fig. 103. (Top) A Brown family homestead, *Ripley* was built in 1805 on a property of the same name granted to William Hackett in 1678. (Bottom) The Dairy and shingled Schoolhouse at *Ripley*. Author, 1961.

Hodges, second son of the first William Hodges of "Liberty Hall." It seems that the *William's Venture* plantation-house was possessed or occupied in 1783 by two sons of Colonel James Hodges of "Liberty Hall"—the reason, no doubt, which caused Swepson Earle in his *Chesapeake Bay Country* to believe that the two dwellings were one and the same. Colonel James Hodges was a member of General George Washington's staff.

In 1806 *William's Venture* domicile was bought by John Humphreys, M.D., and was then commonly called *The Point, Humphrey's Point,* or *Page's Point.*[42]

At first the brick section of the dwelling (Fig. 102) was but a storey and a half, with steeply-pitched roof. The main south gable-end was built of Flemish bonding, and evidence of a former cellar door may still be seen in the brickwork. The early frame kitchen wing or outhouse, off the south gable-end, has disappeared. Evidently the main floor was of the hall-and-parlor variety— the Great Hall having panelled window seats and handsome mantel flanked by closet doors with H-L hinges. The Parlor has a fine 18th-century stairway (Fig. 137) in the northeast corner, with steps to the cellar under it. The turned balusters are very slender and the curved spandrels are walnut; the handrail is reputed to be mahogany. Moreover, the cornices of this room are heavy, carrying two cymas, a fascia, and a quarter-round.

The early front door, which stood in the Parlor, directly opposite the rear door, next to the stairway, has been moved into the Great Room; and the partition between Parlor and Great Room has been removed.

In the early 19th century the brick portion was enlarged to two full storeys, and the main cornices were made up of oversailing courses of bricks. The present frame wing on the north is said to be the fifth addition to *William's Venture*. The Great Room chimney is small; probably it was cut down in size.

The Two Talbot *Clays*

Near the head of the northwest branch of Harris Creek, and close to the water, is the site of old *Clay's Neck* (Fig. 101), a picturesque 17th-century dwelling, razed in January, 1935, by a building contractor who wanted some old bricks. Shortly before its demolition this writer was able to photograph and measure the cottage, which resembled *The Ending of Controversie*, especially in its brick gables and frame sides.

Clay's Neck was originally the homestead of one Henry Clay, of Talbot County, who was involved in 1663 in a lawsuit with a Robert Martin.[43] Moreover, in 1665, he had a writ upon him by William Leeds in an action upon his case to the value of 10,000 pounds of tobacco.

This property was surveyed for Henry Clay on April 24, 1679, in the "Cattails" branch of Harris Creek. In 1684 he and his wife Mary conveyed to James Sedgwick not only his own plantation, but also lands adjoining called "Clay's Neck" and "Lurkey."

Then in 1722 *Clay's Neck* was owned by John Wrightson, who left it to his son of the same name. Nevertheless, John's widow, Mary Wrightson, continued to live on the premises and received a patent for it in 1743. In her will, probated in 1741, she bequeathed to her son Francis her interests in *Clay's Neck* and "Jordan's Folly."[44]

At the time of its destruction, this home was only a ghost of its former self: the west brick gable-end had gone, leaving the floors sagging; and nearly every sash had been pushed in or out. The kitchen wing, of which traces remained in the ground, had been previously moved away—no one knew where. The panelling, with an arched mantel, had been stripped and moved to Easton. The staircase was in the last stages of dilapidation.

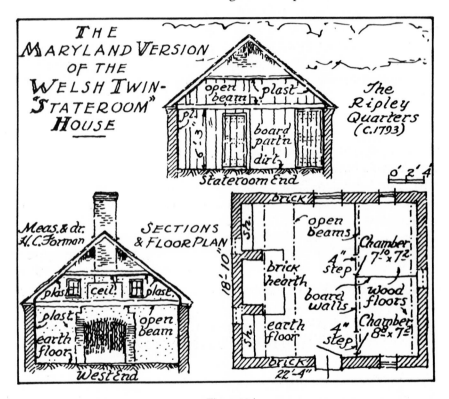

Figure 104

The dwelling followed the hall-and-parlor classification much used in the 17th century—a winding staircase having been in both Great Room and Parlor (Fig. 74, bottom right). The brick eastern gable-end formed an especially quaint composition.

Henry Clay of Talbot County—he was *not* an ancestor of the famous orator of that name[45]—and his wife Elizabeth also owned "Bever Neck plantation" (Fig. 75) and "Clay's Hope" in 1657 and 1662 respectively. This last, sold in 1664 to James Colston (I), was a property of two hundred acres on Clay Creek, a branch of the Choptank River, on which stands the house, *Clay's Hope,* the birthplace of Samuel Alexander Harrison (1822-1890), son of Alexander Bradford and Eleanor (Spencer) Harrison. She was a daughter of Colonel Perry Spencer, of *Spencer Hall,* Talbot County.

Fig. 105. (Top) *Bordlington* is a Georgian brick pile with semi-projecting chimneys which buttress the walls. Author, 1959. (Bottom left) Detail of glazed brick bands. Johnston, 1930s.
Fig. 106(bottom right). *Ripley Quarters* (*c.* 1793). Author.

From its architecture, *Clay's Hope* (Fig. 93) appears to have been erected about 1720–30. It is two-and-a-half storeys high, with small, twelve-pane windows, and Flemish bond. Unfortunately, in recent years the place has been much changed, and the box garden, of two concentric circles, has entirely disappeared. The ancient barn (Fig. 74, bottom left) with its great timbers and "ship's knees" still stands.

Other interesting things about the house are the chamfered watertable or base molding, the brick belt or fascia courses—especially those in the gables,—the stairway inside with vertical-board wainscoting and closed string, and the great beam across the cellar measuring a foot square.

Medieval-Style Great R.
at SPENCER HALL Kent Co.

III.

The Lower Eastern Shore

III.

The Lower Eastern Shore

Cator's Ancient Duplex

SITUATED on the north, cool end of Taylor's Island, this small cottage complex known as the *LeCompte* or *Cator House* (Fig. 107) was evidently in the ownership of members of the Edmondson family in the first half of the 19th century, if the dilapidated gravestones there are any indication.[1] That the place was the residence of Colonel Moses L. LeCompte (d. 1801) in the late 18th century will have to be proven from the land records, because there is no trace of his stone in the family plot. This writer has been told that the plantation-dwelling was last occupied by Mrs. Mollie Cator, an aunt of Senator George L. Radcliffe. For more that twenty-five years, it also has been said, the farm was held by members of the Spilman family. Since the last occupant, transient campers have poached there; and now the house is not fit for human habitation.

It appears evident that in view of the information we have gathered about the place, some of the published statements in other books leave much to be desired, *e.g.,* that the date of the older portion is "1710" and that the frame extension was constructed a half-century ago.

It was fortunate that the writer was able to obtain technical studies and measurements of the *Cator House* a few days before someone tore down the building and left the remains strewn over the ground. At the time of our measurements the dwelling was in extremely poor condition—even the main downstairs floors were covered with straw and manure, so that there must have been more living inside than campers.

That portion of the duplex designated as House I (plan, Fig. 108), had a framework of posts and sills which were identified by Mr. J. Marshall Whiting and this writer as the earliest members, probably of very late 17th-century date. For one thing, there was a tilted outer plate on which the roof rafters rested and even featheredged roofing clapboards, as the detail illustrates.

Fig. 107. A(top). *Cator's* duplex on Taylor's Island was made up of two separate houses set together, the later one being nearest the camera. B(bottom). Detail of joint between buildings and of nogged bricks set on edge. Author, 1954.

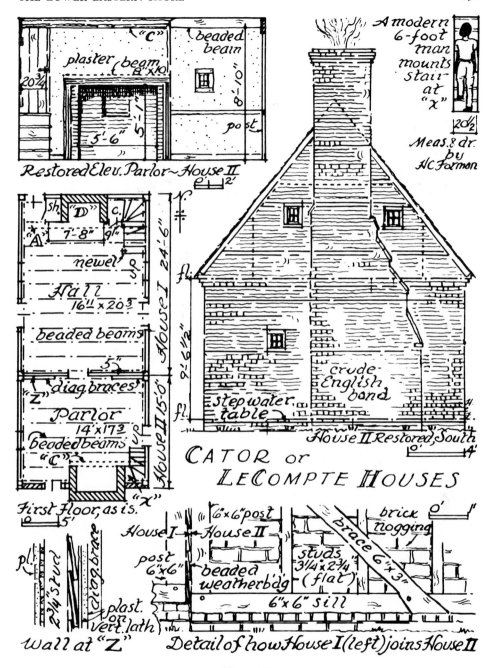

Figure 108

The study of the complex at that time, 1959, was not without difficulties, because House I, comprising a Hall or Great Room and two loft chambers, had been completely dressed over and covered with early 19th-century plaster, millwork and panelling (Figs. 108 & 109).

On the other hand, House II, probably constructed in the early- or mid-18th century formed a separate dwelling which had been moved from another location and shoved up against the south frame gable-end of House I.

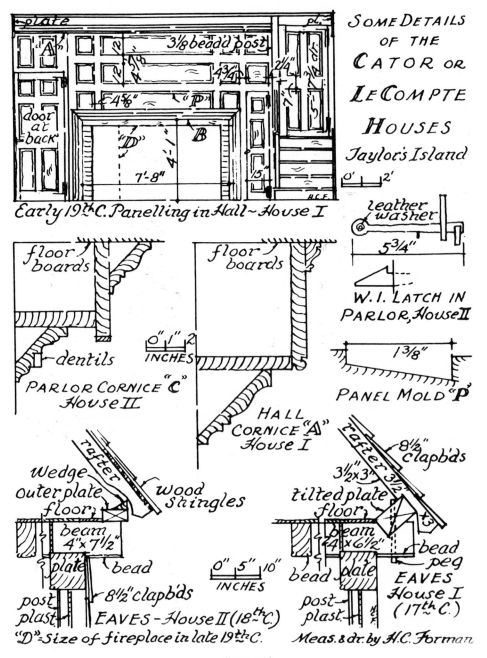

Figure 109

For those with some years of studying old buildings, it was easy to decipher the division between these two buildings where the siding had dropped off, as may be seen in the photographic detail (Fig. 107B).

Curiously enough, when House II was moved up against House I, the studs of the former against the south gable-end of the latter were eliminated, but not the two diagonal braces, which were obviously left in place to strengthen the corner posts. Then hand-split laths, marked "Z" on Fig. 108, were nailed *vertically* to the beaded oak clapboards of House I, both upstairs and down, and plaster put over them.

In the gables of House I the oak clapboards were graduated smaller as they approached the ridge—an optical sophistication common to early buildings.

Having related how House II was moved from elsewhere and placed abutting the other cottage, we are ready to continue to describe House I with its tilted outer plate. At the north end of this section there once stood a tremendous fireplace in the Great Hall measuring 6'-9" in span and evidently still in use when the early 19th-century panelling was installed. How do we know that? The distance between the fireplace bolection moldings originally measured 7'-8", but in the later years of the 19th century it seems that the fireplace proved too large for the occupants of the house who cut it down so that the woodwork around it became only 5'-9" (see point "D," Figs. 108 & 109). At the time, a small closet was formed, as the floor plan shows.

The mantel tree of this big fireplace was 5'-1" above the hearth.

This writer has had the feeling that when the 18th-century House II was moved against the other, the brick gable-end on House II was constructed. This brick of crudely-laid English bonding, later stuccoed over, formed a wall only *nine* inches thick, and was probably an intrusion into House II. So much for a theory. How else can such poor brickwork be explained?

The doorway in this same brick gable-end was put there to afford access to a small shed addition in the shape of an "ell," the roof outlines of which are visible in old photographs.

A conjectural, squarish casement has been drawn (Fig. 108) copying the lie-on-your-stomach casements which once stood high in the brick gable. The size of such casement sash was only 10" by 13". Although very late in date because it projects on both sides of the brick wall, the great chimney of House II is unique in that it has four weatherings or slopes on one side and one on the other.

In House II there are only Parlor and Parlor Chamber. To proceed from one room to the other, one mounts a steep staircase with high risers—each measuring about 9¼". But this stair is only 20½" wide—narrow even for the early days. To go up these steps, a six-foot man, as shown in the corner diagram (Fig. 108) would have to turn his shoulders slightly to the side as he ascended. Some fat people would not make it.

Both the Parlor of House II and the Great Room of House I have exposed interior construction—beaded posts, beams, and plates.[2]

The Parlor also has brick nogging in two of its outside walls—the soft bricks having had to be laid *on edge* in mortar because of the narrow, three-inch space between clapboards and plaster lath. Both the drawing and the photograph show this kind of nogging.

Probably the dormers were later additions to the roofs. It may be noted that although the brick gable-end of House II had been built possibly as late as the 1860s, the earlier style of brickwork—English bond—and brick corbels at the eaves were employed on Cator's duplex. But there were no box cornices on House II until within the last hundred years or so.

The eaves of both sections did show both the rafter ends and the beaded joists exposed on the outside—these members having been drawn as details. It so happened that some of the rafters of House I, cut carefully to fit over the tilted outer plates, were found lying on the ground after having been torn off the building; consequently, they were easy to measure.

The outer plates of House II were not tilted, but nonetheless the builders put in triangular wedges and hollowed out the ends of the rafters to fit them, thereby gaining the effect of a tilted plate.

The end of our Cator duplex story comes with a few technical remarks about moldings. The Parlor of House II has a plain, $2\frac{1}{8}''$ window trim, which surrounds the sash on all four sides. The sash muntin is $1\frac{3}{8}''$ wide.

It will be noticed that there is a difference between the 18th-century Parlor cornice and the 19th-century cornice in the Hall. The one in the Parlor is more compact and has dentils. Then, too, the Hall chair rail is crude, comprising a $3\frac{1}{2}''$ board with a bulbous, $\frac{1}{2}''$ bead molding tacked in its middle, and is fastened to the wall by cut nails of the 19th century. The $7''$-wide bolection molding in the Hall was sleek and suave. The newel post in that room had a thin cap, with its knob knocked off, and $1\frac{1}{8}''$-wide chamfers with lamb's tongues—a medieval characteristic which carried over into the 19th century.

No doubt these technical and minute descriptions, although of interest to antiquarians and millworkers, have strained the reader's patience. But let us not close the chapter before noting a couple of ditties which we found on the gravestones. On John H. Edmondson's tomb is engraved:

> "Weep not for me dear friend
> To grieve it is in vain
> Christ is my hope you need not fear
> We all shall meet again.
>   Meredith Maiker Ball"

And upon Mary Ann Edmondson's stone is inscribed:

> "Sister thou wust mild and lovely
> Gentle as the summer breeze
> Pleasant as the air of evening
> Dearest sister thou has left us
> Here thy loss we deeply feel
> But tis God that hath bereft us
> He can all our sorrows heal."

In those days what a pleasant custom it was to place a poem on a gravestone, so that every time one of the family strolled from Cator's ancient duplex to the little nearby plot encircled by the fence, he or she could find a kindly thought over the remains of the departed. Today we keep so busy with a multitude of the world's distractions that we have little time to think of whence we came or where we are going.

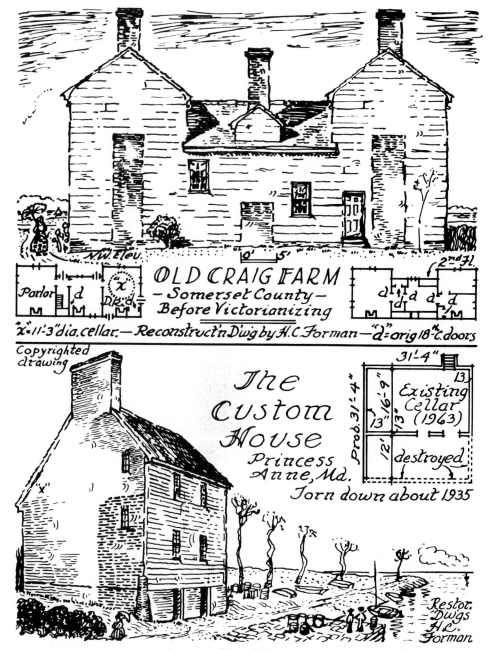

The following labels appear within the drawing:

N.W. Elev.

OLD CRAIG FARM
— Somerset County —
Before Victorianizing

Parlor d D.rd. x

2nd Fl.
d d d d

"x"=11'-3"dia.cellar.—Reconstruct'n Dwg by H.C.Forman—"d"=orig 18ᵗʰ C. doors

Copyrighted drawing

The Custom House
Princess Anne, Md.
Torn down about 1935

Prob. 31'-4"
31'-4"
16'-9"
13" 13"
12'
13
Existing Cellar (1963)
destroyed

"X"

Restor. Dwgs H.C. Forman

Figure 110

Skeleton in the *Custom House* at Princess Anne

One of the picturesque public buildings in Princess Anne was torn down about 1935 before it was adequately photographed or measured. This was the old *Custom House* built on the river bank along Water Street. Fortunately an old view of the edifice remains (Fig. 122); and there is a portion of a cellar extant under a modern warehouse floor, from which restoration drawings

(Fig. 110, bottom) have been made. By working out in reverse the perspective of this building, as exemplified in the old snapshot, we found that the *Custom House* was 31'-4" square as measured in the cellar.

The main east gable-end was entirely of brick, the other sides were clap-boarded. This east façade was marked by a huge flush chimney with five flues and at the main floor, two narrow windows with six panes each. The roof was a catslide, making the edifice two storeys high on the front and one on the rear.

By the time the old photograph was taken, which may have been 1930, a corner buttress had been constructed on the northeast corner to brace the structure against collapsing. The most interesting architectural feature appears to be the area of large checkerboard bond with glazed headers in the brick gable-end, towards the river corner, and extending from the ground to just above the first floor gable-end window, as marked on the drawing. Those were larger bricks than the others in the same gable-end, which was formed of common bond, not Flemish. From the examination of these details we know at least that a portion of the *Custom House* formed an earlier nucleus with handsome, large glazed headers in Flemish bonding. At some time, possibly in the late 19th century, the whole gable-end was plastered over, as the snapshot shows.[3]

When the *Custom House* was in the process of being razed, a human skeleton was discovered under the eaves, marked "x" on the drawing. Inasmuch as that particular triangular eaves' space had been completely sealed with old plaster and lath, one wonders how many decades the bones had been confined in there. A doctor identified the remains as those of a young girl. To someone she may have been "dear as remembered kisses after death."

The Old *Hooper's Island Catholic Church*

In Dorchester County there stands a little, shacky-looking structure of timber, set up on brick piers, and with its interior crammed full of junk and refuse—all that remains of a Roman Catholic Church. The establishment is so plain in appearance that no one passing would give it a second glance.

The diagrams (Fig. 111, top) of this chapel are based on brief notes about the interior, especially the pew plan, made over several years during short visits. All the slip pews had been ripped away, but traces remained on walls and floor. As for the pew widths, as shown on the drawings, they varied from 28½" to 37". Each slip pew appeared to have been roughly 7' long and 33" high to the top of the cap molding.

Around the single room runs a dado of wide, horizontal, beaded boards— on the long sides it is situated under the window sills, but on the short sides, it is higher than the window sills. The plaster is lime with hogs' hair on old laths.

The feature of this little church is the balcony, supported by round wooden columns on square bases—which replaced earlier, square wood columns with

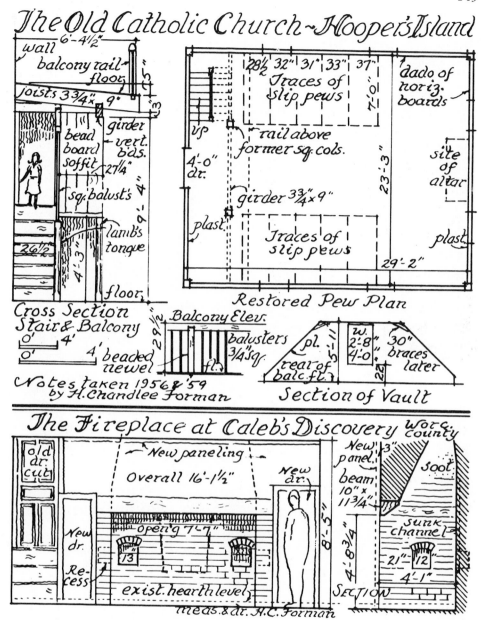

The Old Catholic Church ~ Hooper's Island

Cross Section Stair & Balcony

Restored Pew Plan

Balcony Elev.

Section of Vault

Notes taken 1956 & '59 by H. Chandlee Forman

The Fireplace at Caleb's Discovery Worc. County

meas. & dr. H.C. Forman

Figure 111

staff beads. At one end of the balcony a narrow, 26″-wide staircase with chamfered newel post and lamb's tongues, as well as square balusters, rises to turn on an even narrower landing, to continue upward to the balcony floor. The upper flight curiously has a closed stringer, whereas the lower does not.

What is interesting about this staircase is that no two steps appear to be the same. If you measured the first risers you would find: 8½″, 6½″, 7″, 6½″, 7″, 5″, 8½″, and 9″—as may be seen in our section through the balcony. The first few treads vary from 7½″ through 9″. Further, the first step in the return flight projects out into the landing space—a country carpenter's crude solution to the problem. What naïveté for a year as late as 1819.

Fig. 112. *Old Trinity Church,* Church Creek, Md. (*c.* 1690), is shown after its 1953-1960 renovation and repair. It was constructed of Flemish bond with chevron designs in the front gable and has leaded glass casements and a "circle" at the east end. Author, 1962.

The church is definitely not of the 18th century from the architectural evidence. Further, it appears to have been constructed in two periods. The first, in the year 1819 when Ambrose Marechal, third Archbishop of Baltimore, administered the Sacrament of Confirmation here, is shown by the cut nails and absence of wood pegs in the newel post and other framework. This period includes the two square posts holding up the balcony girder, the balcony rail of yellow poplar, part of the stair, and the slip pews. The main plates of the building seem to have been cut with a circular saw, used about 1830 in this area.

The second period dates from 1867, when Father Edward Henchy altered the church, and includes the existing round columns under the balcony, the boards on the stair, the horizontal board wainscoting on the walls, and the closed stringer.

The church is roofed by a modified tray ceiling, without the sloping ceiling at the ends. Short braces, thirty inches long, were added to the ceiling which give it a peculiar shape. Another curiosity is the landing newel post which has been cut off and is chamfered on three sides only. This post probably went to the ceiling of the balcony. Children could have fallen off the balcony: the rail is less than thirty inches high.[4]

After the exterior siding had been stripped from the framework in 1965, the writer examined the original framing and could not find the slightest evidence of an *early* apse or chancel addition at the altar end of the church. The old framework proved that the original structure was a plain rectangle.

Also visible in 1965 were the four large tree-trunk posts, some eighteen inches in diameter, which had been retrieved from under the church: shades in Dorchester County of the ancient *Cedar Park* tree-post foundations across the Bay.

Notes on *Old Wye* and *Old Trinity* Churches

On December 4, 1953, Miss Katherine Scarborough, of *The Sun*, Baltimore, and author of *Homes of the Cavaliers*, wrote a letter about *Old Wye* and *Old Trinity*, which is herewith quoted in part: "I hope that the errors which befell Old Wye will not be repeated at Trinity. Somehow, this whole restoration business growing out of Williamsburg has me confused. I would be brash indeed to pit my 'feeling' against the opinion of the architects and historical researchers and I do not dream of doing so, but I cannot convince myself that Pre-Revolutionary Williamsburg was as elegant and complete as it has been made to appear. It seems to me like an idealization of what may have been its potential. So does the restoration at Old Wye."

Miss Scarborough shared with this writer the opinion that the renovation in 1949 of *Old Wye* Episcopal Church in Talbot County made that edifice too elegant, overdeveloped, and ornate for its date of construction, 1717–21, only seventeen years after the end of the 17th century.

Fig. 113(top). *Old Trinity* has carved end-boards, and one is shown being nailed to the church. Author, 1956.
Fig. 114(bottom). The garden of the *Dr. Alexander H. Bayly House,* Cambridge, showing Quarters, Smoke House, Kitchen, Pump, and Dwelling. Author, 1965.

Referring to Dr. Elizabeth Merritt's study *Old Wye Church*,[5] called originally *St. Luke's Chapel*, "for it was only a chapel" of ease of St. Paul's Parish,
we find that this building (Fig. 71B) was ordered to be constructed on
October 28, 1717, by William Elbert "either where the Old Church stands or
hard by the same." The specifications of *Old Wye* briefly were 50' by 25' "in
the clear"—meaning inside measurements. Further, the "End building at the
East End"—that is, the Chancel—was to be 18' by 16' in the clear. Those are
approximately the dimensions of the church building today (Fig. 70).

In addition, there were to be three windows on each side of the church, and
two *oval* windows at the West end "above the square"—which means the
square area below the gable or level of the eaves. On the east or Chancel end
there were to be a large *oval* window at the head and a window "propor-
tionable" in each side. Pilasters or buttresses were to be built as were thought
fitting for strengthening the outer walls. The ceiling was to be arched, and the
roof covered with white oak or cypress shingles. In the chancel was to be an
altar table raised three steps high and set about with rails and turned balusters.

In the main body of the church were to be pulpit and reading desk. Consequently, except for pews, *Old Wye* was substantially completed in the spring
of 1721. A diagram of the box pews, finished in 1723, is shown (Fig. 71A) in
"A Register of the Pews at St Lukes Chappell at Wye ordered to be Recorded
by the Vestry September seventeenth Anno Dom 1723."

In 1733 two more pews were constructed, to stand "next the Chancell"; in
1745 all the chapel windows were repaired with new lead, solder and putty,
and all cracked "squares"—that is, rectangular panes—were replaced with new
ones; in 1792 a gallery in the west end with an outside stairway was constructed; about 1845 the west gable, above the eaves level, was removed and
rebuilt with old brick.

In 1949 *Old Wye Church* was repaired, renovated, and restored in part by a
gracious and generous benefactor. In those respects he did a great community
service. Nevertheless, we state advisedly that it is only a partial restoration,
not a complete one. To restore a building means what it says—putting it back
as far as humanly possible, except for necessary modern utilities, *to its form
and condition at an earlier decade or period*. That has not been done at *Old
Wye*. At least the church might have been restored to its 1723 appearance,
the time when the pews were finished.

The plate (Fig. 70) shows the west gable-end with *two* circular windows,
as were placed in the original church, not the *three* circular openings of the
1949 renovation. For years this writer had the feeling that there was too much
crowding of window space in that little brick gable. The design did not ring
true, for there is a large round window flanked by two small ones, with no
Eastern Shore Episcopal church precedent for that kind of design. In truth
the composition was overworked and is *de trop*.

When he first came across Dr. Merritt's booklet, mentioned above, the writer
found that the early specification called for a pair of oval windows only. In
1949, the third oval was added to provide a better distribution of light for the
gallery, but instead of erecting a wrong gable design, would it not have been

better to provide adequate concealed artificial lighting for the gallery? Within the meaning of the term, the western gable has not been restored.

Our photograph of the church purposely omits the front façade. But it does show a handsome Palladian window at the head of the Chancel; nevertheless, the specifications of the early church called for a large oval window there, so that the east end of the building has also not been restored.

Next, it is obvious from the record that the sliding sash windows held leaded panes, not ones with wood muntins, installed in the 1949 work.

At the same time the main entrance door on the west now has a modern enframement of wooden pilasters and entablature holding Greek triglyphs and drops—for Maryland, good Mid- or Late Georgian decoration, but scarcely plain and unsophisticated enough for an Eastern Shore chapel of its date, way down country. *Old Wye* was built at a time when the Georgian style was just emerging on the Shore. Not only that, the pilastered enframement woodwork of 1949 has been fitted awkwardly against a two-inch break-out or projection in the brick wall about the entrance door. The visitor to the church can see for himself how the modern wood abuts the sloping or beveled brick top of this break-out. Obviously there was something else there in 1717–21—some entrance feature of a different kind and of more simplicity.

Most pew plans in parish records are drawn very roughly and are not to be taken literally. In a way they are rough approximations and improvisations of the real layout. Consequently, when the pew plan of 1723 at *Old Wye* is examined, one should not jump to the conclusion that the delineator of that era purposely meant to show an unsymmetrical plan, where the aisles are not balanced and the pews on the north were only half the lengths of those of the central and southern pews. If the reader will look at the plan closely, it will become obvious that the artist started putting the names of the pew holders in the north pews, from numbers 1 to 11, in the usual crosswise manner for a page in a vestry book; but finding that pews numbers 12, 13, and so on, in the south and central ranges, had to have two names in each box, he made the pews double the length and wrote the names in at right angles in order to fit the spaces. In other words, the variations in the sizes of the box pews in the 1723 plan were made for the convenience of the delineator and not because the pews were to be constructed that way.

Besides, the regular style of Eastern Shore church embodied symmetrical and balanced side aisles. The reader may check the pew plan of *Green Hill* (Fig. 116), which was built in 1733, only twelve years after the completion of *Old Wye*. The pew plans of 1730-32 at *St. Luke's Church* in Church Hill; of *St. Martin's Church* (1762), Worcester County; and of *Spring Hill* (1773), Wicomico County, all show aisles symmetrically placed. Even historic *St. Paul's* in Kent County has aisles between the present slip pews exactly balanced, indicating that the original aisles of 1713 between the box pews were also symmetrical.

But in spite of good Eastern Shore precedent, the *Old Wye* aisles were constructed in 1949 unsymmetrically and unbalanced: the north box pews being 5'-4" long, the ones on the south 6'-5½"—measuring from the plaster walls.

The aisles, besides being thrown out of joint, are not even the same widths—the north one being 4'-9" and the south 3'-10". One can be thoroughly sure that early *Old Wye* was never like that.

In designing the pews themselves, Eastern Shore precedent for the period in which *Old Wye* was built was again ignored. A comparison (Fig. 117) of the pew-back top of *Green Hill*, where stand the original pews of 1733 showing an extremely simple molding of two cyma curves, with the existing pew-back top at *Old Wye*, indicates that *Old Wye* backs were done in 1949 in a larger, more curvilinear, and sophisticated manner, appropriate for a church of the very late 18th century—not for a little country chapel as early as 1721. But that is not all: the business of making rounded, instead of right-angled, corners to the box pews, as may be seen in the plan has no precedent in Eastern Shore churches, as far as is now known. The pew plan of *Green Hill* (1733) and of the other Eastern Shore examples cited, adequately show that pew corners were right-angled.

Moreover, the pew plan of 1723 in the vestry records of *Old Wye* shows the pulpit taking up only pew number 6, not filling three pews as was done in the 1949 renovations. Poor William Clayton in box pew 5 and Thomas Emerson in box pew 7 would have been deprived of their legitimate seating areas if the renovations had been made immediately after 1723. The box pews of 1949 are no restoration of what formerly existed at *Old Wye*.

The great coat-of-arms on the interior scarcely adds anything to the church, other than trying to make a small down-country Eastern Shore chapel, built just as the Georgian style was getting a start, into a baronial hall. Remember: the windows of original *Old Wye* were *leaded*. There was still a trace of medievalism in the architecture.

About 1850, *Old Wye* had become a ruined stable, with cows wandering in and out the doorways.

It has been written, and with just criticism, that *Old Wye Church* was "renovated and 'restored' *à la Williamsburg*, but scarcely *à la* Eastern Shore."[6] A very worthy preservation project, the work of 1949 formed a partial restoration, not a whole one.

There is much to write about the recent renovation and rebuilding of *Old Trinity* Episcopal Church (*c.* 1690), also known before 1853 as the *Fishing Creek Church* or *Dorchester Parish Church*, on Church Creek, near Cambridge. These brief notes are by way of introduction and are in no way definitive.

Old Trinity (Fig. 112) was partially restored from 1953 to 1960 inclusive, in memory of Mr. and Mrs. Walter P. Chrysler. The patrons of the church during those years were extremely generous.

Mr. Finlay Ferguson, A.I.A., of Norfolk, Virginia, was architect for the church for seven years, from 1953 until 1959, except for the interim from May 1956 to May 1957, when the writer served as architect, designing, and supervising the installation of, all the exterior woodwork on the old church and the new vestry house. These items include the "duck" end-boards, batten doors, and leaded-glass windows. In 1959 and 1960 a cabinet workman from

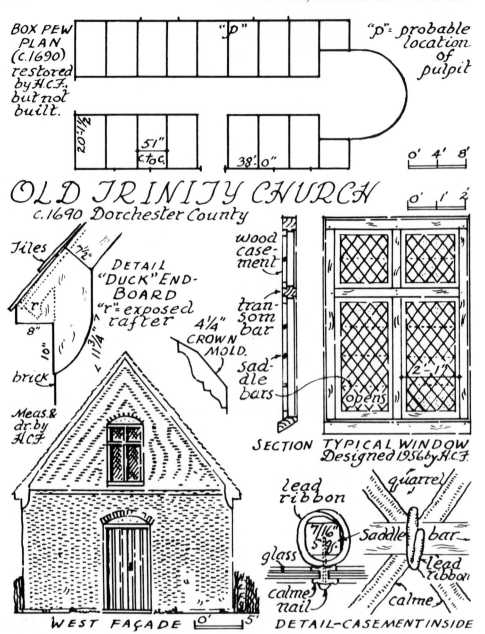

BOX PEW PLAN (c.1690) restored by H.C.F. but not built.

"p" "p"= probable location of pulpit

20'-1½

51" c.to c.

38'-0"

0' 4' 8'

OLD TRINITY CHURCH

c.1690 Dorchester County

0' 1' 2'

Tiles   DETAIL "DUCK" END-BOARD "r"= exposed rafter

7½"   8"   10"   3'4"   1'11"

brick

Meas.& dr. by H.C.F.

wood casement

tran-som bar

4¼" CROWN MOLD.

sad-dle bars

SECTION

opens

2'-1"

TYPICAL WINDOW Designed 1956 by H.C.F.

WEST FAÇADE   0' 5'

lead ribbon   quarrel

glass   7/16" 5/16"   Saddle bar

calme nail   lead ribbon

calme

DETAIL—CASEMENT INSIDE

Figure 115

England designed and built the church pews in the "English manner"—that is, in the style of a church or churches in England.

During the early stages of the work on the fane, Mr. and Mrs. Marion Brewington issued on March 15, 1954, an exhaustive report on *Old Trinity*, from which we take the liberty of quoting. First, the matter of the date of construction. Mr. Brewington examined the transcripts of Fulham Palace, London, in the Library of Congress, Washington, and found records showing that the church was standing by the year 1692. Inasmuch as the church records, which might have shed light on its date, were destroyed many years ago in a courthouse fire in Cambridge, Maryland, probably no one will be able to establish an authentic date for *Old Trinity*. That it was built about 1690 has been understood for many years; therefore it is misleading and unauthentic to erect a sign "*circa* 1675" at the church entrance, as has been done, to claim an antiquity which cannot be proven. The church is not, of course, the oldest church in active use in the United States.

Old Trinity was constructed of Flemish bonding, with chevron design on the front gable (Fig. 115). At the east end is a "circle" or apse. The church is small, comprising a rectangular space inside only 20'-1" wide by 38' long. During the repairs and renovations of the 1950s the south transept or vestry room, which dated from about 1745, was eliminated, not without some protests because of its early date; the pointed Gothic Revival arches and other features of the 1850s were removed; and the original building was then largely dismantled and almost completely rebuilt, numbered brick by numbered brick, around a new steel frame. Concealed steel rafters were made to support the roof, and wood shingles were replaced by fireproof sheathing and clay shingle tiles. With such sturdy construction the church should last a long time.

The windows and doors, by this writer, are conjectural; we had to rely heavily on precedent. As may be seen in the photographs, the windows have leaded glass, comprising "calmes," or lead strips, and diamond panes. But actually the wooden casements could with equal justification have had rectangular panes—they were called "squares" at *Old Wye Church*. Also, there could have been wood muntins instead of lead strips. No piece of calme or leaded glass, either diamond or square, was reported found in the exploratory archaeological excavations around the church by Mr. Ferguson, the architect.

The rafter ends of the church were exposed to view in the 17th-century manner—before the fad for box cornices. The "duck" end-boards (Figs. 113 & 115) were designed and named by the writer, and were derived from those which once decorated old *John's Point*, built soon after 1665 in the same locale. These unusual end-boards were drawn full-size right on the site at *Old Trinity* just as stone masons and joiners designed and built at the sites of medieval churches in Europe. With the publication of this volume there will probably be a rash of "duck" end-boards stuck on ranch houses, and the like, around the Free State.

The double front door, as well as the single door on the South, are battened with vertical quarter-round moldings outside and diagonal boards inside, and were modelled by the writer upon an ancient door existing in Somerset County on the Eastern Shore.

One record which is important about the pews of *Old Trinity* came from the land books of Dorchester County, and describes how one John McKeel, gentleman, on May 8, 1760, assigned to Thomas Manning, blacksmith, all rights, title, and interest which he had in "one pew in Fishing Creek Church numbered Five, standing close on the right hand as one goes in at the front door of the said church." That gives us some idea of where pew five was located.

Fig 116. A(top). An Episcopal church only moderately changed inside and out since its construction in 1733 is *Green Hill*. B(bottom). Detail of the original box pews, designed in native pine with simplicity and dignity. Author, 1964.

In 1840 or 1842 there was record of a gallery at the west end, along with outside steps leading up to it. Becoming dangerous and unnecessary, the gallery was removed in 1850.

No pew plan of *Old Trinity Church* has ever been found. The subject of that pew plan is a lengthy one, and the following are some pertinent observations about it. The existing combination of slip pews and box pews, made in the renovations of 1960, was found not to be worth illustrating here. They were made by an Englishman from London, but not according to Eastern Shore Episcopalian precedent.[7] It is true that in the 19th century the box pews of *Old Trinity* were changed to slips, but that fact has little bearing on the original pew plan.

From what we learn about the orginal pew plans of *Old Wye* (1717-21), *Green Hill* (1733), the Church Hill *St. Luke's* (1730–32), and *Spring Hill* (1773), near Hebron, and others on the Eastern Shore, we know that the early builder or joiner *tended to divide the available space into uniform or regular box pew units.* Slip pews do not appear to have been used at first in early Eastern Shore Episcopal churches. Consequently, the renovations of 1960 at *Old Trinity* do not conform to the Eastern Shore style and fashion as far as the pew plan is concerned.

In short, from present indications, the available area on the north side of *Old Trinity* was divided into nine equal spaces (Fig. 115), the pulpit pew being perhaps a tiny bit greater in width over the *regular unit of fifty-one inches.* Or the pulpit itself could have overlapped a pew back, as was sometimes done, to make the pulpit larger.

The fifty-one-inch pew unit was arrived at by the writer after months of study, and fits like a glove the interior of *Old Trinity*, its windows and doorways. Naturally the dimension is less than the fifty-four-inch pew unit of *Old Wye*, a later church by some thirty years. *Old Trinity* is a late 17th-century building of the most elementary character and design; the sophisticated slip-box pew combination installed there, as well as the elaborate pulpit and sounding board, are not in keeping with the requirement of simplicity. And since the pew plan was not done correctly in 1960, the church has undergone only a partial restoration.

It should be stated that a fifty-one-inch pew unit is too small for the use of contemporary man, but was adequate for early Marylanders.

The Brewington report of 1954 stated that unless *Old Trinity* varied widely from the Council's orders, "it was extremely simple"; that the parochial report of 1724 "confirmed the simplicity" because at that time the church owned no library, vestments, altar cloth, or communion vessels; and that the only trace of interior decoration seems to have been a Table of Marriages. There was then no instrumental music, because the church requested an indentured servant who could act as parish clerk, lay bricks, and sing the new version of the Psalms.

There were long periods of neglect, including once when *Old Trinity* was used as a sheepfold and cattle shed. There was no continuous use of the church

from the time of its erection. There is in existence an early chalice, dating
from 1767, still owned by the church.

One of the very few pieces of evidence about the interior woodwork may be
seen in the crown molding detail, found by Mr. Ferguson among the rafters
of the "circle." It was probably a finishing board between the plaster walls
and the plaster arched ceiling of the main part of the church.

Green Hill—A Church Saved By
Providential Isolation

On a beautiful pine-tree-studded bank of the Wicomico River stands brick
Stepney Church, called also *Green Hill* or *St. Bartholomew's* (Fig. 116).
According to the large glazed-brick numerals in the gable on the east or river
end, the church was constructed in the year 1733. It is situated in Stepney
Parish, formed in 1692 under an Act of Assembly, and in old Green Hill Town
(Fig. 15), a ghost settlement like Dover Town which was in 1706 ordered to
be laid out as a port of entry.

Fortune has smiled on *Green Hill Church* because the vestries over a two-
hundred-year period have not given in much to the urge for "restoration" and
permitted building contractors to "make hash" out of the old woodwork and
brickwork. Perhaps the building has been saved by its splendid isolation and
the conservative-mindedness of its owners. What is especially interesting is
that the building preserved most of its original pew system of 1733 (Fig. 117).
Let the renovators of *Old Wye Church* (1717-21) come down to Wicomico
County and find out what pew woodwork of 1733 looked like on the Eastern
Shore. At any rate at *Green Hill* the proverbial spark or contractor has not
yet caused any havoc.

Like most Maryland crossroads churches, this one is a barn of a place—
simple and forthright in its lines. The belltower probably was of temporary
construction nearby; now there is no trace of it. On each long side of the
church are four large windows with segmental arches, and on the east gable-
end are two more of the same. But on the front gable, over the two doors with
segmental arches, is a six-pane casement window, an intrusion in the wall. In
the upper portion of each gable is a string course or fascia of brick—an
unusual feature.

The interior is one large room 65½' by 40', with an arched vault, the plaster
of which has been covered with narrow Victorian boards. According to our
studies in 1956 there were originally fifty box pews, some of which, dotted
on the floor plan, are missing. Also there has been some patchwork among
the pews, and one pew panel has been cut in half.

Moreover, as the detail drawing of the pew with its wooden fastener button
shows from the brick aisle, the original pew height has evidently been cut
down from forty-eight to forty-four and a quarter inches. That the pew backs
have thus been tampered with is indicated by the absence of the quarter-round

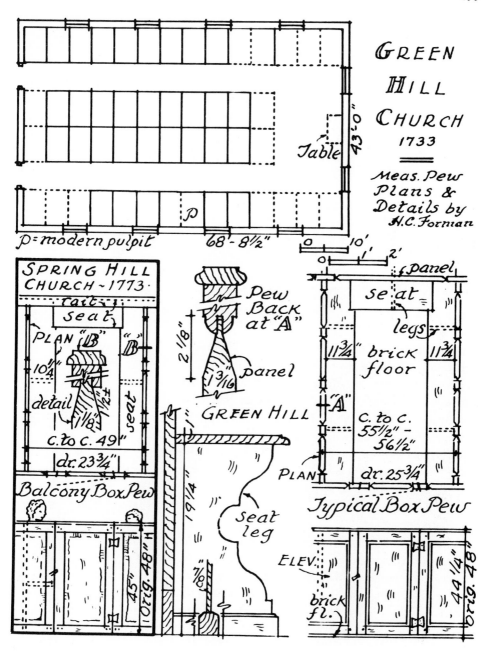

Figure 117

panel moldings at the bottom of each panel—probably cut away at some time. Marks of four-feet high pew backs have been seen on the brick walls.

The pews, as the photograph (Fig. 116B) shows, were designed with the utmost simplicity and dignity. Notice the little capping strip with cyma curves topping the pew backs, as shown at "A" on our diagram, and the wrought-iron butterfly hinges on the pew doors. The seats are old, but some of them may not date to 1733. Probably some time during the 19th century two regular box pews on the south side were turned into a modern pulpit pew. We have

Fig. 118(top). Except for the balcony box pews, *Spring Hill Church* (1773) has suffered changes and amputations to a great degree. The center door is an intrusion. Author, 1964.
Fig. 119A(bottom). West side of *Buckingham* showing segmental arch and buttress. Author, 1954.

had this pulpit pew examined by experts in old woodwork. It has press nails and rotary saw marks. In 1956 it was about fifty years old, certainly not over seventy-five.

The pulpit itself is modern except for three ancient back-board panels. Even the pulpit door is modern with an old panel brought from somewhere else. The reading desk is all modern. In short, the entire pulpit pew is a fairly recent intrusion into the church.

Where the original pulpit stood is a moot question. Usually it was on the north side of a church. Keen eyes today may detect at a point on that side that the exposed woodwork of the pews is of lighter tone than that of the average pew, a condition which might indicate a change of woodwork.

A church earlier than 1733 is shown by a letter "C" on the plat of Green Hill Town and Port made in 1707 by William Whittington, county surveyor, and is reported to have stood about one hundred yards northeast of the present church.

In the same Stepney Parish is the frame *Spring Hill Church* (Fig. 118) near Hebron, built in 1773, just three years before the outbreak of the Revolutionary War, and used as a Chapel of Ease. This structure has actually suffered so-called "restoration" of one kind or another, without any feeling for the ancient woodwork or design. It is different from *Green Hill Church* in its balcony and round-arched windows.

Unfortunately some persons have made kindling wood out of portions of the center pews, which have been cut down four or five inches, and their back boards canted. The front pews in the center have been cut down a whole foot. Moreover, all the box pews downstairs have been changed into slip pews. The atmosphere of the old church has gone. There is no trace of the original position of the pulpit. But the sounding board of the present pulpit appears to be 18th-century.

It is the balcony of *Spring Hill* which stores the real interest in this sanctuary, even if the area up there is used as a warehouse. The original box pews are set end-wise to the balcony railing (*see* detail, Fig. 117, left) and average forty-nine inches from center to center—a very narrow space to sit. The seats, too, are narrower than those at *Green Hill*: they are like bookshelves, ten and a quarter inches wide. They have no molded edges, and have plain, not curved, board leg supports.

Probably forty-eight inches high at first, the balcony pew backs have been cut down by three inches. Their panels are crudely cut and omit the quarter-round moldings, as at *Green Hill*. The doors were hung by butterfly hinges. Some believe that these box pews were brought from somewhere else, but the evidence cancels that theory.

The front of *Spring Hill Church* would look better if, instead of the single modern door in the center, the two original front doors were carefully put back in place. But it would be a large and expensive undertaking to reconstruct the whole church to its original shape and layout.

Fig. 119B(top). From the Southeast, *Buckingham* shows corner buttress on left and widening crack at right. C(bottom). The Great Room with paneling behind plaster and stair door hanging by one hinge. Author, 1954.

Fall of the House of *Buckingham*

On the Lower Eastern Shore a ruined brick dwelling of the hall-and-parlor type still stands, probably erected soon after the American Revolution, and having the distinction of a sloping brick corner buttress, dating almost as early as the building. This is *Buckingham,* sometimes called *Ironshire* (Fig. 119B), a lonely and deserted sentinel keeping its last watch.

Obviously, soon after the place was constructed, the southwest corner started to crack off and had to be supported by a neat, battered buttress (Fig. 119A), the brick courses of which match those of the main walls. What appears to be a similar crack has developed within recent years on the southeast corner, and now widens year by year. At grade level the buttress projects outward on each side about nine inches, as may be seen in the floor plan (Fig. 120).

For reasons of space we have not drawn restored elevations of the other three sides; nevertheless, the long sides possessed front and rear doors of 3'-6" widths with segmental arches, as well as square-headed guillotine windows four panes wide and six high.[8] All gable-end windows were evidently seg-mental-arched; although only one of the four has its arch bricks in place—an example which helped our drawings of the south elevation.

On the east the main front has Flemish bond with glazed headers; the north gable-end, now covered mostly by a 19th-century kitchen-curtain wing, has English bond; and the other two sides have common bond. A stepped water-table runs around the house.

At the time of measuring *Buckingham,* the end-boards, probably curved, had disappeared, but the cornice moldings were still there to record on paper.

The floor plan comprises two rooms downstairs and two up, with a single winding staircase and no cellar. The first two are evidently the Great Room and the Kitchen, which possesses a fireplace seven feet in span. Unlike the smaller fireplace with sloping jambs in the Great Room, the one in the Kitchen has jambs at right angles, in the prevalent fashion of kitchen fireplaces. A small underground pantry or buttery, lined by brick walls, was discovered under the kitchen floor. It is a three-foot deep pit, "p," immediately in front of the fireplace. In the gable-end a kitchen doorway evidently opened out to a series of outhouses. One is still standing—a small structure covered by wood shingles, the function of which was not immediately recognizable.

Besides the buttress, the main feature of old *Buckingham* is the Great Hall panelling (Fig. 119C), in wretched condition at the time of our studies. Antique hunters and decorators will have a difficult time finding that wood-work. In the first place, the panelling had long ago been completely covered by lath and plaster—probably for the sake of warmth. The vertical-board partition between the two downstairs rooms had also been covered over in the same way.

In order to see the panelling all across the fireplace end of the Great Room, it was necessary to squeeze into the closets and even into the broken-down fire-

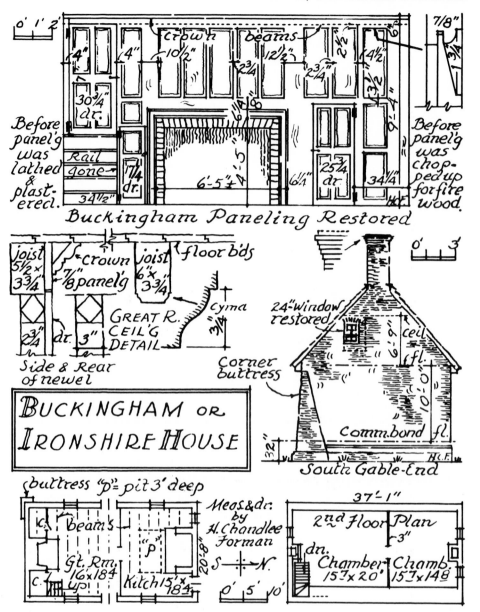

Figure 120

place itself, with its chimney bricks ready to fall on one's crown, and to make studies from behind the woodwork. Our drawing is based on measurements taken on the backs of the panels.

On our early visits to *Buckingham* the steps and stair door in the Great Room were in place; but on later trips, the steps had disappeared, and the stair door swung outward, suspended by one hinge. Large areas of pine flooring—exposing ¾ tree-trunk joists,—some of the panelling, and other pieces of millwork had vanished to make firewood in certain miserable hovels in the immediate neighborhood. Gradually, stick by stick, plank by plank, all the *Buckingham* interior woodwork faded away into the abyss of Time.

Because of its few very wide styles or vertical members and the irregular spacing of its panels, the Great Hall panelling was rustically designed. The lower staircase steps lacked a railing, which had disappeared before our studies commenced, but one of the newel posts, with a shaped diamond-head (*see* detail), was found to be part of the stair door jamb. The shaped head abutted the floor joist against which the panelling was nailed. We have illustrated both side and rear views of this newel post, to give an idea of what the missing newel on the first floor may have been like.

Downstairs the ceiling is beamed. As our ceiling detail exemplifies, the beams have rare cyma edges, and the top of the panelling was decorated by a crown molding against the underside of the boards on the second floor. Also, against the joist over the fireplace the Kitchen had another crown molding, of somewhat different profile from that in the Great Hall.

The fireplace in the Great Room had a bolection molding; but the kitchen mantel had gone, so we do not know its appearance.

The steps in the upper part of the staircase were steep, there being six treads in thirty-six inches, or six inches to the tread; and there was no railing, as far as could be seen, to offer protection against a fall down the stairs from the chamber above. There were no dormers, and this chamber was lit only by one lie-on-your-stomach window.

The door in the three-inch-thick plaster partition between the bedchambers is designed for small persons; it is only 29" wide and 5'-5" high.

Thus ends the short story of Fall-of-the-House-of-*Buckingham*.

Burned Just Yesterday—*Old Craig Farm* of Unique Design

Even to its wealthy city owner, this ancient retreat (Fig. 121A & B) on the Lower Eastern Shore had little value—no doubt because on the surface the place seemed to be Victorian. Nevertheless, the singularity and *bizarrerie* of the *Old Craig Farm* struck this writer at once upon the occasion of his first visit in 1954. Unfortunately, he waited eight years to find time to take measurements and make careful studies of the farmhouse. When on May 22, 1962, he visited the spot again, *Craig Farm* was nothing but two chimneys and a pile of ash and debris. "Burned just yesterday," sadly related the nearby farm-hands. The old, old story had been told once more: *Fire*.

In order to get dimensions for floor plans, the writer had to wade through foot-thick beds of black and white ashes to measure the brick foundation. Then, from those dimensions, his former rough outline of the rooms, and the photographs, the restoration drawing (Fig. 110, top) was made showing the appearance from the rear—before it was Victorianized.

This Late Georgian dwelling, probably of 1795-1800 date, had been incrusted with Victorian "pilaster-ettes" at the main corners, wider entablatures

Fig. 121. A(top). Rear view of *Old Craig Farm*, built about 1795–1800, and later Victorianized. Author, 1954. B(center left). The front of the house with later octagonal porch. C(center right). *Old Craig Farm* after burning in 1962.

Fig. 122(bottom left). *Princess Anne Custom House* before its destruction around 1935.

carrying friezes, overhanging rakes, diamond windows in the peaks of the front gables, twin-windows on the front façade, and an octagonal front porch. Although all the brickwork was common bond, some of it was varied by a bit of glazing here and there on the front foundation of the western wing.

It was on the interior that the *Craig Farm* revealed its early origin. Still hanging in place were seven 18th-century, six-panel doors, marked "d" on the block plans (Fig. 110, top). In the Dining Room the "d" marked double china closet doors. All these old doors were hung on H-L hinges with leather washers. The remainder of the interior woodwork had been changed to Victorian—even the stairway had circular turns of that style.

Under the Dining Room floor there was a round storage cellar, eleven and a quarter feet in diameter, probably reached by a trapdoor in the floor itself. The circle, dotted at "x" on our plan, was built of old brick covered by two coats of plaster.

The composition of the rear of the abode formed one of the most unique designs of this nation: a low "hyphen" connecting two-storey gable-ends with exposed chimneys flush with the walls. Curiously, in the center of the composition, on the roof of the "hyphen," a narrow chimney projected out from a miniature, blank gable. The general design was reminiscent of *Gunn's Run,*[9] Charles City County, Virginia; but that example had no centering miniature gable to give it an individuality of its own.

Opposite this tiny gable was one on the front of the house to match; although incrusted with wide Victorian eaves, painted darkly, this one on the front was actually a dormer—the small guillotine window with twelve square panes having been either the original, or a copy of the original.[10]

One wonders if the owner of the *Old Craig Farm* will ever have a regret that this cottage of exceptional design was allowed slowly to deteriorate as an ordinary tenant house, followed by fire and obliteration, and that he permitted such an interesting example of Americana to disappear for all time.

Fassitt's "Carmel" Plantation

One of the small 17th-century homesteads in Worcester County was a place known as "Carmel," comprising buildings and improvements on 2,000 acres laid out for Colonel William Stevens on the northernmost part of Sinepuxent Neck. In 1696 "Carmel," along with its "houses, edifices, gardens, woods," and 500 acres was sold by John Johnson and Persey, his wife, to William Fassitt. Later, in 1745, there was a description in the land records on which this writer's very conjectural view (Fig. 123) was based. This account is found in a survey of Capt. William Fassitt, Jr., eldest son of the man of the same name: "The plantation whereon his father dwelt—one old dwelling house forty foot [with] two brick gabel ends—new kitchen twenty foot framed— one new thirty foot barn, one log'd house, and one old milk house."

Besides the above, there were "two apple orchards containing three hundred and forty trees—fencing [of] eight hundred panels—yearly rent five pounds ten . . ."

Our sketch is based only on the above vague description and on 17-century precedent of the lower Eastern Shore. Nothing in the diagram is to be taken literally. To our knowledge no excavations have been made at "Carmel"; therefore nothing is known of the size and layout of the foundations. The Elizabethan knot garden would have been appropriate at that era. The view is across the sound to Assateague Island.

Figure 123

In One Family 263 Years—*Liberty Hall*

A few miles south of Princess Anne this old homestead stands in a park of large trees beside a creek branch of the Big Annemessex River. It is so isolated in the woods that the early owners must have liked all sylvan things. Its first floor plan is much like that of *Kingston Hall* in the same neighborhood.

We have understood that *Liberty Hall* dwelling-house (Fig. 125) is situated upon a land grant called the Armstrong patent of June 1, 1667. Cecilius Calvert, Lord Baltimore, issued to Matthew Armstrong, mariner, of Boston, in New England, 250 acres by assignment from Lt. William Smith—probably the carpenter of that name who owned a house in St. Mary's City—and another 250 acres by assignment from Randall Revell. At any rate, out of these two parcels totalling 500 acres Matthew Armstrong got "Armstrong's Purchase" and "Armstrong's Lott"—both lying on the north side of Annemessex River.

One Daniel Curtis, a Quaker from Virginia, who became a planter in Somerset County, Maryland, obtained on April 17, 1672, the Armstrong patent from Hannah Armstrong, of Boston, a widow, and former wife of Matthew Armstrong.

It is interesting to learn, after trying to decipher the old deed of 1672 in its 17th-century script that the Armstrong tract bordered land having a house, formerly in the occupation of William Boist, deceased, and also land called "Salisbury," formerly in the occupation of John Rhodes.

Granted in the Armstrong patent to Curtis were "rooms, cellars, sollets [?], halls, parlors, chambers, houses, housings, court yards, closes," as well as "fences, woods, underwoods, tymbers, or tymberlike trees." Further, Curtis received one half of the stock of cattle and hogs "and other things being in joynt stock and accompt (always provided a negro woman excepted)."

The plantation remained in the possession of members of the Curtis family from that time until 1935—a total of 263 years.

In 1680 an inventory was made of Daniel Curtis' property. In his late 17th-century home were among things the following: feather bed with some furniture, two cattail beds, four blankets, two rugs, a square table, and four flag chairs.

There were only two pairs of sheets, two pillows, two tablecloths, six chests including a "wainscot" chest.

Lumber occupied both the Kitchen and the Milk House. Among the kitchen effects were a brass stew pan, a spit, dripping pan, gridiron, a cask of molasses, and three iron pots with hooks. There were also a gun and three pistols, and a small number of tools and animals. And there were tobacco tongs. That was about all which the Curtises had for comfort and use in a primeval wilderness.

The last Curtis owner of *Liberty Hall* is reputed to have been a gay dog, losing the plantation on a bank mortgage because he spent all his money on horse racing and other diversions.

One of the owners was John Curtis who died in 1864. But which Curtis built the existing main part of the residence in 1795 is not yet known. Within the building are portions of an earlier house—how early, no one knows. The wing on *Liberty Hall* dates from about 1840.

Most of the downstairs rooms have low panelled dados, dentilled cornices, and fireplace mantels with dog ears. Such fireplace decoration includes friezes with guilloches, flutes, and flanking S-scrolls (Figs. 140 & 144). The wide front door is of two leaves of battens, with diagonal boards on the inside. The curved broken pediment over the front door is recent and does not belong there.

The main portion of the abode is Late Georgian; in spite of the late date, 1795, the Federal style appears to have passed it by in its solitary isolation in the forest.

Fig. 124 (top). *St. Giles* box garden. Author, 1958.
Fig. 125(bottom). The property on which *Liberty Hall* was built in 1795 was the Armstrong patent of 1667. The wing dates from about 1840. In 1680 Daniel Curtis left an early homestead on this tract containing cattail beds, flag chairs, and several other items. Author, 1958.

Cross-House and Cross-Garden: *St. Giles*

The early 19th-century garden layout at *St. Giles* (Fig. 124), a homestead begun in 1820 by John Harris and owned later by members of the Bounds family, revolved around an axis. This imaginary central line runs down the middle of a cedar-lined entrance driveway from the main road, through gateway posts with shaped finials, along the center of a cruciform house and boxwood garden at the rear, then crosses a stable yard and passes through the middle of horse and cow barns.

The origin of the name *St. Giles* comes traditionally from that of a church near Coventry, standing in a part of England from which many settlers emigrated to the section of the Eastern Shore surrounding the plantation whereof we write.

For another garden of the same period, but not laid out symmetrically, the reader may refer to the garden plot of *Burley Manor* (1832–33) in *Tidewater Maryland Architecture and Gardens.*

The *St. Giles* habitation was erected in the form of a cross—at least so it is believed—with an open porch on the front and an enclosed one at the back.[11] While these wings are not original, they are said to replace ones of approximately the same size. Further, on the West the low curtain wing and one-and-a-half-storey kitchen with great chimney have been superceded by a modern structure of about the same area and location.

In the garden plan (Fig. 126) a circular driveway has been very lightly indicated in front of the mansion as was customary in a formal layout, but the present owners have indicated that no such circle stood there within their memory.

The original box garden at the back of the dwelling evidently used to form a knot garden of four rectangles. Parts of these oblongs are now missing, but the plan shows how they may have looked, and illustrates the paths, now laid down with brick. In one corner stands a Lily of the Valley tree, and there is also a Franklinia tree—one of the genus Gordonia, a rare specimen, descendant of those found by John Bartram in 1790 along the banks of the Altamaha River.

On the west side of the garden stands a small clapboarded pump house, where earlier stood a well-house surrounded by lattice-work walls.

Another fenced enclosure about the same size as the garden lies to the East and was formerly the vegetable garden; but today it is adorned with boxwood walks, flower beds and goldfish pool. Other boxwood walks, large trimmed yews, trees and shrubs have been added to the front lawn.

In the stable yard, outside the two enclosures described above, and near the fences, were the Meat House, Wood House, and Necessary—the last two being one shanty. The two-storey Bath House with great tub on tall feet was moved from a location between the enclosed back porch of the domicile and the present millstone, marked "m" on the plan, which had been brought from the

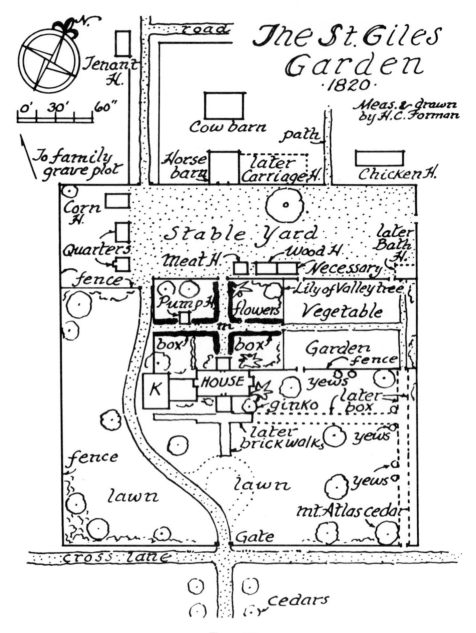

Figure 126

water grist mill on the property. Obviously the Bath, a Victorian affair, had been a later addition to *St. Giles* house because it blocked the main axis of the garden.

On the West of the stable yard is an existing Quarters building with an old chimney, which was formerly occupied by a man who took care of the horses. Also there is a Corn House, which probably replaced an older one. Between those two outhouses at one time stood another Quarters hut, which has vanished.

The old Horse Barn is small, some 22′ by 25′ and has a hayloft. The cattle were sheltered in a Cow Barn which once stood to the rear of the Horse Barn, at some distance to allow room for farm wagons, but which stands today against, and in line with, the Horse Barn.

A local touch is given by the tombstone in front of the old Horse Barn which reads: "Bob Faithful Horse Died Oct. 7th 1909."

Undoubtedly there were other outhouses, such as a Milk House, which have gone without a record of them.

The family grave plot stands off in a tangle of vines in a field at some distance behind the site of the old tenant house and is said to contain the stone of John Harris, the builder of *St. Giles*, who at one time lived in an earlier habitation which was situated near the bank of Rewastico Creek. The place where that homestead stood is still marked by a great old pear tree. John's father, Stephen Harris, came from Somerset County.

Look on *Meekins Plantation* as Dross

One ancient domicile of the 18th century, difficult of access and isolated on the lower Eastern Shore, is *Meekins House* (Fig. 127A), a name given by this writer, who could call it as justifiably the *Tubman-Tyler-Creighton House* because of certain tombstone names in the family plot.[12] Among these particular moss-covered stones is that of William R. Tubman which reads as follows:

> "Farewell my dear and loving wife,
> Contented may you be,
> Look on all below as dross,
> Prepare and follow me."

In damp, mosquito-infested country, we came through the pine woods to discover suddenly a good example of a Late Georgian, beaded-clapboard residence of two and a half storeys with cellar, built in the 1780s or '90s. The place is now the haunt of ghosts, or lovers—the latter having inscribed their names on the old plaster. Although 40'-2" long and 28'-2" deep, the structure is no fancy home; it is fairly plain throughout.

One enters the front door facing the water by a wide doorway with a 16-pane transom above it. In the passage is a stairway with scrolled step-ends and square newels and balusters, and the side of the steps is divided by small triangular and rectangular panels.

The Great Room is large: 27' long by 16' wide. The small fireplace with dog-eared mantel has a span of three and a half feet—big enough for medium-sized logs. On the right-hand side of the fireplace is a closet, wood-lined, with one door over another.

From indications of the masonry in the cellar we found that on the other side of the stair passageway from the Great Room there were not two rooms and catercornered fireplaces, as today, but one long room, a dining room, with one fireplace able to take at least four-foot logs. At the southeast corner of

Fig. 127. A(top). River front of *Meekins House* (1780s–90s) on an isolated neck. B(bottom left). Last year's leaves are strewn in the stair passage of *Meekins House*. Author, 1957.

Fig. 128(bottom right). The ancient checkerboard bond part of *Golden Quarter,* built 1761 by Ebenezer Campbell, before it was changed. Author, 1934.

this room stands a corner cupboard with fluted pilasters, and at the southwest corner, a small, secondary staircase to the second floor.

Upstairs the rooms are arranged in pairs on either side of the passage, and a small chamber for a child, eleven feet square, lies at the front of the passageway. The two chamber mantels are handsomely carved, the one on the north having a dog-eared bolection trim surmounted by a frieze with three reeded panels, and the other, in the southeast chamber, having been drawn on the floor plans (Fig. 129). The southwest bedroom has a cupboard with superimposed fluted pilasters without caps.

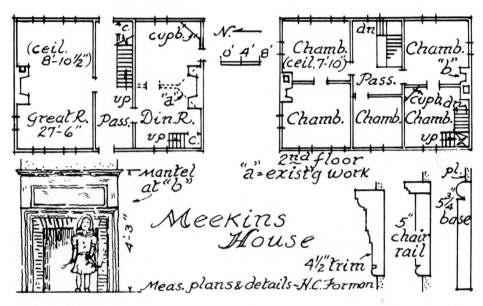

Figure 129

The typical window trim, chair rail, and baseboard have also been drawn, and one can see at a glance how plain they are—the work of country carpenters.

Three Transitional Brick Gable-Enders

On the lower Eastern Shore the *Bishop Farm* (Fig. 130), also known as the *Peacock House* or the *Chevron Brick-End Dwelling*, is a small, storey-and-loft affair of which three sides are timber-framed. As in most early Maryland homes, the dormers were later additions. For years the Great Room has been stuffed with bales of hay, so that measurements of the panelling were extremely difficult to obtain. Nonetheless our drawing (Fig. 132, top) illustrates fairly well what remained of the woodwork about the Great Room fireplace. There are five rectangular panels, and an arched panel, above the fireplace itself, but the mantel had disappeared, so that a wide bolection molding had to be shown conjecturally.

Fig. 130(top). The *Chevron Brick-End House* or *Bishop Farm* is Hangover Transitional of about 1790 and had three tiny windows in the brick gable-end. Author, 1957.

Fig. 131(bottom). The Great Hall fireplace in the *James R. Tilghman House* (*c.* 1710–30). Haislip, 1963.

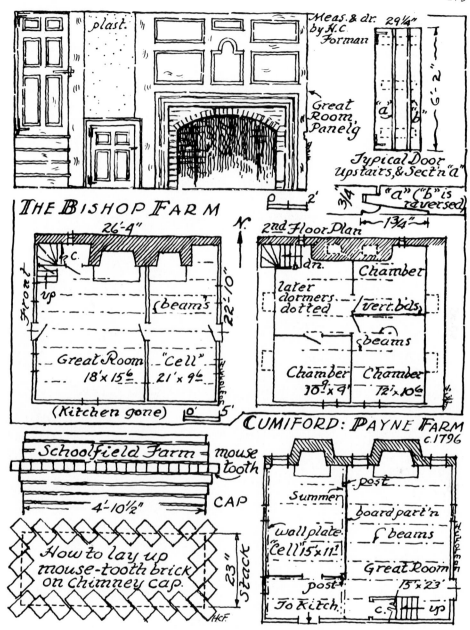

Figure 132

The three-foot high closet door with its trim overlapping a face board of the mantel area forms a picturesque feature; on the other hand, both that door and the one on the staircase had disappeared, so they also have been drawn by conjecture. It is curious that the surface of the plaster was found to be almost flush with the old panelling.

Upstairs are a passageway and three chambers, all separated by vertical boards with small beads. But on the other walls, and on the sloping ceilings, there is horizontal board wainscoting. All the rooms had open beam ceilings.

Fig. 133A(top left). Cornice and end-board of *Schoolfield Farm* (1795). Author, 1961. B(bottom left). Brick gable-end of *Schoolfield Farm*. C(bottom right). The *Schoolfield* Great Room.

Fig. 134(top right). The *Honga Windmill,* a Dutch type of mill with movable cap and blades with sails, before destruction. Weymouth, 1952.

An interesting feature in the loft is the use of the batten door (*see* detail) with two quarter-round vertical moldings, one the reverse of the other, and with a small width of slightly less than thirty inches.

Some time during its long existence the abode had one of its lie-on-your-stomach windows widened in the brick gable-end, as the photograph shows, and the downstairs small window was blocked with brick. The kitchen was evidently a separate outhouse which has gone, and there is no cellar.

It has been told that the *Chevron House* was owned over the last hundred years by members of the Bishop family, but there is no graveyard plot to prove the theory.

Another cottage built on the same plan as, and resembling, the *Bishop Farm*, is a place called the *Schoolfield Farm* (Fig. 133B). Before its changes it was a typical lower Eastern Shore example of Hangover Transitional style. Its rooms were stuffed with bales of straw. The graveyard to the north of the dwelling contains the stone of Sarah Schoolfield (1812–1895) and others.[13] In recent years the property belonged to Charles Schoolfield, and before that, to his parents, Sam and Mollie Schoolfield.

A brick tile with the date "1795," drawn (Fig. 135) from the ground by this writer, had been inset in the brick gable; consequently the year of construction is well authenticated.

In the late 19th century a large frame addition of Victorian style was built against the west gable-end; also an outshut and porch were constructed to cover up the south or main front of the original house. The kitchen probably stood on the west side where the Victorian wing now lies. The dormers are of the same later vintage.

A lumber company, for profit, had ripped out the panelling of native pine in the Great Room (Fig. 133C) and the little "aisle" or "cell" room behind it, before this writer's first visit in 1957. The missing cupboard had a round top to fit into the existing, empty, circular arch.

Unlike the *Bishop Farm*, the *Schoolfield Farmhouse* possessed a staircase, rising, not from beside the fireplace, but from the back portion of the Great Room. The steps have gone, yet evidence of them is visible in the second floor boarding. There is also a brick cellar, lit by small windows with vertical wooden bars.

Upstairs is a narrow, transverse stair passageway having knee-wall closets, and two chambers, one having a fireplace. The lie-on-your-stomach sash have two panes in the upper and four in the lower.

The interesting chimney stack has a mouse-tooth brick course, the secret of its layout being shown in the detail. The main cornice has dentils and carved end-boards.

The third dwelling, *Cumiford* or the *Old Payne Farm* (Fig. 136A), has a crudely built-up brick gable-end of common bond. In an adjacent field is a single gravestone with the name of Wheetley Dennis, born the 19th of July, 1772, and died, the 18th of March, 1813.

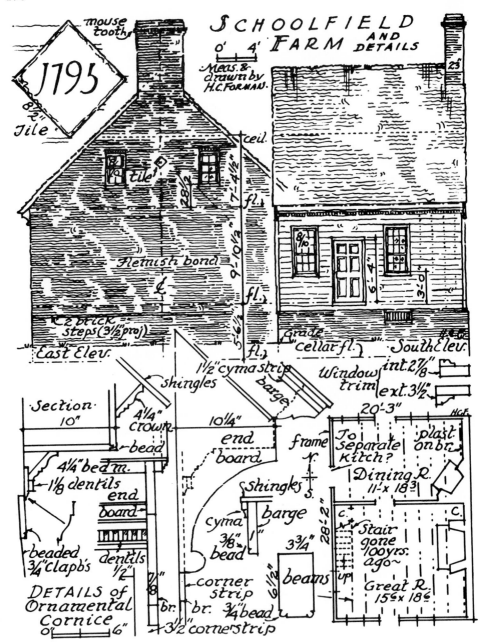

Figure 135

The floor plan (Fig. 132, bottom) is slightly different from the two examples described above. For one thing, there are outside chimneys with sloping or bevelled sides. The Great Hall is divided from a little back "cell" or "aisle" by a board partition and summer beam, and has an ell space at the back of the stairway—a kind of passageway between the former kitchen outhouse and the "cell," which was used as a dining room.

Rising from the Great Hall in a straight flight, the open stairway has slender turned balusters on a closed stringer, and the side of the stair is marked by large triangular and rectangular panels. The mantel in this room is carved with dentils, and the beams and wall plates are beaded timbers. The walls are brick-nogged for insulation, and the beaded clapboards are feather-edged, with nine and a half inches of them exposed to the weather.

Upstairs at *Cumiford* one of the two loft chambers has a fireplace, adorned by a narrow bolection molding. The typical door is six-panelled, with a later type of molding, the cyma.

From its architecture we have dated the habitation about 1795—the date of *Schoolfield Farm* several miles away across the forests.

Tenants have unfortunately made the interior of *Cumiford* into a shambles by deliberately wrecking partitions, stairway, mantels, and the like.

The *Bacon-Townsend Mansion*—
Georgian Arboretum

This manse displaying twenty-four-paned sash windows stands in a wild spot of park-like woods on the lower Eastern Shore. Because of the condition of the edifice, its architecture has been difficult to record properly on paper; likewise, because of its isolated situation in a forest country, its history has been not easy to trace. The earliest known owners, a couple named Bacon, are reported to have been buried in the field behind the house. Nevertheless, the only stone located by this writer is a marble foot marker with the letters "JCB"—presumably a Bacon. Other owners, it has been said, were Teackle Townsend, and later, his grandson, Irving Townsend, although we cannot vouch for the accuracy of the report. From another source it was learned that Elijah Townsend once possessed this elegant homestead with the elaborate modillioned cornices and heavily-scrolled stairway. In any case, the house is a Georgian prize, uncared for and unkempt—long forlorn, perhaps a quarter of a century without occupants. Its size makes it a competent barn. There was so much straw in the front passageway that it was impossible to ascend the stairway to the second floor.

The approach or north front (Fig. 139A), as well as the rear, shows evidence of original two-storey porticoes, now gone. The reader may note that in the photograph (Fig. 141A) the front cornice, decorated with dentils, modillions and end-boards, has a triangular piece taken out of it over the central window on the second floor, and the marks of a roof upon the siding. There are further nicks and notches on the clapboards which indicate that the porches were narrow ones—tall and slender.

At either gable-end the chimney was divided by windows and was arched together in the loft, as is clearly seen in the photograph of the west gable (Fig. 141B). On the east gable-end there were two outside doorways, with marks about the dining-room door of a curtain or colonnade of unknown vintage. Halfway between these two doorways was the cellar entrance, leading to a dirt floor area and, under the main stairway, a small, thirty-one-inch-wide

Fig. 136. A(top). Another brick gable-ender is *Cumiford* or *Old Payne Farm*. The chimneys are splayed in plan, with necking bands thicker than usual. B(bottom left). The pine staircase with closed stringer in *Cumiford*. Author, 1956.

Fig. 137(bottom right). The stair with delicately-turned balusters at *William's Venture* or *Humphrey's Point*. Author, 1957.

fireplace of cater-cornered shape. From this broken-down cellar the writer rescued fragments of the ornamental spandrels or consoles of the first- and second-floor stairways.

The stairs on the first floor had a heavily-turned newel post, its top and bottom being square blocks. On every tread were three turned balusters, and there were heavily-molded nosings and decorated scrolled-leaf spandrels. This was a stair fit for a prince—lost in the Eastern Shore backwoods.

A complete stair spandrel or console on the second floor was pieced together, something like a Chinese puzzle, and is drawn and photographed here (Figs. 138 & 139B). The hand-wrought nails were countersunk, with white lime putty in the holes to cover the nailheads.

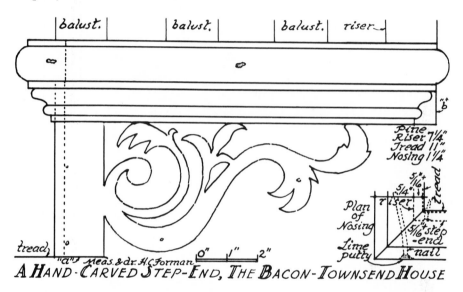

A HAND-CARVED STEP-END, THE BACON-TOWNSEND HOUSE

Figure 138

Because each spandrel was handcarved, its thickness was not uniform and varied from $\frac{3}{8}$ of an inch to a little less than $\frac{5}{16}$. Each spandrel was slightly different, the local variations keeping the stair from looking mechanically-built, like today's product of the millwork factory. In the drawing it is interesting that the piece of pierced scrollwork was made part and parcel of the vertical strip at the left, marked "a," and the horizontal strip above, marked "b." There was one coat of paint remaining on the whole step—a bright blue.

While we succeeded in salvaging a complete scrolled spandrel from the second floor, a whole one from downstairs was not to be had; but we do know that there was the similar scrolled spandrel design, yet different in detail, especially in the leaf pattern at the termination of the scroll. There was the same complicated nosing molding; nevertheless the original paint was different: light chocolate.

It would cost more than $8,000 to reproduce these two stairways in the *Bacon-Townsend Mansion.*

Going on with our detailed description, we cite the wall in the front passageway having a dado of two, very wide, horizontal boards with chair rail,

Fig. 139. A(top). Traces of the former slender two-storey portico may be seen on the wall and modillion cornice of the *Bacon-Townsend House*. B(bottom). Actual pieces of a second-floor console or step-end placed on an ink drawing of step. Author, 1955.

and door and window trim possessing double dog-ears. The other rooms downstairs followed suit. Only one mantel in the domicile had not been stripped. This one had tumbled through the second floor and was found leaning against the front passage wall in a disheveled state. Because of blocks of wood set in the brickwork, there were obviously overmantels, the design of which will probably never be known.

It is estimated *Bacon-Townsend* was constructed some time between the end of the American Revolutionary War and 1800—probably near the turn of the century. It is not too late to restore the house, although it will be soon. It would be dangerous to be near the sagging front facade when it slides off the brick foundation.

Love's Labor Lost at *Tilghman's*

According to Henry Adams, history is only a catalogue of the forgotten; and this little brick-and-frame dwelling lies in that category. It was in the Tilghman family of the lower Eastern Shore for several generations. The Reverend William Tilghman, of *The Entailed Hat*, belonged to the same clan. But the building was forgotten by the people of the State of Maryland—unfortunately, as we shall soon find out. Let those who sincerely regret the stripping and demolition of this ancient building in 1963 by a bona fide museum in the Carolinas stand up and be counted.

Like *Genesar* down on the Atlantic Ocean shore, this *James R. Tilghman House* had some features unique in the Free State; but Maryland, sad to relate, will never have more of this homestead than what is recorded here (Figs. 142 & 143A). The opportunity which the State and its people had for preserving and renovating this abode, with its mantel tree high enough for a man to stand under and its Jacobean bracketed shelf and its unique batten door, has been lost forever. Two centuries or more from today, how will people feel about Maryland's lost opportunity?

The *James R. Tilghman House*—we have presented this nameless cottage with that appellation because a gentleman of that name owned it in the 1870s —formerly belonged to members of the Henderson and Dryden families, and reputedly was a part of the George Dennis estate.

When destroyed and left a pile of rubble and twisted planks by the museum, the house was in fair shape. Although badly weathered, it had been used seasonally for years as a tenant house. Some of the panels about the Great Room fireplace and the entire middle, cross-partition downstairs had already been lost to the house—reportedly taken by a lumber company—but who can tell? The commercial interests are very strong.

From its architecture the *James R. Tilghman House* was Transitional in style, and according to this writer's judgment, dated 1710–30; the museum will probably label the building 17th-century, although it was not. It is the fashion to claim that an object is older than can be proved. It is true that there are Hangover Medieval features, like the post-and-beam construction on the in-

Fig. 140(top). Stair with question-mark spandrels and paneled dado at *Liberty Hall* (1795). Author, 1959.

Fig. 141.   A(bottom left). Cornice details at *Bacon-Townsend House*. Author, 1955. B(bottom right). Divided chimney at *Bacon-Townsend House*.

terior and the brick corbels on the outside, but one end of the cottage is two rooms in depth, conforming to the "Late Cell Type" of the Transitional Style; and the Great Room wainscoting (Fig. 145) obviously was of the multi-panel type of the Transition rather than of the standard vertical-board type of the Medieval Style.

Then, too, the ornate bolection molding around the fireplace in the Great Hall did not date before 1710.

Other Hangover Medieval features (*see* details) are the four small segmental arched windows in the northwest brick gable-end, which from the evidence of the wood frames had tiny casements; the tilted outer plate; and the unique batten door on the northeast side of the domicile.

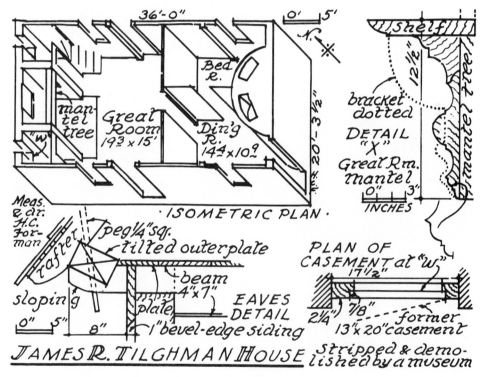

JAMES R. TILGHMAN HOUSE

Figure 142

This door was made up of three wide planks separated by two narrow plank moldings, of which we have drawn a profile, resembling those on a door at *Old Bloomfield*, Talbot County. The three batten boards have the refinement of being rounded on their outer surfaces, as shown on another detail in the same drawing. Also the reader may examine the sketch of the fine sliding and tapered wood bolt, which penetrated a hole two inches deep in the great house-post, decorated with cyma-curved edges. The knob for sliding the bolt had disappeared. As if the wood bolt were not enough for fastening, a wood stop was used at the top of the door, as shown in our view of the door on the inside.

The outside of the door had been worn down by countless raindrops. Showing how strong and relentless had been the elements against the dwelling, the

Fig. 143. A(top). The *James R. Tilghman House* was built between 1710 and 1730 in the Transitional Style of Late Cell Type, but in 1963 a man-made hurricane struck it. B(bottom left). A *Tilghman* gable-end window which held a small wood casement. Author, 1956.

Fig. 144(bottom right). *Liberty Hall* Dining Room. Author, 1959.

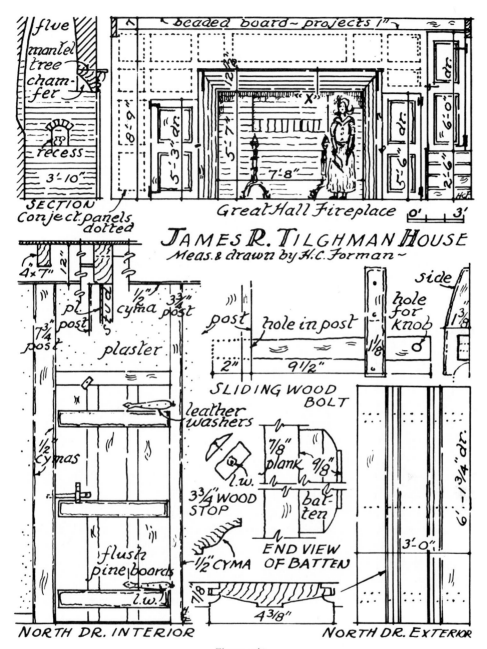

Figure 145

bevel-edged siding boards on the northeast side had been thinned down from the standard one-inch thickness to a half inch. Even the casement window frames in the northwest brick gable-end had been worn considerably by the weather.

The Great Hall fireplace (Figs. 131 & 145, top), flanked by closet doors, had an opening 7'-8" wide, as well as a mantel tree, a great timber over a foot square, which stood 5'-7" above the hearth. In other words, any person that height could stand inside the fireplace. That height, by the way, was normal for men or women two centuries ago, before they began to eat so much at better balanced meals.

Note that there was no brick showing around the opening of the fireplace: the bolection molding, formed of a torus and two scotiae, came to the very edge of the mantel tree and the brick jambs.

The mantel shelf with its two brackets exhibiting Jacobean curves was outstanding—one of the few examples where a very early shelf still stood in position in a fireplace.

Through the big fireplace we have drawn a section to show a brick-arched warming recess, which was built in either jamb. At the rear of the fireplace was a four-inch deep smoke channel to help guide fire sparks and fumes up the broad flue, for in those days they did not build throats and smoke shelves. In the two other downstairs rooms the fireplaces were on a circular plan, as the isometric drawing (Fig. 142) illustrates.

Although both these last two Tilghman fireplaces were concealed at the time of our measurements, the one in the larger room, presumably the dining room—because there was an outside, gable-end door leading probably to a kitchen wing or kitchen outhouse, now gone—was about 4'-6" in span, and had its hand-carved mantel stripped away by the museum in 1963.

The doorway between Great Room and Dining Room is shown on the diagram where the owner of the property remembered it to have been in the panelled cross-partition.

At the time of measurements the loft had had its cross-partition removed. Inasmuch as there were no original dormers, and no windows in the southeast brick gable, the entire upstairs was probably lit and ventilated by the two little lie-on-your stomach windows in the northwest brick gable. At the time of the writer's visits, there was in the southeast gable a small, squarish hole, with jagged brick edges and no sash—a true *wind-hole*, probably closed by a curtain to keep out the winter winds. In size this hole was smaller than the lie-on-your-stomach window in the opposite gable.

It is of course possible, but not probable, that a tiny window had been built originally in the southeast gable and had been enlarged at a later time, therefore accounting for the jagged sides of the wind-hole. But to this writer there was no visible evidence of a segmental arch, like the arches of the opposite gable-end.

The original wood casement sash, now gone from the brick gable, was roughly 13" by 20" in size and one inch thick. The roof was one of the steepest in Maryland: 52 degrees to the horizontal.

These are the good and rare things which the Free State has lost.

A fireplace similar to *Tilghman's* is at *Caleb's Discovery*, a homestead near Berlin, which was constructed in two brick sections, the older being one-and-a-half storeys and possibly built as early as 1720 or soon after. The larger part is locally believed to have been an addition constructed by Judge William Tingle, who is reputed to have died in 1824. The place also belonged at one time to a member of the Powell family. The whole house has been stuccoed with lines imitating ashlar masonry, a 19th-century embellishment.

The great fireplace (Fig. 111, bottom) in the older part is the attraction. Seven and a half feet in span, it has four arched warming recesses, but most of the woodwork about it is new. The great mantel-tree, a foot wide, was visible before being covered by modern paneling. Since the above was written, another large fireplace has been discovered in the house.

The original name of this property is not known, according to a noted land surveyor of Worcester County. Nevertheless, a recent garden tour brochure gives the name of the land grant as "Hillard's Discovery."

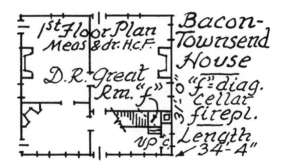

The Dining Room of *West St. Mary's Manor* contains an oak press cupboard, an oval gateleg

IV.

Southern Maryland

IV.

Southern Maryland

17th-Century House in a Brick Cocoon—
Cedar Park

THIS account of the evolution of *Cedar Park* (Fig. 150B) in Anne Arundel County has been written after studies of the structure over an eleven-year period, beginning in 1953. But previously, in 1932, this place was measured in part for *Early Manor and Plantation Houses of Maryland*.

Further, Mr. J. Reaney Kelly has described well and adequately the historical and topographical aspects of *Cedar Park* and touched briefly upon its architecture in the article, "Cedar Park, Its People and Its History," published in the March, 1963, issue of the *Maryland Historical Magazine*.[1] The plantation has been owned by members of the Galloway, Sprigg, Mercer, and Murray families.

According to Mr. Kelly, it is "not clear when or by whom the original installation, now the frame-interstructure of the present Cedar Park house, was built." At this date no one has been able to find out who erected it or when it came into being. But Mr. Kelly shows "firm documentation on the size and appearance of the old dwelling during the period between 1690 and 1736." The date 1690 is the year when Richard Galloway II obtained possession of *Cedar Park*, and 1736 the time when he died.[2]

The dwelling is situated upon a rolling meadow once used as a deer park. Also, a yearly meeting of Friends was held in 1684 in the "house of Benjamin Lawrence," which may have been the present *Cedar Park* house.

In the evolution of the ancient domicile we find that there are three chief developments: first, the *medieval* house of about 1690, marked Phases Ia and Ib on our plates (Figs. 146 & 147); second, the *Hangover Jacobean* house,

189

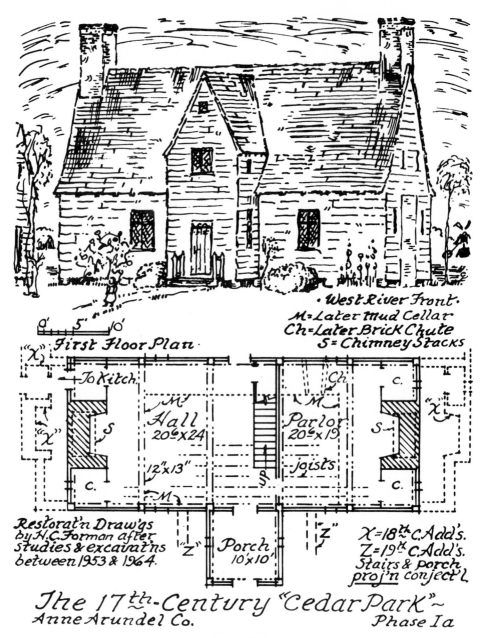

· West River Front ·
M = Later Mud Cellar
Ch = Later Brick Chute
S = Chimney Stacks

First Floor Plan ·

Restorat'n Draw'gs
by H.C. Forman after
studies & excavat'ns
between 1953 & 1964.

X = 18th C. Add's.
Z = 19th C. Add's.
Stairs & Porch
proj'n conject'l

The 17th-Century "Cedar Park"~
Anne Arundel Co.   Phase Ia

Figure 146

dating *after* 1736 (Phase II, Fig. 148) ; and last, the house with the *Federal Style*, octagonal front wing and other 19th-century additions, some of which are indicated in floor plans and photographs (Figs. 148 & 150A).

Mr. Kelly coined well the words, "frame-interstructure of the present Cedar Park house," because the medieval dwelling, built to the shape of a "T"—a cross-house—has been pretty well enclosed and covered over by the later Jacobean habitation, except for the original front porch wing which has vanished. The plate showing Phase Ia represents a cruciform building of the same style and pattern as *Old Bond Castle*, which hitherto we termed "the most

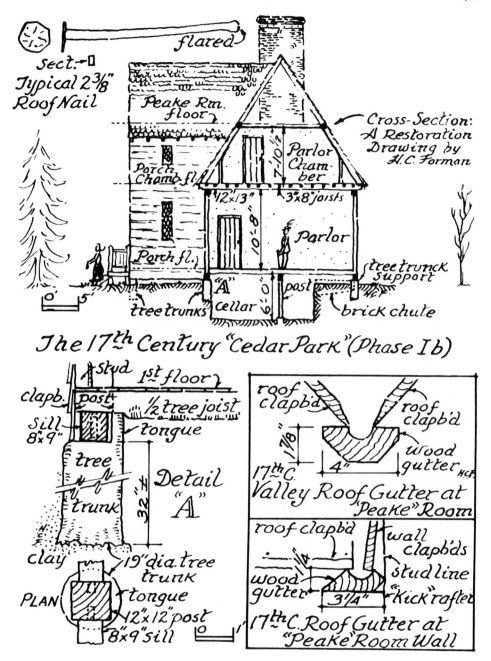

The 17th Century "Cedar Park" (Phase Ib)

Figure 147

significant rural edifice of Maryland." Actually *Cedar Park* was a timber-framed storey-and-a-half edifice built of five ten-foot sections in length, with the end-chimneys inside the gable-ends and a tall, narrow, enclosed front porch wing, ten feet wide,[3] on the water façade.

The house is unique in having a framework of vertical posts and main sills resting on rounded, tree-trunk piers, about nineteen inches in diameter and with crude butts, sticking into the ground (Figs. 147 & 153B). Mr. Kelly indicated that posts and butts were one piece; but the writer thinks the posts

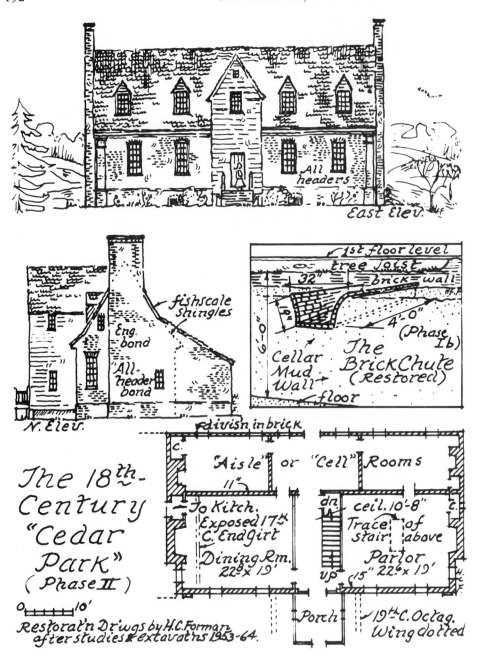

Figure 148

rested on top of tree-trunk piers, which have a lip or tongue on the interior side to keep the posts and main sills from slipping.

Usually in timber-framed construction the posts rest directly on the main sills, but at *Cedar Park* they come down on tree-trunk piers, and the sills are mortised into the posts, as the detail "A" in the drawing shows.

This method of wooden piers set in the ground used 275 years ago for a substantial building like *Cedar Park* is today found in shacklike or flimsy buildings.

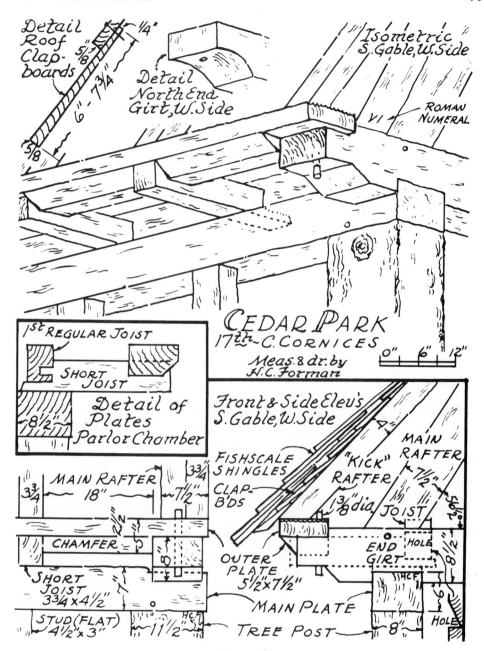

Figure 149

When we look at the framework more carefully, we find that the corner posts form great trees adzed down to a size of 8″ by 11½″ and the intermediate posts marking the ten-foot sections already mentioned, are even larger—8″ by 13″.

More interesting features are the half-tree joists supporting the first floor (detail "A") and the main cornices of the Phase Ia house which were not boxed, as they were in the 18th century, but left with the beam ends exposed to view. The roof, one of the steepest in the State, has an angle of 56½ de-

Fig. 150. A(top). The Federal wing with curious two-storey octagonal portico. Author, 1954. B(bottom). *Cedar Park,* Anne Arundel County, showing the 18th-century house before the Victorian trimmings and addenda were removed and the whole place renovated and modernized in 1962. At extreme left is Federal-style octagonal wing. Engle.

grees to the horizontal, and evidently always had a "kick" front and rear, because the gable-end girts and summer beams (Fig. 149) project a foot out
from the wall framing.

It could be argued that because these projecting beam ends have angular
undercuts at the south end of the house and semicircular undercuts at the
north end, the original abode was only one room and loft; nevertheless, it is
entirely possible that this difference in cutting was simply a very early idio-
syncrasy or naïveté.

To examine the framework further, we note that although the regular joists
of the second floor (shown dotted) run longitudinally with the edifice, there
are at right angles to them small joists about two feet long which project
beyond the walls at the eaves level, and help support the *outer* plate upon
which the short "kick" rafters sit. Why the eleven notches were cut at the end
of the outer plate, as the diagram shows in two places, has not been deciphered.
The Roman numerals were, of course, incised for purposes of pre-fabrication,
and we have shown a "VI" on an end-girt rafter.

At any rate, we can be sure that construction details are difficult for the
reader to assimilate; but let him or her be reminded that this is the first, fairly
complete account written of the finest 17th-century roof ever found in
Maryland.

As the floor plan shows, the Hall and the Parlor have two heavy end-girts,
as well as four great summer beams or summer trees, even larger than the
girts. All these rest on the big corner and intermediary posts already described.
Then there are subsidiary members, like regular joists and studs. The longitudinal joists rest in mortise holes, $4\frac{1}{4}$ inches square, cut in the girts and
summer beams. It is interesting to find that these holes are about eighteen
inches on centers and are splayed back into the girders: in other words, the
hole does not go back square, but beveled, to take a joist which also is beveled
(Fig. 149, bottom).

Following the five-section layout of *Cedar Park*, the roof is divided into five
compartments by heavy rafters, and there are also subsidiary rafters. At the
ceiling level of the second floor there are purlins, and where the vanished front
porch used to be, there is still another purlin just under the roof ridge.

Oak clapboards, which are original hand-rived, feather-edged boards, are
still in place on both roof and walls of the Phase Ia dwelling, and a detail of
these clapboards is shown. These vary greatly in size, the average measuring
$7\frac{1}{2}$" in width and 5' in length. The clapboards are also feather-edged at the
ends and overlap each other about $3\frac{1}{2}$ or 4 inches. The wrought-iron nails
(Fig. 147, top) have rose-heads, flared ends, and average $2\frac{3}{8}$ inches in length.

The evidence of where the original chimney stacks went through the present
roof of *Cedar Park* is still visible from the inside.

Two kinds of wooden gutters (Fig. 147) were located during an examination of the valley rafters of the vanished original porch wing. One gutter ran
between the roof of the main house and the roof of the porch which has gone.
The other went from the house roof to the upper wall of this porch. These are

Fig. 151. A(top). Woodwork of the 18th century in the Dining Room, formerly the Great Hall, *Cedar Park*. Engle. B(bottom left). *Cedar Park* Quarters. Author, 1954.
Fig. 152(bottom right). Detail of Sasche view of Annapolis (*c.* 1859) showing *Adams-Kilty House* and Stable, and the gambrel-roofed *Jonas Green House*.

probably the first actually authenticated gutters of the 17th century ever found in the South.

The restoration drawings of the 17th-century homestead show as conjectural the main stairway, the casement windows with diamond panes, the exposed chimney-brick in the gable-ends, the location of the kitchen outhouse, and how far the front porch projected outward from the main building. It is possible that the original stairs could have been winding ones inside the chimney closets, which were capacious.[4]

In Phase Ib some slight changes were made in *Cedar Park*. For one thing a cellar six feet deep below the floor of the early house was dug out of the primeval mud, as shown by the dotted lines, "M," on the floor plan. To get down to the cellar there were probably some crude steps, such as a ladder, descending from the Hall or Great Room, and there were wood posts put in to support the longitudinal girders.

Probably in Phase Ib a sloping and tapering-in brick chute was constructed in the crawl-in-space between the cellar and the rear, or west, wall. This has been marked "Ch" on the floor plan and has also been sketched. Not all the chute is there today. The later brick foundation wall had been built across its entrance on the west side; and on the east or inner side a modern oil furnace was set up in 1962, thereby breaking up most of the remaining portion of what may be the only known old chute in the South. What the 17th-century colonists used the chute for is anybody's guess.

In Phase Ib some brick foundation walls appear to have been constructed between the tree-trunk piers in order to support better the sagging main sills of the house and to close in the cellar and crawl-in spaces. Also at that time the existing fish-scale shingles, about seventeen inches long, were nailed to the oak roofing clapboards.

When Richard Galloway II, the husband of Elizabeth Talbott Lawrence, died in 1736, an inventory was made of his estate, listing furnishings and possessions by rooms. Naming the rooms was customary in early Maryland. There were at *Cedar Park* in that year seven rooms listed besides a kitchen and a store, which were undoubtedly outhouses. In the main house there was the Hall, known also as the Great Hall or Great Room. In it were large and small oval tables, a dozen Russia leather chairs, an elbow chair, and an easy chair with cushions, as well as a tea table and large bookcase. This must have been the place for living and dining, near the Kitchen, at the south end of the building. The Parlor with its two beds and their furnishings, a looking glass, small table and old trunk—equipment for a bed chamber—must have been by itself at the north end. In addition, the enclosed Porch was off the Great Hall.

Upstairs were Hall Chamber and Parlor Chamber, containing bedroom furniture. The Porch Chamber, a small area, was evidently used in 1736 for storage because of its thirty-two chairs, feather bed and bed furnishings, as well as two chests of drawers. Last, there was the Peake Room, having bed and its furnishings, table, looking glass, spice box, and glass case. This must have been a tiny, cramped space obviously above the Porch Chamber because

Fig. 153. A(top left). Jacobean decorative, stuccoed, brick pilaster, *Cedar Park*. Author, 1954.
B(top right). Rotted tree-trunk pier in *Cedar Park* cellar. Engle.
Fig. 154(bottom). *Adams-Kilty House* in Annapolis (*c.* 1783-84). Author, 1964.

of available window space. The great six-foot-wide end-chimneys of the dwelling left no room for windows in the upper gables.

The original aspect of *Sudley* or *Cumberstone* in the same general neighborhood had several similarities to the Phase Ia house at *Cedar Park*, as may be checked by the plan and photographs in *Early Manor and Plantation Houses of Maryland* (p. 101). Also resembling *Cedar Park* was a cruciform house reputed to have been constructed in 1664 in Prince George's County—*The Woodyard*.

In the magazine article already cited Mr. Kelly well summed up the cocoon-like quality of the medieval *Cedar Park* as follows: "The original frame house with its steeply-pitched roof has been absorbed in the present brick structure." True enough: except for the roof, it was encased in a brick shell.

The Hangover Jacobean house, illustrated by Phase II, dating after 1736, the time of the Galloway inventory, was marked by several features which will be taken up one at a time.

First, the gable-ends, north and south, were extended outward some four feet—marked by "X" on Fig. 146.

Second, three brick "cell" or "aisle" rooms were added on the rear or west side—a feature of the Transitional Style.

Third, the change of the old clapboard walls on the front façade and gable-ends was made to new brick ones—*except for the front porch wing*, which was probably never brick, as may be seen in the second restoration drawing (Fig. 148). The brickwork on the front and the lower portions of the gable-ends was all-header bond, possibly reflecting an Annapolis fashion of the time. On the front façade at the ends were built Jacobean pilasters, with caps and bases, for decoration only (Fig. 153A); for, like Seneca, you could say they supported nothing; and the cornice itself was boxed in with a large plaster cove. English bond decorated the upper gable-ends and the "cell" west wall. The medieval house was thereby almost completely enveloped.

Fourth, other changes were made, such as the installation of dormers. In making a new Hall fireplace, a pilastered mantel and paneled overmantel (Fig. 151A) were installed. Also a cross partition, or what the English would call a screens, was constructed to close off the Hall from the stair area.[5] The 17th-century end-girt of the original Hall was never removed and still showed on the ceiling. It has been marked on the floor plan. For some reason, the similar girder in the Parlor did not show below the plaster ceiling.

There were at least two puzzling features found in the Hangover Jacobean or Phase II house. What Mr. Kelly called "possibly a balcony" in his article appeared to be a stairwell opening in the ceiling of the Parlor, just north of the transverse summer beam. This probable former stair has been dotted on our plan; and it is possible that for some reason a partition once cut the Parlor in two.

Then there is a vertical break in the rear, or "cell" wall, marked "division in brick," which lines up with the above-mentioned 17th-century end-girt in the Hall. Some may argue that back "cells" or "aisles" were added to the medieval house, Phase Ib, only to be lengthened at the rear to make a longer domicile.

The third major development at *Cedar Park*, Phase III, occurred in the 19th century and was marked by the tearing down of the old frame porch and porch chamber and the building of a long octagonal brick-and-frame wing in the Federal or Early Republican Style. This occurred some time between the period when an owner, John Francis Mercer, served as Governor of Maryland, 1801–1803, and his death in 1821. Moreover, this addition, carrying an octagonal porch with a smaller porch above it, was probably already in existence when President Monroe and some of his cabinet members in 1818 visited *Cedar Park* for two days in May.

The hole in the habitation left by the 17th-century porch wing was 10′-10″ wide. The octagonal addition completely covered up this gaping aperture because it was 8′-6″ wider.

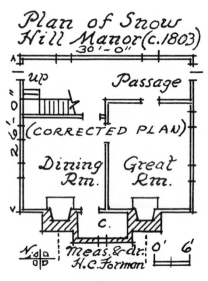

Figure 155

In studying this dwelling-plantation, set in its park lands, one learns that persons who occupied the great chamber in the octagonal wing, fit for the reception and stay of a president of the United States, had to walk a distance of 145 feet through the house to reach the unheated "necessary" house, one of a variety of 19th-century agglomerations beside the south gable-end. One of these additions was a frame structure which may have been half of an old school or academy (*c.* 1825), which originally stood as a separate entity to the north of the homestead.

One old photograph shows Victorian lobed trimmings on dormers, cornice, and west porch—an addition. Of the early outhouses only the Quarters remains (Fig. 151B).

The much-needed renovations and modernizations of 1962 were not always in keeping with the tradition of the old house, as for example, the modern type of cornice end-boards constructed at that time.

Even after eleven years of study we are sure that *Cedar Park* has more secrets and puzzles to unravel. This copyrighted account is in no way definitive.

An Archaeological Find Near the
Leonard Calvert House[6]

In the exploration of St. Mary's City it sometimes happens that an isolated find occurs which appears to have no relation to any other specific known portion of that buried town. While searching for the remains of Gov. Leonard Calvert's house, *East St. Mary's*, probably later called *Smith's Town House* (revised site), in the Governor's Field, the writer in 1940 accidentally stumbled upon a refuse pit, probably 17th-century in date, containing a number of interesting artifacts which shed light upon the articles belonging to the early colonists of Maryland. The pit was completely excavated and its contents were recorded.

The Calvert house was a large frame residence, built soon after the Governor's Field was patented in 1634 to the first Governor, Leonard Calvert, brother of the Second Lord Baltimore. Whether some of the objects thrown into the pit came from this historic mansion is not known, but there is always the possibility.

The location of the find is about 125 feet south-southeast of the site erroneously known today as *Smith's Town House* and about sixty feet from the boundary between the Governor's Field and the Chapel Land. The walls of the trench are of hard sand and clay, the floor of sand and gravel. Roughly triangular in shape, the pit is not large, nor deep, but ample enough to contain two graves if there had been human burials.[7] Inasmuch as animal bones, some of which were charred, came from nearly every part of the cavity, and the earthenware recovered was already in fragments before it was thrown in, the probability is that the pit was used for refuse disposal and not as the mud cellar of a building.

The rich fill of earth in the trench contained also charred timbers and oyster shells.

As may be seen in the inventory published in the *Maryland Historical Magazine* article already mentioned, the principal objects (Fig. 156) from the excavation present a good but partial view of the equipment of the early settler in that section of the country. A fragment of quarrel, or leaded window pane (Fig. 11), from a casement is the second such piece of glass found in Maryland. Since quarrels were generally employed in America before 1685, and less frequently after 1700, it would appear that the date of most, if not all, of the artifacts recovered is 17th-century. As a counterpart to the piece of quarrel, there was discovered a strip of lead calme, the first of its kind brought to light in the State. In the early casements such calmes held the quarrels in place.

Other objects of note came from the pit. There is a green glass button with raised points and traces of silver paint upon it. Probably used for spirits or ointment, a yellow glazed pitcher was found with incised designs probably of swan and peacock. The vessel has no handle and shows signs on its marred

Fig. 156(top). Artifacts from early colonists' refuse pit near the *Leonard Calvert House* site, St. Mary's City: branding iron "K," Indian flint spear point, plaster with leaf pattern, second quarrel fragment found in Maryland, green glass button, 3¾" high yellow-slip pitcher, and others. Author, 1940.
Fig. 157(bottom left). Slave door to kitchen loft at *Dorsey-Birch House.* Author, 1965.
Fig. 158(bottom right). *Cherry Grove,* of George Taylor. Ferguson, 1940.

Fig. 159(top). W.P.A. model of destroyed *St. Mary's Chapel* (1634–38), St. Mary's City, based on drawing in *Jamestown and St. Mary's* by authority of the writer.

Fig. 160(center). Crude earthenware bowls (9″–11″ diam.) from Pit near *Leonard Calvert House* site. Author, 1940.

Fig. 161(bottom). Dilapidated *Hickory Hill,* Prince George's County. Ferguson, 1936.

Fig. 162(top). "St. Michael's Manor" comprised 1500 acres patented by Gov. Leonard Calvert in 1634. The one pictured, standing on the manor lands and known by that name, is not the original manor-house, but a dwelling built around 1800. Author, 1964.

Fig. 163(bottom). *St. Barbara's Barn,* St. Mary's City, before it was chopped into firewood. Author, 1934.

foot of what seems to be premeditated chipping, as if a child had once upon a time been amused by making mutilations. The crude earthernware bowls (Fig. 160) are marked on the outside with shallow ring groovings, and have been pieced together by the writer. There is a front door footscraper and a garden hoe and shovel. An inhabitant of St. Mary's City whose name began with "K" possessed the branding-iron with that letter (Fig. 31). Such irons were often used for branding cattle or hogsheads of tobacco. A bit of plaster with the incised leaf pattern (Fig. 6) decorated the wall of a house.

Other items of interest in the inventory were the chocolate-brown glazed earthenware cup, with mottled effect of black and yellow, and its handle gone; a stoneware cup or jar fragment with a face of an Indian or African in relief on blue and gray field; Indian flint spearhead; pipe bowls and stem fragments with fleur-de-lis designs.

Among the bricks from the pit were orange or red Dutch bricks and brick-bats, and yellow Dutch brickbats. These bricks were smaller and harder than the usual English Statute bricks in St. Mary's City, and were similar in size, 7⅜" long by 1⅜" thick, to those found earlier by this writer in the great fireplace of ten-foot span in the *Secretary's Office* of that buried town, as described in *Jamestown and St. Mary's: Buried Cities of Romance*.

The Original *Charles' Gift*—Home with a Buried Jetty

So well publicized has been *Preston* or *Preston-at-Patuxent*, erroneously named "Charles' Gift" by a former owner, Hulbert Footner, because he liked the term, that scarcely a person has heard of the early, authentic *Charles' Gift* house (Fig. 164), standing today in an isolated spot on a bluff of the Chesapeake Bay. For *Preston* and *Charles' Gift* were never the same plantation, because they were on different bodies of water. By the time anyone wishes to purchase the original *Charles' Gift*, it will probably be too late to do anything about it. With his scythe Father Time has been standing by for decades, and besides, the neighborhood boys have done the rest.

In the Rent Rolls of Maryland we found that "Preston's Cliffs" or "Charles' Gift"—also "Charles' Guift" or "Charles's Gift"—comprised a thousand acres surveyed on May 5, 1652, for Richard Preston, a man known as the "Great Quaker," upon the west side of Chesapeake Bay. The boundary of this property began at a marked cedar standing in a branch. When resurveyed for Richard Ladd in 1687, the land was found to contain not 1,000 acres, but only 616.

"Charles' Gift" very early had a house upon it, for in 1691 Captain Richard Ladd willed to the church which was built upon the "hornes of the Clifts" the dwelling-plantation, *Charles' Gift*, for maintenance of a minister. It is possible but not probable that the framework of the early portion of the existing abode incorporates Ladd's cottage of 1691. Nevertheless, no interior trim found in the house has a 17th-century profile: it has all been changed.

Fig. 164(top). This is the authentic *Charles' Gift*. The larger chimney at left is part of the
earliest structure. Author, 1938.
Fig. 165. A(bottom left). The so-called "plank house," *Aquasco,* is a log structure. B(bottom
right). Unusual dovetail joints of "plank house." HABS.

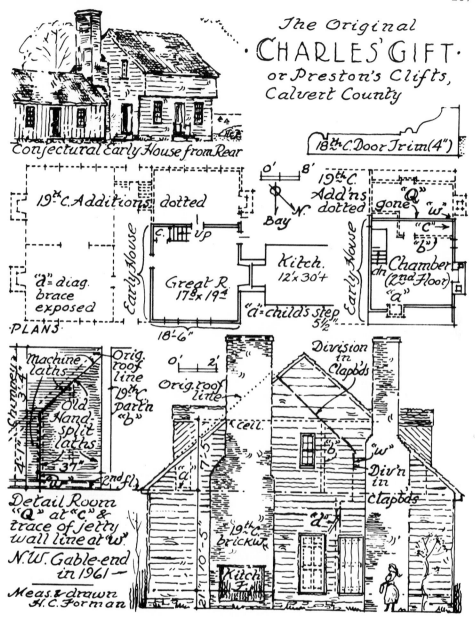

Figure 166

In 1723 the tract was possessed by Abraham Skiptin for Dorman's orphans who had 277 acres, Christopher Dungorman who held 100 acres, and Gabriel Deminian with 239.[8]

This existing *Charles' Gift* domicile on the shore of the great Bay is one-and-a-half storeys high, frame, with two rooms on either side of a central passageway, which is eight feet wide (Fig. 166). Except for the little early cottage with what appears to have been a rear jetty or overhanging second floor, now completely embodied in later work, the mansion is mid-19th-century in date or even of Civil War period with interior trim of Gothic Revival style.

The early homestead with its front toward the Bay was a tiny arrangement

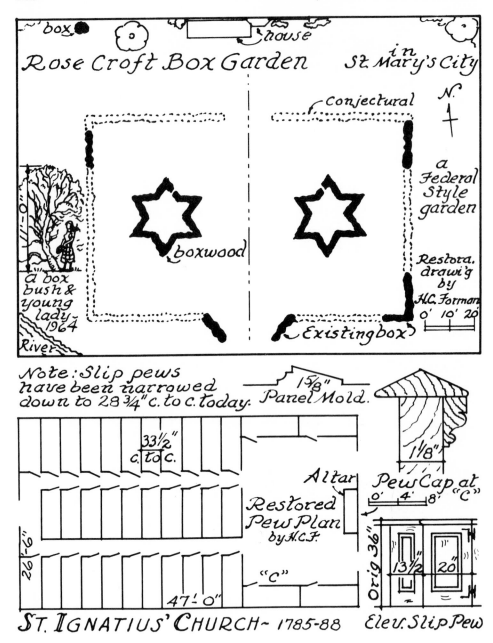

Figure 167

of room and loft, reached by a winding staircase. The newel post had an octagonal knob and lamb's tongues. The Great Hall measured only 20'-6" by 18'-6". There was but one chimney, now replaced by later brickwork, which contained the Great Room fireplace, 4'-4" in span; that of the kitchen out-house, 4'-8" wide; and that of the solitary chamber, 2'-9" wide.

In the Great Room has been set a typical 1780-90 period mantel, carrying a pulvinated frieze, and what remains of the old door trim appears to date from the same period. One of the doors has T-hinges; another has H-hinges with leather washers.

The most interesting feature of the entire structure is the outline of part of the roof of the original cottage upon the northwest gable-end. Now this is what happened there: when the mid-19th-century extensions were added, the entire roof was set at a little less pitch, and the builder, instead of nailing all new clapboards against the northwest gable, left most of the old ones in place, and tried to match them with new ones when the gable was extended, as the drawing shows.[9] By working out these details graphically, one finds that the upper storey of the early house must have overhung the lower by about sixteen inches, making a rear jetty (marked "w") closely resembling that at *Huntingfields* (Fig. 213A) in the same neighborhood.

The entire *Charles' Gift* is now a shambles, interwoven with vines and trees, and has not long to survive. Before this writer was able to sketch the octagonal-knobbed newel post, it had disappeared along with much of the interior trim. Of the kitchen wing only the fireplace remains, gaunt and forbidding. In 1953 a couple of barns with catslide roofs were standing, but they too have gone.

The child's step, marked "a" on the floor plans, was presumably built to permit infantile peeps through the dormer window toward the Bay, and the clothing pegs in room "Q" are two interesting features in the mid-19th-century additions.

This little account is a good-bye to the original *Charles' Gift* house in Maryland. Many a person would have liked to own such a home, distinguished by a rare, overhanging jetty.

West St. Mary's Manor and Its Knot Garden

How far this ancient seat, about which much has been written, has been resurrected since it was the *McKay House* may be seen in the photographs (Figs. 25A & 169), the older of which was taken in 1932 by the writer when the owner of the place, McKay, ran a still in the Great Room and fearfully kept the door to that room always locked. The house has been restored over the years as a setting for appropriate William and Mary furniture and decoration.

"West St. Mary's Manor" is the earliest grant of land known to have been recorded in Maryland. On May 9, 1634, it was granted as a 2000-acre tract to Capt. Henry Fleet, who helped in the founding of St. Mary's City. He built there the original manor-house of which no vestige remains. In 1640 this manor was owned by Thomas Cornwaleys and by 1644 by the Lord Proprietary. The size of "West St. Mary's" was extended to include several manors, making a seigniory. Thence, it became known as the "Honour of West St. Mary's."[10]

In 1644 Lord Baltimore had animals at "West St. Mary's" listed as one boar, four sows, and ten pigs. Also William Braithwaite's inventory (1644) of His Lordship's goods remaining there included a feather bed, three stock beds, two bolsters, a green and two white rugs for the bed. Two wooden platters and three wooden trays graced the table. A skiff supplied transportation across the river to St. Mary's City.

Fig. 168(top). *St. Ignatius' Church,* St. Mary's County, was built 1785–88 by Father James Walton, S.J., with square sacristy added in 1817. Author, 1964.

Fig. 169(bottom). *West St. Mary's Manor* is a Transitional example built probably between 1700 and 1730, with a conjecturally restored knot garden in appropriate style. Inset photograph was taken by the author in 1932.

In 1762 Surveyor Jesse Lock made a plat of the manor, which now appears to be missing. Along with the plat was made a record of the lands and improvements leased to tenants, which is extant. The dwellings and outhouses were listed by size, as in the following example: "No. 2. Lease to Benjamin Woodward. March 1729. 91½ acres. One old dwelling house 32' by 16', two brick chimneys . . . one granary 16' by 12' with one tobacco house 32' by 20'." Of the fifteen leaseholders, possibly one of their houses may fit the size of the existing *West St. Mary's Manor*, which from its architecture was constructed some time between 1700 and 1730, in the Style of the Transition, of Late Cell Type.

That habitation represents a good specimen of what may be accomplished with an old place after years of devoted labor by the owners, with expert and professional supervision, and with meticulous care in every detail, both inside and out.

The wooden elliptical arch dividing the stair passageway (Fig. 170) had its prototype in England. One example of about 1600 stands at *Tintinhull House*, Somerset, where the archway is located at the foot of the stairway.

The late Mr. Alden Hopkins, landscape architect of Williamsburg, Virginia, laid out the garden as a knot made up of plain squares of boxwood, a small amount of topiary work, brick walks, a wood bench or two, and a picket fence.

Tower-Chimneyed *Elizabeth Hill*

In lonely grandeur this ancient monument stands on a hill a mile back from the main road and well out of sight of it. Miss Frances Benjamin Johnston, the photographer, "discovered" this place in the late 1930s when already it was a somber, abandoned structure. The photograph of *Elizabeth Hill* (Fig. 172A) depicts the dark gauntness of this house.

At the time of her visit the frame chimney-pent was mostly hidden by an "ell" wing which has now disappeared, along with the pent itself. Consequently the towering chimneys, estimated to be forty feet high, are now exposed to view.

The chief interest of this lonesome bower is in its being a good example of the persistence of the Medieval Style of architecture for about two centuries after the founding of St. Mary's City. The house appears to date from the 1820s or 30s, and technically may be called Hangover Medieval. But there are some more luxurious features than the Medieval had to offer: downstairs sash of six lights over nine; eight-foot high ceilings on first and second floors; a broad stairway of one flight, instead of the usual boxed stair with winders. At the top of the stair the well curves around by the newel post, now gone, as shown in the floor plan (Fig. 171).

There was ample space on the second floor for four bedchambers and a passage. Even so, there was never a closet for clothes.

In a cubbyhole off this passageway a ladder mounts to what this writer has called the "supra-attic," but which seems to have been known in early times

Fig. 170. At *West St. Mary's Manor* the open-well stair of 1700–30 has simplified step-ends, block-and-turned balusters, and a rail terminating in a scroll above the newel post. The William and Mary walnut lowboy came from Pennsylvania. Blagojevich, *c.* 1963.

as the "Peake Room,"—a bare, unfinished space with two windows, at the top of the roof.

Between parlor and dining room, which are of about equal size, is the double-door feature characteristic of many early 19th-century homes—representing the first attempt to break out of the tight, enclosed-room plan of an earlier day in favor of open spaciousness.

While the general shape and mass of *Elizabeth Hill* may be Medieval, the moldings will be found to have progressed beyond the Georgian stage, and are early 19th-century in style. One of these is the typical door trim (*see* detail), which the reader may see possesses a steep "cyma" and flat recessed "fasciae" or planes. The stair spandrels are of the plainest S-shape, and the balusters, now stripped away, were rectangular in section. The oblong raised panels of the front door and of several other doors have quarter-circle, instead of the usual right-angle, corners.

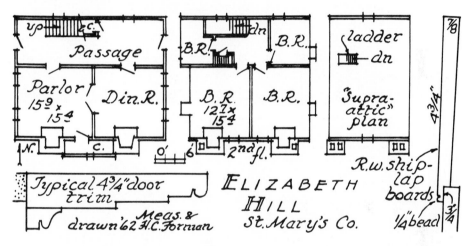

Figure 171

Then, too, the parlor mantel (Fig. 172B), found lying face down on floor rubbish by this writer, has twin fluted pilasters at each side; and each pair of pilasters holds a Gothic pointed arch in relief. Also, in the frieze are a rectangular, sunken panel in the center and pointed-arch panels at the sides. In that way the Gothic Revival bore down lightly on a domicile with Medieval Style roots.

The exterior siding is made of random-width boards, $7/8$″ thick at the upper edge, $5/8$″ at the lower. The edge bead is very small—only $1/4$ of an inch (*see* detail). The shiplap boards were put on with cut nails, at the time when wrought-iron nails had become too expensive to use, and cut nails had superseded them.

Elizabeth Hill resembles the *Driscoll Farmhouse*, or *Old House on the Bay near Trap*, which was discovered by the writer in 1932 and was first published in *Early Manor and Plantation Houses of Maryland* (1934). There is the same "ell" covering up a chimney-pent between tall stacks.

Fig. 172. A(top). Built in the 1820s or '30s, *Elizabeth Hill,* St. Mary's County, follows medieval characteristics of the 17th century in Maryland. Note chimney-pent hidden by addition. Johnston, 1930s. B(bottom left). The Parlor mantel, *Elizabeth Hill.* Author, 1962.
Fig. 173(bottom right). *Loch Leven,* a Compton home. Ferguson.

There are echoes, besides, of *Elizabeth Hill* in the design and layout of *Snow Hill Manor*, which was illustrated in *Tidewater Maryland Architecture and Gardens*, and a floor plan of it given there. While the *Snow Hill* parlor and dining room are of about equal size, and there is a transverse passage, like *Elizabeth Hill*, there are two differences: the stair was set in an alcove in this passage and there is a stair landing. Further, the *Snow Hill* chimney-pent was brick, 9″ thick, and projected 18″ out from the chimney. We acknowledge the error made in drawing the chimney-pent in the above volume (p. 134), and present here the corrected version (Fig. 155). The date mentioned, "1803," was carved on two 6″ by 7″ bricks, located about in line with the top of the *Snow Hill* chimney-pent.[11]

Who knows whether or not the poet Edwin Arlington Robinson had in mind a dwelling like *Elizabeth Hill* when he wrote:

> "They are all gone away,
> The House is shut and still,
> There is nothing more to say.
>
> Through broken walls and gray
> The winds blow bleak and shrill:
> They are all gone away.
>
> There is ruin and decay
> In the House on the Hill . . ."

Forgotten *Old Friendship*

In the lower part of Southern Maryland stands an early messuage (Fig. 175A) of antiquarian interest. Occasionally one runs across these little medieval-styled cottages with their quaint gable-ends—built in a manner now long forgotten, but which was appropriate for the time in which the builders and occupants lived. This one with picturesque chimney and brick penthouse is named *Old Friendship*.

The original dwelling comprised only Hall and Hall Chamber above. The kitchen was separate. At point "a" on our floor plan (Fig. 176) are marks on the plaster ceiling of a corner china closet, now gone, as well as a staircase to the upstairs chamber. It is interesting that the house corner post inside this former closet was chamfered to allow more room for china. Shown dotted on plan and elevation, the brick chimney-pent did once form a storage closet next the fireplace, which has a five-foot span.

The other downstairs room, the Parlor, and the Parlor Chamber, form the addition, as the plan indicates. The huge outside chimney at that end of the building has disappeared, but its stone footings were located by the writer, and have been marked down accordingly on the drawings. Further, the brick foundation of the existing hearth, ten feet long, is visible (*see* point "x") in the crawl-in space under the Parlor floor. It is evident that this ten-foot length indicates a greater fireplace span than the present boarded-up opening with mantel indicates.

Fig. 174. (Top) Built in the mid-Georgian style, *Mt. Lubentia*, Prince George's County, has had its wing heightened, dormers and walk added. (Bottom left) Main doorway, *Mt. Lubentia*. (Bottom right) The Dining Room china closet, *Mt. Lubentia*. HABS, 1936.

Fig. 175. A(top). *Old Friendship* is a brick-nogged frame cottage, the right half of which formed the first house. B(bottom left). Mid-Georgian woodwork in the Parlor, *Old Friendship*. C(bottom right). Board-and-batten woodwork in Hall Chamber. Author, 1957.

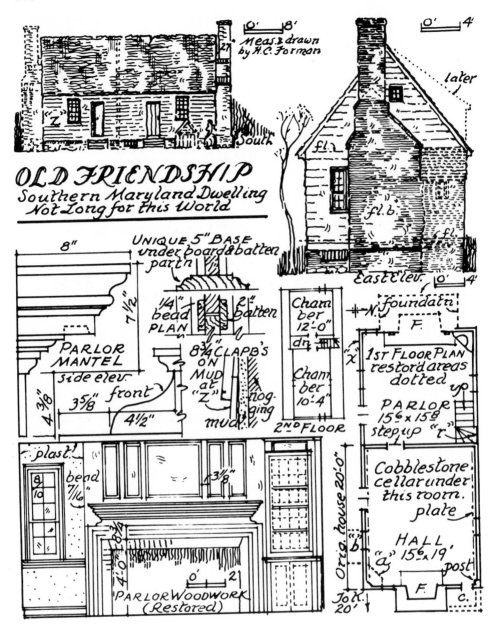

Figure 176

The whole edifice is brick-nogged; and at point "z," on the first floor plan, the outside wall was found to have a layer of mud between the beaded clapboards and the nogging, as has been drawn in the detail. Point "b" on this plan marks the outside cellar stairs.

The upstairs woodwork in the two bedchambers (Fig. 175C) appears to be of the same date as the stairway, which is a crude insertion in the abode, and later than the Parlor and Hall woodwork. In these chambers the chair rail and the batten or muntin pieces (*see* details) are plain board strips beaded on both edges; but what seems to be unique is that the plank partitions in the passage rest on flat, wood base boards cut with cymas, as another of the details illustrates. Contrary to the usual method, this partition is not nailed to the floor with shoe moldings to conceal the cracks.

The doors in the partitions are only five feet and five-and-a-half inches high—scarcely tall enough for today's children. But the stair is hardly of a size for modern men: it is only twenty-six inches wide, and has winders. An interesting feature is that at the point before the stair turns, there is a three-inch deep recess in the outside wall—no doubt to give extra space for the turning of pieces of furniture being carried on the stairs.

At some time in the 19th century the north eaves were raised about four feet; but strangely enough, the alteration made no better headroom in the east chamber, because the old ceiling was preserved, as shown in the photograph.

A kitchen outhouse once stood about twenty feet from the east gable-end and measured, according to our soundings, about 20′ by 24′. Such is *Old Friendship*, forgotten and forlorn.

Six Southern Maryland Dwelling-Houses of the Transition

When one is directed to *Mansion Hall* down a lonely road through the woods, a large building would naturally be expected, in conformity with the name; but this hut is one of those tiny, very late 17th- or early 18th-century examples, of medieval hall-and-parlor arrangement and with transitional "cells" or "aisles" added at the rear (Fig. 180, right). When this addition was constructed, a little, squarish window was found to peek out from behind a chimney, as may be seen in the photograph (Fig. 177A). The weatherboarding is shiplap, and the walls are brick-nogged.

Some of the windows at *Mansion Hall,* other than the square ones mentioned, are but two panes wide, the upper sash being four panes, the lower two. At the same time there are batten doors and low ceilings.

Several years ago the writer discovered in this habitation the first Jacobean staircase (Fig. 177B) found in the State.[12] Jutting out from a little winding stair in a corner of the Great Room, and below a door made up of two wide battens on H-L hinges, are three steps having a handrail with medieval profiles and splat, or flat-shaped, balusters, cut jigsaw-like. There is a closed string and a square newel post with a shaped finial. While in 1940 there were two whole balusters, nine years later all of them had been knocked out of the railing, probably to be burned for firewood. Today there are no balusters.

A winding path at *Mansion Hall* leads to pine woods where the wreck of a burial ground remains. Mrs. Helen West Ridgely in her book, *Historic Graves of Maryland and the District of Columbia,* well expressed the situation when she wrote about one Maryland plantation that they had to pass through a barnyard as the shortest way across a field to a rise of ground, where in a copse lay the dead.

Fig. 177. A(top). In spite of the name, *Mansion Hall* is a small Medieval hall-and-parlor cottage, with Transitional "aisles" added at the rear. Author, 1953. B(bottom). The remnants of the first Jacobean stair found in Maryland has splat balusters, hand rail with Gothic profile, and shaped newel post. Author, 1940.

This writer gives forthwith the names and dates of those stones which could be found, because someone, some day, may be glad to have the record. The oldest stone visible above the vines is that of Captain John F. Gray, who was born on November 24, 1771, and who passed away June 26, 1830. It is curious that each Gray who had possessed a wife had one by the name of Elizabeth.[13]

In this area the first John Gray owned "Gray's Addition," 100 acres surveyed for him in 1682, adjoining the land of Richard Harrison. He also held (1725) "Lee." In 1716, he willed to his sons Richard and William the (unnamed) "dwelling plantation" with 398 acres—probably *Mansion Hall*.

Another early tract was "Bryerwood" or "Briarwood," comprising 650 acres surveyed in 1665 for Gerrard Fowke on the south side of "ye main fresh or run that falls into Mattawoman Creek. This land being in Pangaya Manor, [was] granted him at 30 bushels of Indian corn per annum." On March 5, 1685, Gerrard Fowke conveyed "Bryerwood" to Thomas Mudd. In 1725 this parcel of land was owned by Colonel Philip Hoskins, whose son of the same name was a joiner by trade.

For one or two generations, the dwelling, *Bryerwood* (Figs. 178 & 190), situated upon that acreage, has been the refuge of tramps and squatters; and when not occupied by them, a lonely house in desuetude. On warm summer days masters of the osculatory art scratched their names on the plaster, as for instance: "LOVERS—WF LOVES MH." Even the termites have eaten through the great 8″ by 11″ girders in the cellar, which contains a large fireplace.

The floor plan (Fig. 180, bottom) and photographs of this lodging show an example of what this writer has called "Transitional of the Late Cell Type"—that is, having "cells," symmetrical gables, and no catslide roof. Thus *Bryerwood* is a more advanced phase of a house with "cells" than is *Mansion Hall* with its asymmetrical gables.[14]

The exterior walls and interior partitions of *Bryerwood* are well nogged; and where the plaster has fallen and exposed large bare spaces of brick, the appearance of the wall is like half-timber work. The habitation has certain refinements, like the watertable of double curvature (*see* detail), and a separate passageway for a transitional stairway, so that the date of building is probably in the second quarter of the 18th century.

The stair itself (*see* detail) is wainscoted with beaded pine boards laid diagonally to follow the slope of the steps, like those wainscots at *St. John's* in Charles County and at the Law Office at *Havre-de-Venture*. At *Bryerwood* there are no dormers: a small gable window suffices to ventilate each of the four chambers upstairs.

On a hill on this farm stands an early 19th-century house; in its graveyard are stones of McDaniel and Penn.[15]

Still a third transitional example is *Federal Grove* (Fig. 179), a two-storey-and-loft seat which once belonged to members of the Brown family. Actually

Fig. 178(top). *Bryerwood,* a good example of "Late Cell" stage of Transitional style, has chimney-pents and stands on Pangaya Manor. Ferguson, 1940.

Fig. 179(bottom). *Federal Grove* has quaint motif of brick pents flanking one of the chimneys. Author, 1955.

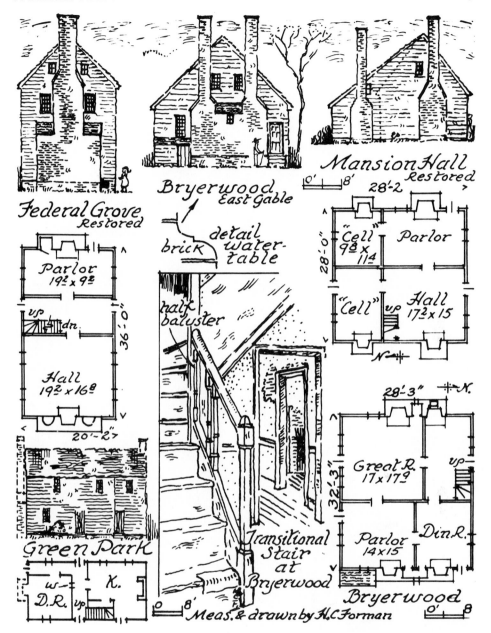

Federal Grove Restored

Parlor 19ᵉ x 9ᵉ

Hall 19ᵉ x 16ᵉ

Green Park

D.R. W. K.

Bryerwood East Gable

brick detail water-table

half baluster

Transitional Stair at Bryerwood

Mansion Hall Restored 28'-2"

"Cell" 9ᵉ x 11ᵉ   Parlor

"Cell"   Hall 17ᵉ x 15

28'-3"

Great R. 17 x 17ᵉ   up

Parlor 14 x 15   Din.R.

Bryerwood

Meas. & drawn by H.C.Forman

Figure 180

the building belongs to the style of Hangover Transitional, since it appears to have been constructed some time between 1795 and 1810. This, it may be noted, is a specimen of a Maryland home which "went vertical instead of horizontal."

The chief interest of *Federal Grove* lies in its two picturesque gable-ends, the west one having been drawn to scale (Fig. 180, top left). Note that there is a small brick pent on each side of the western chimney which houses a semi-circular closet with arched heads and curlicue shelves. Further, the east end (Fig. 182B) has but one pent, a regular closet with door, but no window, and

Fig. 181. A(top). Home of a Signer of the Declaration of Independence, *The Retreat* has an unusually-designed chimney-pent, now changed. Ferguson, *c*. 1940. B(bottom right). The early type of stair at *The Retreat*. Author, 1940.

Fig. 182. A(center left). Brick nogging at *Federal Grove*. B(bottom left). East gable-end, *Federal Grove*

with shelves and two drawers. The Parlor has a great panel over the fireplace.

Nearby stood an ancient abode known as *Rose Mary Lawn*, which was burned. It is supposed to have resembled *Federal Grove*.[16]

A fourth example of the Transition, *Green Park* (Fig. 180, bottom left), follows the sprouting-upward trend of *Federal Grove* into a full second storey, while keeping to the one-room depth. When writing of *Green Park*, we refer specifically to the timber-framed wing (*c.* 1700-30) of a large brick mid-19th-century building. This wing, by the way, originally stood in the garden in front of the site of the present brick edifice, and was later removed to form an addition. At that time the free gable-end of the wing was constructed of brick in a bonding similar to that of the brick house.

Notice that the passageway at *Green Park* has a boxed stair in an "ell." The little window marked "w" on the floor plan may have been used as a pass-through to the dining room.

The frame house may have been built by a son or grandson of Gov. Thomas Greene, whose home of 1639 was at "Greene's Freehold" or "St. Anne's" in St. Mary's City. It is understood that after 250 years and more *Green Park* still belongs to persons by the name of Green.

A fifth domicile of the Transition is the little-known place called *The Retreat* (Fig. 181A), once the property of Daniel of St. Thomas Jenifer, a framer of the Constitution of the United States and member of the Continental Congress. From 1775 to 1776 he was president of the Maryland Council of Safety and from 1777 to 1781 first president of the Senate of the Free State. His grandnephew, Daniel Jenifer, was United States ambassador to Austria, and also lived at *Charles Towne*, Charles County.

The Retreat has especially picturesque chimneys with weatherings at different angles and pent window. The first floor is divided into a transverse passage on one side and two rooms on the chimney side. In an "ell" off the passageway is an open stairway with simple spandrels and turned newel post with tall crowning or shaped knob (Fig. 181B). As was done in several other Charles County homesteads, the bottom step was placed on the diagonal to project beyond the line of the stairs.

The old kitchen, from all indications, was not in the present rear wing of the house—which contains too small a fireplace for kitchen use—but was in a separate outhouse to the east of the chimney-pent.

Daniel of St. Thomas Jenifer was a close friend of George Washington, who on June 3, 1763, was a visitor at *The Retreat*.

The original Daniel Jenifer—and there were several of the name—owned "Laurell Branch," 1,000 acres surveyed for him in 1669 next to "White's Field" in Port Tobacco Hundred.

Planter's Delight (Fig. 183), the last Transitional habitation of this Southern Maryland group, is a very late 18th-century example of the "Late Cell Type," which at some period was almost doubled in length by an addition. It is of course possible that the place is as late as 1810. At any rate it appears

Fig. 183(top). *Planter's Delight* was built some time between 1790 and 1810 and had lost a pair of end chimneys when photographed. Author, 1940.

Fig. 184(bottom). The interior of *Elverton Hall,* a nitroglycerine victim, made use of the circle, semicircle, and ellipse for decoration. HABS, 1936.

to have been constructed on a property of the same name surveyed in 1659 for George Thompson, and possessed in 1725 by Peter Mills, who married the widow of Ignatius Wheeler. Without the twin chimneys, which blew down at the end of the addition, and in its dilapidated condition, *Planter's Delight* has lost much of its distinctive appearance.

In the old days a nearby plantation-house called *Stoke Hill* stood on land surveyed for John Wheeler and later was owned by Philip Lynes of St. Mary's City, but nothing is known of its aspect.

The Dynamiting of *Elverton Hall*

In Prince George's County an excellent example of the Federal or Early Republican domestic style was old *Elverton Hall* (Fig. 185A), located near Mullikin. More particularly, the overall design of this building was what was known as "Post-Colonial," a phase of the Federal Style of architecture which this writer has called "Hangover Georgian"—a more graphic expression for the persistence of the Georgian Style into the 19th century. "Colonial" can be made to mean a lot of things.

Elverton Hall probably dated between 1840 and 1860 and formed a squarish brick pile with later, marble-floored porches, wooden jigsaw cornices, and a rear frame wing with inset second-storey porch—all Victorian additions. The design of the front is interesting because it shows what could happen to the typical Georgian façade after the year 1800 had passed. Here the usual front door had sprouted side-lights and oval transom; and more important, the five windows were also widened by side-lights. As a result the brick flat arches over these windows were very wide, perhaps six feet, since they had to cover the side-lights on the flanks. The photograph of the front shows all four chimneys intact, but one dormer missing.

The writer was not able to make a measured plan of *Elverton Hall* between the time of his first visit and its destruction about a year later. But we did find that the stair (Fig. 185B) was boxed in on the side of the entrance passageway. One started upwards by climbing six winding steps in a 90° turn. Curiously enough, the narrow column of a newel post was not attached to a hand rail with balusters, but abutted the jamb of the stair door, as the picture indicates. The fifth riser, too, bulged out in order to receive that slender post— a unique method in this country of designing a newel.

As in many other Hangover Georgian buildings, the interior made use of the circle, semicircle, and ellipse for decoration. The two rooms (Fig. 184)— perhaps parlors—show free use of the elliptical arch and vaulting, as well as circles on the ceiling and in the door trim, and a semicircular fan transom. The downstairs passageway had three fan-lights over doorways. Although the door trim had profiles and corner circles of Victorian design, the window jambs were panelled in the Georgian manner.

Fig. 185. A(top left). *Elverton Hall,* Prince George's County, formed a good example of what happened to the Georgian Style by the 1840s. HABS, 1936. B(top right). Front stair with unusual newel. Wilfong, 1952. C(bottom left). Main front of *Elverton Hall* after dynamiting. Wilfong, 1952.

Fig. 186(bottom right). Weatherbeaten *Hard Bargain,* Prince George's County. Ferguson, 1940.

By the year 1950 *Elverton Hall* was still standing; nonetheless one corner of the brick portion had been blown away, reportedly by an attempt to dynamite tree stumps in the neighborhood. Then weather entered the mansion through large holes. To a new owner this damage by the elements was discouraging, because he decided to get rid of the whole pile at once. In the spring of 1952 a tremendous charge of dynamite left the structure a heap of rubble, glass, and fractured timbers. We were not there, but the tremors may have shaken the United States Capitol.

One friend of *Elverton Hall*, who supplied two photographs of it, has well written: "The ghost of *Bond Castle* has a compatriot if there's such a place as an architectural Valhalla." But *Bond Castle* never suffered the shocking fate of TNT.

Three Southern Maryland Two-Storey "Penters"

The St. Mary's County type of chimney-pent, or closet with one-slope roof beside the chimney, sometimes comes two floors high. There are examples in St. Mary's County, as at *Woodlawn* and the *Davis House;* but also Prince George's County possessed at least three known ones. For brevity, we call them "two-storey penters."

The first of these is a destroyed edifice, *Hatton's Mansion* or *Chapel Hill* (Fig. 189), which once stood near Fort Washington. Although the roof above the double-storey brick pent in one photograph resembles one with a hip, actually the gable had fallen backward as the roof started to collapse. At the other gable-end there is a single chimney, which, as the evidence of the wall indicates, had a small one-storey pent. The mansion was brick-nogged, so that where the wide bevel-edged siding boards have fallen off, the wall construction resembled half-timber work.

Hatton's Mansion passed away, as Mr. James C. Wilfong, Jr., once well stated, "too early for the motor age to bring restoration help past its door."

Another specimen of the same type of homestead is *White Hall Farm* (Fig. 192), of the Marburys, having a two-storey brick pent with one window above the other, and the appearance of an 18th-century building, although the interior woodwork is later. Notice how the brick is laid up in the Flemish bond and how much smaller are the second floor windows than those on the first floor, except in the chimney-pent, where the reverse is true. The little kitchen wing nestles picturesquely under and at right angles to the great chimney-pent, rising upward like a strong buttress. Wilfong called this establishment a "structural curiosity" and related how "one circles the house and comes upon the surprising chimneys, unseen from the road."

The third example is *Spring Hill* (Fig. 191) with a windowless two-storey pent between chimneys. Again Wilfong had appropriate comments: "it is a large frame rectangular dwelling of no interior pretension, but possessing a very unusual exterior chimney treatment [which would] delight the eye of any

Fig. 187(top)   Almost forgotten by mankind is brick *Ohmerest* on its Southern Maryland river. Note early plaster necking band. Johnston, 1930s.

Fig. 188(bottom).   *Grovehurst* unfortunately has disappeared from Prince George's County. HABS, 1936.

Fig. 189. (Top left) "I tell the tale as 'twas told to me": the writer never had an opportunity to visit *Hatton's Mansion* before its end. Ferguson, *c.* 1936. (Top right) *Hatton's Mansion*, Ferguson, *c.* 1936. (Bottom left) Another view of *Hatton's Mansion*. HABS, 1936. Fig. 190(bottom right). View of *Bryerwood*. Ferguson, 1940.

Fig. 191(top). At one end *Spring Hill* has a windowless double-storey pent. Author, 1953.
Fig. 192. (Center) *White Hall Farm* contains small apertures in the pent. Author, 1940.
(Bottom) Another view of *White Hall Farm*. Wilfong, 1950.

artist. . . . This house was built probably in the 1790s, [a theory] based on its interior woodwork, but neither its present nor former owners can authenticate that date. Confusion with another *Spring Hill* [which has] now disappeared from the western ridge of the Patuxent, near *Mt. Pleasant,* makes tracing its early history difficult."

Finally, *Spring Hill,* the two-storey penter, may have a plain stairway in the main passageway, but the newel post is unique in its design—something like a four-way triumphal arch on four posts, with a heavy top of torus and cavetto profiles.

The Nottingham Town Ghost Houses

In 1939 an "ace" reporter for the *Times Herald,* of Washington, D.C., wrote of his visit to Nottingham—or West Nottingham, as it was once called—situated on the Patuxent River. Some of his words about that formerly flourishing port are too good to miss:

"When you drive into Nottingham, you don't see anything but a couple of houses and a barn sitting in tobacco fields, with the blue waters of the Patuxent at the foot of the fields.

"It's difficult to picture in your mind colonial ladies dismounting from their coaches to stay overnight in the big Nottingham hotel on the way from the South to Philadelphia and New York . . . But they used to be there. Cotillions were danced in the hotel every night, ships laden with silks, satins, powdered wigs, and pipes of Madeira and port bobbed at anchor in the harbor and near-by in a mansion lived young and handsome [General] Robert Bowie, soldier statesman, with his bride, Priscilla Mackall with whom he [had] eloped when she was 15, he 19.

"All that used to be there. But it's gone now. All that's left is the sepulchral, silver-grey ruin of Robert Bowie's house, gaunt, ravaged, tumbling down, haunted by courtly memories.

"We walked to the front door. It had been ripped out, wainscoting and all. Inside, crumbled plaster lay on the floor, a bed spring, a lawn mower, empty tin cans, cobwebs and dust. Wasps and flies buzzed. Weeds clutched at its foundations. It was a sad sight.

"Sloping away from the shaded house were fields in which I could see ruins of old houses, parts of which had been sold to antique collectors, parts burned by fires through the centuries, overgrown with bushes and weeds."

Next, the "ace" reporter told of an old negro called Ambrose, "who [some years previously had] lived in the back rooms of the [Robert Bowie] mansion" and "must've been a hundred if he was a day." Ambrose is reported to have said: "I can remember when there was a big town here, full of doctors and businessmens, and McCuppen's tavern was a-flourishin' and they wouldn't let the slaves drink out of the town spring 'cause the water was cold and'd give 'em cramps so they couldn't work in the fields."

Fig. 193 (top and center). The *Gov. Robert Bowie House*, known as *The Cedars*, was a focus of attention for architects and antiquarians. HABS, 1936.

Fig. 194 (bottom). Near Largo, Prince George's County, stands 19th-century *Chelsea*, of hand-riven framing, and with an early "farmer's porch" across the entire front. Wilfong.

Fig. 195. A(top). In the *Gov. Robert Bowie House, Nottingham*, the Parlor plaster frieze had
rinceaux, egg, and leaf designs. B(bottom). The passage with hand-carved stair. What were
the preservation societies doing at this time? HABS.

Fig. 196(top). The left-hand section of *Old House* near Ardmore on "Three Sisters" tract has one of the steepest roofs in Maryland. Wilfong, 1952.

Fig. 197(center). In the knot garden of almost solid boxwood squares at *Hard Bargain*, Charles County.

Fig. 198(bottom). *Lower Notley* or *Rozier House*, with spurious names, originally had a gambrel. Wilfong, 1953.

The above-mentioned mansion was the *Governor Robert Bowie House,* otherwise called *The Cedars,*[17] the *Berry House,* or *Nottingham Farm* (Fig. 193), which Mr. James C. Wilfong, Jr., and this writer together visited in October, 1952. In a letter at that time written to the editor of the *Maryland Historical Magazine,* Mr. Wilfong remarked that this dwelling "had been ruinous for a generation, but even in its declining years it remained a point of attention for architects and antiquarians for its notable lines and proportions. It was no doubt the oldest [then existing] building [of a half-dozen somnolent residences] in Nottingham, and considering its historical background, it seems the more regrettable that disinterest finally brought about its end." In the photograph is to be seen a typical frame, two-storey-and-loft abode with out-side twin chimneys at one end. But inside there was a fine, though steep and narrow, open stairway, with carved step-ends and saddles on the hand-rail. Also there was at the foot of the stairs a front doorway with fan-light and side-lights (Fig. 195B), which had been boarded across securely; and a classical plaster frieze (Fig. 195A) was of the richest.

At the time of our visit, Mr. Wilfong noted that "only its brick foundations marked its two-hundred-year-old site." It seems pathetic, he indicated further, that the untimely end of this mansion occurred—because in 1950, two years before, it still stood. What were the preservation societies doing at the time? Was not the fine old home of a governor of Maryland worth a few dollars and a little care, for survival? Wilfong went on to declare that "with the destruction of this edifice one more bond between the 18th century and the 20th has been irretrievably lost."

Another of the known buildings in Nottingham was *Harmony Hall,* which as far back as 1936 had only a vine-covered chimney left standing.

Standing in the vicinity of the old settlement is a two-storey domicile of early 19th-century vintage called *The Plantation* or *Dr. Gibbons House,* noted for its fine kitchen chimney with ample weatherings of stepped brick on three sides. Although the seat is plain and typical of its era, it is located on a hill with a fine view, and traces of a large garden remain.

The Western Shore Has Spyglasses, Too[18]

As we have seen in a previous chapter, a real "spyglass" or "telescope" structure must have the roof lines at about the same pitch; the outside walls make somewhat regular setbacks; and theoretically the sections of the building could collapse neatly into each other. If the building looks like a "telescope," but does not meet these specifications, it is a "neo-telescope."

No one has seen all the old "spyglasses" in Maryland, and nobody will ever see them all—too many back roads, hidden fields, and woodlands. Consequently, when we meet with two "true" examples, we should, to be fair, designate them as "among the best" rather than "the best" in Maryland.

Brick *Hard Bargain* (Fig. 197) in Charles County, pictured in several books, was commenced about 1768 and was later given by Gwynn Harris of one of

Fig. 199. A(top). Buttressed by its own studs, you could look through the ribs of *Chestnut Hill,* Charles County, like those of the ship in *The Rime of the Ancient Mariner.* Owned by members of Talbot, Edelen, and Hamilton families, the largest section dated about 1800–20. B(bottom left). View of staircase, *Chestnut Hill.* Author, 1949.

Fig. 200(bottom right). The quaint brick end of *Carthagena.* Michael, 1933.

the neighboring plantations, "Mt. Tirzah," to his brother, Tom Harris. When the writer in 1930 visited *Hard Bargain*, the house was in a bare and decrepit condition; since then, the Maryland renascence has given it, as well as many another early dwelling, a bright renovating and face-lifting. Aesthetically the telescope sections are nearly perfect, and the little square milk house near the end of the building neatly finishes off the picture. Another brick plantation-house in the same county, *Dent's Palace*, built perhaps in the 1770s, belonged to members of the Dent family and is on its exterior much like *Hard Bargain*, but extends in the reverse direction.

"Palace" is a rare appellation in English America; but Maryland had the earliest one in the Colonies—the *Palace of St. John's*, the home of the Third Lord Baltimore in St. Mary's City.

In Baltimore County are two "telescopes" or "neo-telescopes" which we discovered back in the 1930s: One, *Taylor's Hall* (Fig. 224), near Cockeysville, belonged to the family of which Joshua F. Cockey was a well-known member. This abode is unique because the smallest section, believed to be over 260 years old, and the middle portion are both constructed of squared logs with the adze marks showing upon them. The largest part is a typical limestone Baltimore County seat of the early 19th century. The other example, *Hereford Farm* (Fig. 235), where the middle segment is a stone gambrel, was built at Hereford soon after 1714 by John Merryman of Clover Hill, and is described in Part V of this book.

As the reader may have already guessed, the Maryland "spyglass" could have its sections built in any order, or even all at once. Nevertheless the popular impression seems to be that the parts were constructed in the following order, "A-B-C," where "A" is the smallest segment and "C" the largest, as at *Taylor's Hall*, already mentioned. On the contrary, you could have a formula like "C-B-A," where the biggest portion "C" came first, as at *Hard Bargain* in Charles County.

At *Woodlawn*, the Sellman House,[19] in Anne Arundel County (Fig. 212), the middle section came first, resulting in the combination, "B-C-A." Making up the mathematical formula for *Castle Hall* (Fig. 63, center left) is left up to the reader.

If you searched long enough you might find a "telescope" built all at once. A few years ago, Mr. J. C. Wilfong, Jr., discovered in a ramshackle condition down some byway near Nottingham in Prince George's County an early 19th-century weatherboarded example called *The Valley* or *The Valley Farm* (Fig. 201), one of the Contee habitations. It was almost a perfect example of its type. Evidently the owner, whose housing sentiments must have had a strong archaeological flavor, replaced his formerly burned (1806) telescopic lodging with an entirely new one, the three divisions of which were erected simultaneously.

Other interesting "spyglasses" are *Wyoming,* the Marbury home in Prince George's County, which is pictured in several books; *Tudor* or *Tudor Hall* in Anne Arundel; and *Abraham Scott Jr.'s Mill House,*[20] built about 1770 on "Regulation" in the Western Run Valley.

Marylanders must face up to the fact that their early buildings including "telescopes," are being permitted to disintegrate and vanish in large numbers without a record of any kind made of them. Our eighteen-year-old snapshot of *Chestnut Hill,* a Charles County residence of "spyglass" type (Fig. 199A), shows what has happened, and is happening, to large numbers of "spyglass" specimens.

Figure 201

This writer's estimate, based on our surveys over a 35-year period, is that each year in the Free State about 500 structures built before 1800 go the way of the wind. The rate of destruction must be increasing each year because of the accelerated expansion about our great cities and small towns. And in all the desuetude, the brutal alterations, the evanescence, the "spyglass" houses of Maryland, many of which are works of art, have suffered no more, no less, than any other kind of habitation.

Two Post-Revolutionaries: *Ellserlie* and *Pleasant Prospect*

The large tract of land known as "The Partnership" contained 1,500 acres surveyed in 1680 for Major Nicholas Sewall and John Darnall, and lay in Collington "Hundred" on the "easternmost fork" of the "western branch" of the Patuxent River. Today the property is known as *Partnership Farm* or *Ellserlie* (Fig. 205). The single gravestone copied off by this writer reads as follows: "Here lyeth the Body of Elinor Hall Daughter to Benj. & Mary Hall of Charles County Maryland who Departed this Life on Friday ye 17 day of July An[no]1702 Aged 5 years 9 months."

The mansion where little Elinor lived is two-storey brick, with a floor plan of two rooms on either side of a central passageway, and the broad stairway takes up a small alcove or "ell" in the passage. The best woodwork in the house is the elliptical arch on fluted Doric pilasters which divides the passageway into two parts (Fig. 206B). The jambs and soffit of the arch are panelled and have rope mouldings.

One should never date the erection of the house from a gravestone, as some writers have done. This place is, of course, not "before 1702,"—not even 1750, if the architectural evidence is read correctly. The earliest portion of the structure is what remains of the outer brick shell. Although the brick walls were at one time stuccoed over and have been extensively repaired, Flemish bond with glazed headers, and English bonding below the watertable are visible. Some of the windows have gauged or rubbed flat arches; others do not. The narrow, two-pane-wide windows in the west gable-end are curious. The reason for this may be that examination of the brickwork and fenestration of the west gable-end leads one to suspect that the whole wall is a replacement. The main or south façade originally had gauged flat arches over the windows, and is now decorated with a belt course four bricks wide (Fig. 206A). The cornice with modillions and the roof swallow-tail, or "kick" out, are modern.

The front doorway with side-lights of horizontal diamonds and transom light with vertical diamonds belongs to the early 19th century. Even though the brickwork might indicate an earlier date, the floor plan and interior woodwork give evidence of a time of construction of about 1780-90. A dairy is the only outhouse left.

Something on the same order of design and period of building is the brick, two-storey domicile, *Pleasant Prospect* (Fig. 204), ancient seat of members of the Contee, Hill, and Duckett families. Like *Ellserlie* we encounter a floor plan of two rooms on either side of a passageway, Flemish bonded brickwork, and rubbed brick arches on some of the windows. The hipped-roof wing and curtain, both of brick, are more modern.

Pleasant Prospect was probably erected by a man called "Johne Clarke," whose name still remains in the brickwork of the garden façade.

Fig. 202(top). A chapel of ease for Christ Church Parish, Calvert County, *Middleham Chapel* (1746–48) has transepts bonded into main walls, one serving as vestibule with door, the other having only a window. The cornices, windows, belfry, interior decoration, and pews are Victorian. Johnston, 1930s.

Fig. 203(bottom). *Grovehurst* mantel with dancing girls and fruit basket. HABS.

Fig. 204(top). *Pleasant Prospect* (*c*. 1780–90), Prince George's County, presents Victorian gable and farmer's porch. HABS.
Fig. 205(bottom). The earliest part of *Partnership Farm*, or *Ellserlie*, is what remains of the outer brick shell. Wilfong.

Fig. 206. A(top). Brickwork on garden front of *Ellserlie* or *Partnership*. HABS. B(bottom).
Passage has woodwork of about 1780–90, later than original abode. Author, 1938.

Fig. 207. (Top left) Close-up of swags and urns. Author, 1939. (Right) An interior door at *Pleasant Prospect*, Prince George's County, shows Adam influence in swags and urns. HABS. (Bottom left) Double-curvature water-table. HABS.

Originally the main stairway led up from the present rear alcove of the Great Room: the present stair in the central passage is of the 19th century. The front door has bolection moldings on the exterior, but horizontal batten boards on the inside; and there is a good fan-light. Some of the interior doors (Fig. 207) downstairs are in the Adam tradition, having entablatures with stubby flutes on the corona, as well as friezes with plaster garlands and urns.

Upstairs, the window jambs project out into the rooms to allow space for folding shutters. In the "bridal chamber" over the Great Room is a good example of a sleigh bed.

The plantation apparently has only one outbuilding, a wood smoke house.

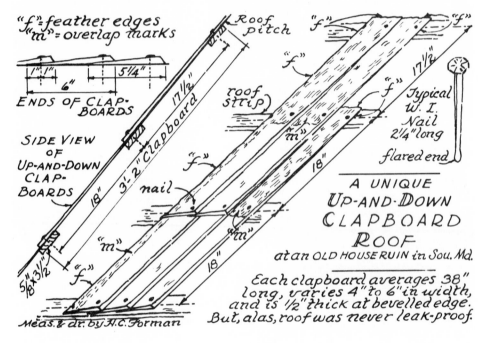

Figure 208

Big House, Little House, Colonnade, and Kitchen: *Hickory Hill*

In very bad condition stands an old Clagett farm in Prince George's County by the name of *Hickory Hill* (Figs. 161 & 254). There is a persistent rumor in the locality that a new owner is about to begin a "restoration." Unfortunately, the homestead is reached only on foot or horseback through long woods, so that there might be difficulty in trucking building supplies for the work.

According to the Rent Rolls, "Hickory Hills" was surveyed in 1703 for William Hutchinson on St. John's Creek, and in 1707 was owned by William Hutchinson, Jr.

The plantation-dwelling there comes close to filling the formula, "big house, little house, colonnade, and kitchen"—where the "colonnade" is actually a curtain or covered passageway.

Presumably the "little" house and kitchen outhouse were constructed first as two separate buildings in the late 18th century. The curtain was then added, and in the early 19th, the largest section.

The interior woodwork is undistinguished, except for a mantel with fluted pilasters and reeds in both frieze and bedmolding.

In this habitation the cedar shingles have fluttered so much that the wrought-iron nails have worked loose and stand up on the shingles. If the reader should ever succeed in exploring about this farm, he will find the great beams and gray planks of the old barn lying flat upon the ground. In Maryland the out-buildings are first to go.

Another abode near *Hickory Hill* was *Exeter,* of the 18th century, having in the Great Room a corner cupboard with wooden latches and a break-your-neck stair shut off by a tiny door.

What's in a Name—Call It *Beall's Pleasure*

In earlier times called *The Beaver Dam* or *The Dairy*, this two-storey-and-loft brick house known as *Beall's Pleasure* (Fig. 211) was designed on the lines of *West Hatton* and *Waverly* in Charles County, Maryland. It has the elliptical-arched door and leaded transom of *Waverly* and a brick curtain wall rising between the twin chimneys, as at *West Hatton*.

The five hundred acres of "Beall's Pleasure" were surveyed on October 20, 1706, for Colonel Ninian Beall, and lay on the east side of Cattle Marsh Branch. Records at Upper Marlborough, the county seat of Prince George's, show that this property was bought in 1794 by Benjamin Stoddert, who was the first secretary of the Federal Navy, and who in 1781 married Rebecca Lowndes of *Bostwick* in Bladensburg, Maryland. Since Benjamin Stoddert's grandfather settled on a plantation in Charles County known as "Friendship," it might be a coincidence that there appear in *Beall's Pleasure* some Charles County mansion design characteristics.

Further, a cousin of Benjamin Stoddert by the name of Major William Truman Stoddert, owned *West Hatton,* in Charles County.

The common bonding of *Beall's Pleasure* appears to indicate a late date of construction—what could be 1794 or a little later, and to disprove the theory that the house was built before the ownership of the Stodderts. But there were improvements on this property in 1776 when Charles Wallingford of Anne Arundel County conveyed "Beall's Pleasure" to James Crawford, of Prince George's County, mentioning "buildings, orchards, fences, pastures."

In some letters written after 1794 by Rebecca (Lowndes) Stoddert to one of her relatives, she refers to *Beall's Pleasure* as *The Beaver Dam*; but on June 20, 1796, she wrote a friend, Eliza Gantt, as follows:

"I hope soon to see your Mama at The Dairy, no longer the Beaver Dam, remember, with you and I. There is something low and vulgar in the Beaver

Fig. 209(top and center). The early 19th-century *Brookefield* has wide entrance doors with elliptical transoms. Two of the old outhouses are shown. Author, 1963.

Fig. 210(bottom). *Wetherill's Mill,* Harford County, has four doors, one above the other. Johnston, 1930s.

Fig. 211(top). A Charles County type of mansion is *Beall's Pleasure*. HABS, 1936.
Fig. 212(bottom). *Woodlawn,* a Sellman home, never belonged to the Contees. Begun in 1735, it was owned by the Sellmans for seven generations, until 1915. Author, 1955.

Fig. 213. A(top). Two views of the jetty and what we have named the "Bridge of Sighs,"
Huntingfields. Author, 1960. B(bottom left). The flower garden. Scott.
Fig. 214(bottom right). Modern upstairs passage-bath in old home, Onancock, Va. Author.

Dam, but The Dairy sounds well. Clarissa Harlowe, I think I shall call myself—you recollect her dairy."

It was Samuel Richardson who wrote *Clarissa Harlow,* published in 1748, in which the heroine, Clarissa, inherited from her grandfather a place called the "Grove," fitted up with a spacious dairy. Some years later Marie Antoinette constructed an elaborate dairy at Versailles and dressed her servants as dairy maidens.

None of the rooms of *Beall's Pleasure* seem to have been panelled, but the interior woodwork, while simply carved, is very effective. The eight mantels are also plain. The stairway at one time was widened, and the den room has new panelling.

The storey-and-a-half kitchen wing of brick is of recent date and does not well fit the habitation. The old frame stable was moved and renovated into a cottage and the box garden was laid out in rectangles.

Huntingfields, Bridge and Jetty Household

This dwelling, the original name of which may have been *Lowrey,* was owned by John Stanforth, who according to the date on his stone,[21] died in 1815. From the Stanforths the place went to their descendants, the Sommervilles, and then to members of the Williams family.

At *Huntingfields* (Fig. 213) is one of the three known existing early "jetties" or overhanging storeys in the Free State. It may be recalled that old *Bond Castle* once had five jetties, possibly the most ever counted in an American 17th-century building. Further, *Huntingfields* has a unique two-storey curtain or covered passage which the writer has taken the liberty of naming the "Upper Deck" or the "Bridge of Sighs."

Today the habitation forms a right angle, one arm being 77'-6" in length, the other 42'-6". From the nucleus this structure evolved in a complicated manner, which we have traced through four phases (Figs. 215 & 216).

In renovating the house in the 1950s the present owners found that section "A" may have included an earlier construction comprising only the parlor and the main part of the stair passage adjoining it, thus forming an overall area of 24' by 16'-6", and possessing one chimney. But the theory of an earlier stage could not be fully proved without taking apart most of the walls of "A." The "old" kitchen outhouse, "B," once had an outside chimney measuring 6'-6" wide and now preserves a winding staircase which appears to be about the oldest woodwork in the entire domicile.

One of the cleverest ideas occurs in the "Bridge of Sighs": a dormer at the rear of the roof of section "A" (Fig. 216) was lowered slightly and opened into a doorway to receive the tunnel or narrow passage, "Z," of the "Bridge," extending over the room leading to the dining room and measuring on the inside only two feet and eight inches in width. By that change an easier way was made to go from one building to another without using the stairs. Be-

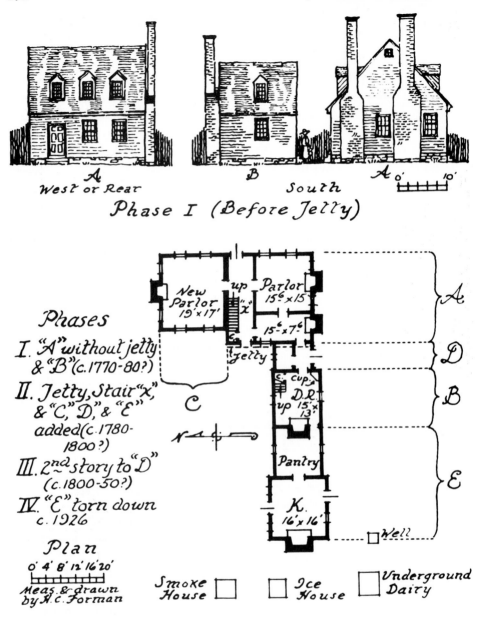

Fig. 215. Reconstruction drawings of *Huntingfields*, Calvert County. For over a century it has had four main phases of development.

cause of the position of the dormer in question, the "Bridge" was erected well off-center of the "curtain" below—a charming naïveté which the visitor might not notice until seen drawn in a diagram.

The final period of change, Phase IV, covers the last 115 years or thereabouts, that is from about 1850, and includes a long period of complete neglect; the tearing down about 1926 of the "new" kitchen and pantry "E," as well as the dining room chimney; and the renovating work of the 1950s. An old, faded photograph shows the "new" kitchen and was used in making the drawings. The kitchen itself seems to have been set on "tarnations"—farmer's lingo for boulders.

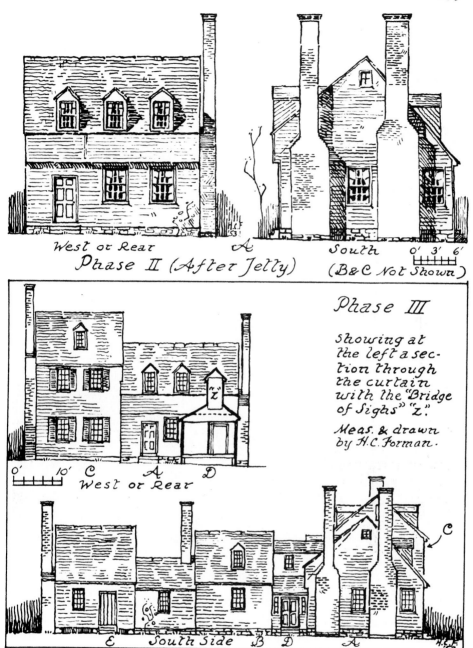

West or Rear   *A*   *South*   0' 3' 6'
Phase II (After Jelly)   (B & C Not Shown)

Phase III

*Showing at
the left a sec-
tion through
the curtain
with the "Bridge
of Sighs" "Z."*

*Meas. & drawn
by H. C. Forman.*

0'   10'   *C*   *A*   *D*
West or Rear

C

E   *South Side*   *B*   *D*   *A*

Fig. 216. *Huntingfields* is an example of how a little Hangover Transitional style house grew to
form a train of additions 120 feet in length.

Among the outhouses was an underground brick dairy, smoke house, ice
house, and well. In *Tidewater Maryland Architecture and Gardens* is drawn a
Huntingfields Quarters, sixteen feet square, with vertical shiplap boards on two
sides and bevel-edged siding on the other two. The antique chaise house also
has boards of vertical shiplap. The pair of old barns are sheathed on roof
and sides with four-foot handriven clapboards, seven inches wide, laid horizontally and overlapping each other at the ends as well as the tops, in the
manner of the early clapboard roofs.

St. Thomas' Hill, Sheathed in False Gothic Dress

There will never be another unique specimen like this eyry, perched bald and bold on its Prince George's County hilltop. At the time of the writer's visits, the homestead (Fig. 218) stood in terrible shape and was occupied by a half-witted tenant. In fact, that occupant is reported to have firmly believed that his lodging was actually constructed in 1732, no more, no less. We judged that he was mistaken by approximately 125 years; because from the architectural evidence it seems obvious that the largest, or two-storeyed, section was constructed first, probably about 1850–60—although 1865–70 may be just as correct. The frame wing with boulder foundation to the north (Fig. 217) was built up against the original tall structure, covering the clapboards. Then later, the curtain and kitchen wing of soft brick was placed against this addition—in fact, built up against the clapboards of the addition.[22]

Figure 217

Further, the walls of this curtain-kitchen wing were constructed of very soft brick, stuccoed over, and scored with grooves to imitate ashlar masonry—dressed stones, as our drawing shows. Even the kitchen chimney was treated that way.

On the main cornices are the dog-tooth designs of the Romanesque style, and "drops" of the Gothic style. These "drops" are found on several true Gothic buildings in New England, such as the *Parson Capen House* at Topsfield. But at *St. Thomas' Hill,* the "drop" and dog-tooth decorations are Gothic Revival—Medieval Revival, it should be stated, dressed up over an early Maryland form—the "big-house, little-house, colonnade-and-kitchen" motif.

Fig. 218 (top and bottom). Although decoration covered it with a false Gothic dress, *St. Thomas' Hill,* Prince George's County, even as late as perhaps 1870, is an example of "big house, little house, colonnade, and kitchen." Note pendants or drops at corners. Author, 1953.

Fig. 219. The Dining Room of the *Adams-Kilty House*, Annapolis, is twenty feet square. Note that the mantel is unlike Buckland's style. Warren. The molded plaster cornice (top) is not as ornate as that in the *Hammond-Harwood House*. Author, 1965.

The *Adams-Kilty Town House*
with the Great King-Post

This elegant brick house (Fig. 154) in the city of Annapolis has had many owners. The property on which it stands was lot no. 52 in James Stoddert's 1718 plan of the town. "I have resurveyed for Mr. John Gresham one lott . . . lying on the northwest side of Charles Street . . ." reads Stoddert's certificate of survey. Gresham also received at the same time the adjoining, triangular lot, no. 53, and also no. 55, lower down Charles Street "where it cuts the wharfage."

In 1772 John Gresham of Kent County, Maryland, died leaving to his brother Thomas Gresham and heirs his three lots in Annapolis "between the Lot of Daniel Dulany and the printing office." From Thomas Gresham the premises went to William Adams, gentleman (d. 1795), of Somerset County, who on February 28, 1786, leased to Thomas Brooke Hodgkin of Annapolis lots 52 and 53 "with the brick dwelling house on one of the said lotts already erected and built" for the term of twelve years at an annual rental of forty pounds. The interesting thing about the lease was that Hodgkin was not only to repair at his own expense the rooms, which were then "impaired," the doors, and the windows, but also to construct near the house a water pump, meat house, wooden stable, room for a carriage, post-and-rail fencing and a garden. The implication is that in 1786 the mansion had been lately completed, because it had been obviously built without the necessary accoutrements such as water and outhouses and fences; and it would take only a year or two or three in an unoccupied dwelling of that time for the rooms, doors, and windows to become "impaired."[23] It seems evident that the mansion was constructed about 1783 or 1784.

In 1789 Gen. John Davidson owned the lot, improved by "one brick house 40 x 40 [the size of the existing house], stable and carriage house frame 20 x 15 [shown on Sasche view of Annapolis, Fig. 152], smoak house 15 x 20 brick." Then in 1802 the place was bought by William Kilty, the Chancellor, in 1818 by Francis Hollingsworth, and in 1823 by George Wells. In the 1950s it was bequeathed by Stanley John Reynolds to the Society for the Preservation of Maryland Antiquities.

The great king-post holding up the pyramid roof (Fig. 249, bottom right), the plaster barrel vault over the upstairs small stair passage, the cellar kitchen fireplace of six-foot span and with flanking oven, and the opening-in cellar casements on H-hinges are all of interest. A photograph of the 1880s shows two freestanding columns flanking a front door with round transom and broken pediment: there was once probably a small hood or porch roof over that ornamental entrance.

It is pretty obvious that the domicile was not by William Buckland, who died in 1774. The first floor plan (Fig. 249, bottom left) is not the reverse of that of the central section of the *Hammond-Harwood House*; because, unlike *Hammond-Harwood*, the two front reception rooms are approximately the same size, the stairs passage is in a different location, and the two rear rooms *both* have access to the front passageway. Also the plaster cornice in the dining or ballroom (Fig. 219) does not have the two leaf moldings of that of the *Hammond-Harwood House;* and besides, workmen used plaster molds over and over for years in any way they saw fit. A chair rail or a window trim can not be labelled Buckland's because the *Hammond-Harwood House* has them: such small details formed a common vernacular used widely by many joiners of the period.

After all, how could Buckland have actually built the *Hammond-Harwood House* when the owner, Matthias Hammond, did not get the deed to the lot until March 23, 1774, and Buckland died in December the same year?

V.

Upper Bay Counties

V.

Upper Bay Counties

Baltimore's *Frontier Fort*—Who Can Tell?

A VERY OLD stone structure owned by the City of Baltimore on the east shore of Loch Raven about two miles above the Dulaney Valley bridge is known as the *"Old Fort."* Because of its aspect and similarities to *Fort Garrison* in Baltimore County, this structure was presumably a frontier fortification—though no one has been able to prove the theory. Whether it was one of the three forts ordered constructed in March, 1692, by the Governor's Council in Maryland has not yet been shown. Tradition has it that in later times the so-called fortification was used as a jail and a still house. Situated among miles of forests, what a lonely spot for a prison.

The floor plan (Fig. 220, top) of the *"Old Fort"* is a rectangle 28'-6" long, with a dirt floor and with the north gable-end askew. Why the rear side is two feet longer than the front façade has not yet been determined. Some early vagary or improvisation?

Although one-storey-and-loft high, the building has two tiers of flared loopholes for use of guns. These openings all spread outward except the one over the smaller doorway, which is squared with the wall and appears to be a later opening.

The cornices, tapering barge boards, and roofing materials do not appear to be original; but there is an old sheathing board under the wooden shingles which is fifteen inches wide.

The upstairs possessed loopholes so close to the floor boards, which have disappeared, that men truly had to lie on their stomachs to see or shoot from them.

Fort Garrison likewise has two doorways on the front, each flanked by loopholes, and gable loopholes as well. There was, too, the same kind of field stonework with large quoins at the corners.

259

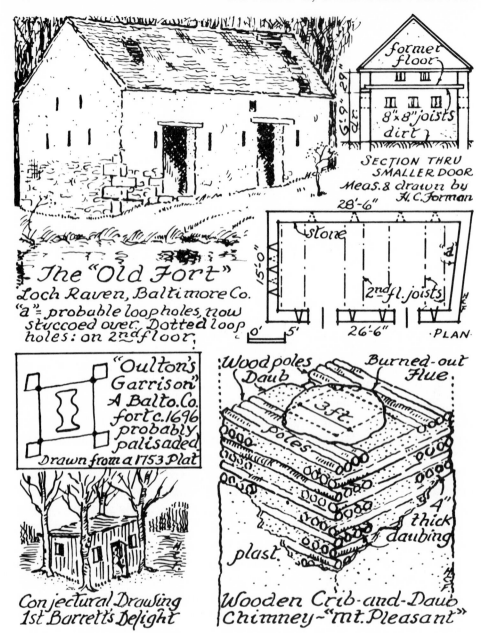

Figure 220

There once stood in Baltimore County a fort with four flankers, probably palisaded, with the name of *Oulton's Garrison,* which has been drawn (Fig. 220, center left) from a plat of 1753 in the Maryland Historical Society. The fort was constructed on a property of the same name, comprising 340 acres and surveyed in 1696 for Capt. John Oulston. Presumably *Fort Garrison* stood near it. At all events it is interesting to find the shape of a pioneer fortification in Maryland.

From One Primitive Baltimore Shelter
to Another

A property patented to John Barrett in 1704 and sold in 1718 by his widow to John Talbot, of West River, was "Barrett's Delight." The original homestead on that land stood in the part known as "Benjamin Ridgeley's Field," and was built of split timbers erected in the shape of a square, with four great living trees as corner posts—a primitive, frontier shelter. We have given (Fig. 220, bottom left) some conjectural idea of it.

Although the present *Barrett's Delight* dwelling-house, belonging to members of the Ridgely family, was built in 1824 amidst a group of earlier outhouses, the most interesting structure still standing on the place is a gambrel log house (Fig. 250, bottom left) constructed in 1775 by Thomas Todd on the portion of the farm known as the old *Todd Place*. The logs have been covered with modern siding, as is often the case, and an ell wing with chimney has been destroyed.

The *Todd House* downstairs comprises only one great room with an ancient corner cupboard with panelled doors opposite a winding staircase—one of the steepest in Maryland. Fourteen winders rise in a circle to the second floor. Anyone falling from above would drop almost a vertical nine feet.

The larger bedroom upstairs has a closet with half-slatted door with wrought-iron thumb latch. Since this homestead held a large number of children, the closet was undoubtedly used as a second bedchamber.

Another primordial edifice in Baltimore County was the wooden chimney in the pre-1730 frame section of the plantation house called *Mt. Pleasant* or *Fort Pleasant*, which stands near the Carroll County line. Before it was partially razed, the stone fireplace used to be 12′ in span, 5′ deep, and 5′-6″ high—a giant. The flue above rose straight up through the roof and was made of a cribbing, or cribbage-and-daub work, which we have tried to draw (Fig. 220, bottom right) from descriptions of a former owner of the property, Mr. J. Marshall Whiting. Rows of wood poles had been laid crosswise, crib-fashion, allowing for a three-foot-square flue for smoke. Each layer of poles was put down in clay and chopped straw, called *daubing*; and there were approximately four-inch-thick beds of daub between the layers.

When taken down, the flue was found to have burned into a rough circle, as the diagram shows. The walls of this section of the home were reported to have had grass and clay filling between the studs.

Turner's Hall with Dixie-Style Verandahs

This unusual mansion is believed to have been erected in 1785 by Thomas Johnson on a tract of land by the name of "Turner's Hall." The house, built in the Federal style, is known by that name, or by the name of *Twaisky Hall*, and was called the *Ferguson House* when in 1851 it came into the possession of Thomas J. Ferguson.

A glance at the floor plan (Fig. 221) shows that the villa was erected in the form of a "T," with porches around the tail of that letter. Further, the verandahs are triple-decked. Perhaps the mansion (Fig. 222) belongs more to Mobile Bay or Mississippi than to the Free State.

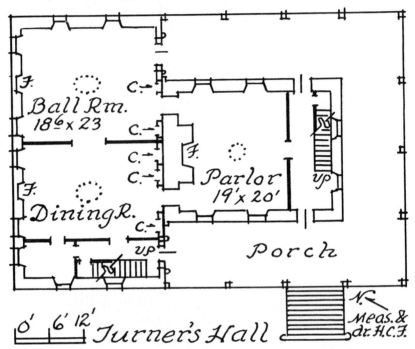

Figure 221

Beginning at the cellar, which is level with the ground, we may visit five storeys. In fact the verandahs extend around two sides of the basement, but on the first and second floors they encircle three sides. On the north the head of the "T" comprises a large penthouse or lean-to, three storeys high, with no porches. *Turner's Hall* is unique in Maryland.

The walls of the edifice are two-foot-thick solid stone. As for the windows, they are mostly all askew, some of the lintels having sunk as much as three inches on one side. The shutters are panelled, but of course they are not original.

The approach to *Turner's Hall* was from the southeast, and the visitor would obtain the whole effect of the triple-storey porches as he rode or drove

Fig. 222. *Turner's Hall* has salons with Adam-style plaster ceilings, triple-storey porches, and large penthouse. Author, 1938.

Fig. 223(top). Baltimore County is noted for its fine barns. This is the *Gorsuch Barn,* at Verona, with its hourglass brick louvres and one arched and pilastered cupola, still extant. Johnston, 1930s.
Fig. 224(bottom left). Telescopic *Taylor's Hall.* Author, 1939.
Fig. 225(bottom right). *Friendship,* before 1790. Wollon.

up the lane to the grove of giant oaks beside the porch stairs. Having gained the main verandah floor, he would have the choice of four entrance doors to enter the mansion. Immediately opposite the front steps is a doorway to the little, narrow front passage—the doorway itself having fluted pilasters on an elliptical plan and pediments which are also fluted. The transom is square and leaded. Two of the other entrance doorways have elliptical-leaded transoms and sidelights ornamented with flower motifs in lead calmes.

The front passage, only six feet wide, extends from cellar to loft—five storeys; the walnut rail, plain curly-maple balusters, and double-scrolled consoles of the stair extend up all the way. Off this passage is the Parlor or Living Room, which was once used as a library and has a plaster ceiling design of a circle with garlands on the outside and rosettes inside. Almost like pilasters, the corners of the chimney-breast wall are fluted, and the cornice is reeded, with rosettes at the corners. As in the rest of the main floor, the window jambs are deep and sloping. The fireplace has a heavy marble mantel of Civil War days.

From the Parlor one passes into either the Ball Room or the Dining Room (Fig. 221) by passageways which are nearly six feet thick through the wall. These two salons are of about the same size, 23' by 18'-6". Like the Parlor, the Dining Room has off it a narrow, backstairs' passage, with a cuddy under the stairs probably once used as a powder room.

As one enters the Ball Room and the Dining Room, he may notice that the doorways have been sunk into the jambs, which are quarter-circles in plan, and that flanking these doorways on either side are very shallow closets.

The plaster ceiling motifs in Dining and Ball Rooms are somewhat similar in design: a rope oval with knotted ribbons, six-pointed stars, anthemions, and rosettes. Over the doors are plain plaster panels ornamented with garlands and beaded necklaces hanging from rosettes. The house is a decorator's dream.

The back stairs give access to three small chambers with knockheads, the center one of which probably did not have a window in the early days. Over the Parlor is a large master bedchamber, with entrance doors on the second floor verandah a little less ornate than those below.

The third floor comprises one room lighted by interior windows unusually placed in back of the dormers—the dormer space between the sash being enough closet area for a heart's content. The fourth floor, actually the fifth storey of this *maison extraordinaire*, contains a peak loft chamber perched high under the ridge of the roof and lighted by one small window through the chimneys.

The only outhouses remaining are the stone slave quarters, spring house, and dairy.

Baltimore County Spyglass—*Taylor's Hall*

Off to the southwest of this "telescopic" homestead (Fig. 224) are the gravestones of several Cockeys, the oldest of whom, Joshua F. Cockey, died October 9, 1821, at the age of 57.[1] At one period *Taylor's Hall* was owned by Thomas Cockey Deye (1728–1807), an intimate friend of Charles Carroll of Carrollton.

The earliest section, the one-storey log kitchen, with huge stone chimney, possesses logs fairly well squared off by adzes and tied at the corners by shallow notches. The owner of the house believed that this section dated from 1665–1670, but proof was lacking for the theory.

Then came the middle part, two-and-a-half-storey log, complete in itself, and with joists showing flush with the walls on both first and second floors. The window frames project from the walls, as they do on Nantucket and other Massachusetts buildings. Inside the log portions the original woodwork has been replaced by that of the 19th century. A very steep winding staircase leads to the garret.

Finally, as the third stage of development, a typical early 19th-century limestone building, of Beaverdam stone, was added, probably by Thomas Cockey Deye.

Picturesque *Philpot* Eyrie

The old *Philpot House*, known by the name of *Rockford*, overlooking Loch Raven in Baltimore County, has an approach which makes a vivid impression. Climbing a very steep hill, you come upon a huge, square kitchen chimney, then a moss-covered shingle roof of the stone portion of the house, and finally a sharp, brown gambrel roof of the part behind. The stone courtyard wall and stone quarters house are revealed. Behind the domicile three grassy "falles" look down upon the lake.

The original habitation (Fig. 228), built of brown fieldstone, now stucco-covered, comprised only a Hall or kitchen-living room and a Parlor. Hall Chamber and Parlor Chamber stood above. Later a small porch, now enclosed, a square dining room, and a couple of closets were added to the rear or southwest side, under a catslide roof.

But even at that time the edifice appeared not to be large enough to house the members of the Philpot family; consequently the original stone part was lengthened about 1800 by the addition of a long gambrel-roofed frame section. The joining of the two structures of about equal width and length proved to be not particularly successful. Because the ceiling heights varied, the meeting of the open roughhewn ceiling beams is irregular. On the northwest side the weatherboarding overlaps the old stone part for some eleven and a half feet. No doubt the overlapping was for insulation purposes and to keep the joint covered between the two constructions.

On the floor plan (Fig. 226) we have endeavored to illustrate some of these points. The date of the stone portion is unknown—possibly the first quarter of the 18th century. The newspaper, *Jeffersonian*, of Towson, Maryland, has indicated that the stone section and the quarters at *Rockford* were standing when one Brian Philpot acquired the place in the early 18th century. The last member of the family to own the plantation was Kitty Philpot.

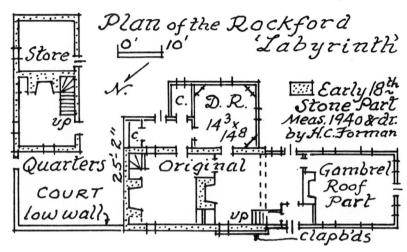

Figure 226

Homes of the Suttons of Spesutia: *Garden of Eden* and Others

When the United States Government acquired vast stretches of land along the Harford County shore, it foredoomed some old homesteads and other structures built by the pioneers and those who came after them. One family which was prominent in Spesutia Lower Hundred is that of Sutton. While the earliest member may have been buried in the yard of the first Spesutia church (*c.* 1671) at Gravelly, located on or near the Bay shore, many later Suttons were interred in the present *Spesutia Episcopal Church* yard at Perryman.[2]

One of the early Suttons was Oswin Sutton, Sr., who according to the first census was living in Spesutia Lower Hundred in 1776, aged fifty-six, with a wife Tabitha and nine children, a baby orphan, and three negroes.

Oswin's son, Jonathan Sutton, Sr. (1761–1825), who married Sally McCracken, was known as "farmer," and appears to have been the first Sutton to have owned a brick plantation-house, of which a photograph (Fig. 229) remains. That was *Bush Point*, also known variously as *Abbey Island, Old Plantation*, or *Holly Grove*. When at a later time that honored edifice was treated with a coat of rough stucco, it acquired a fifth name, *Gravel Dash*. Situated on "Sutton's Cove," it formed two sections of about equal length, both two storeys and loft high. The larger portion, with modillion cornice, was built in the 18th century; the smaller part, with its little second floor

Fig. 227(top). The Horse Stable at *Clynmalira Manor,* Baltimore County, has square brick pierced
louvres for decoration. Johnston, 1930s.
Fig. 228(bottom). *Rockford,* Philpot homestead, has an original stone part lengthened by a
gambrel-roof wing. At left is Quarters. Author, 1939.

windows having upper sash only one pane high, may have been only a few years earlier.

Other owners of *Gravel Dash* or *Holly Grove* included members of the Hollis family, of which Clark Hollis is reputed to have been buried there in 1812, and the noted Philadelphian, Morris Clothier, who used the place seasonally in 1916–17. In 1918, having been taken up by the Aberdeen Proving Grounds, this oldest existing Sutton homestead was used as a model for testing bombs, and its stucco façade became pitted, they say, like the craters of the moon. Other explosions went through the roof to show extent of damage.

Fig. 229. *Bush Point* or *Gravel Dash*, Harford County, was owned by Jonathan Sutton, Sr. Sketch by author after faded photo taken before 1916 by F. H. Middleton.

Jonathan Sutton, the elder, owned also "Fanny's Inheritance,"[3] "Palmer's Point," and "Palmer's Neglect," near Swan Creek; and "Boothby's Hill," in the same area as *Gravel Dash* house. Of Jonathan's three sons Samuel Sutton (1795–1878)[4] continued in the ownership of *Gravel Dash*, was reported to have had a mug of beer every morning for breakfast, and was in 1841 a vestryman of *Spesutia Church*. Further, he served thirteen times in the State Legislature.

The second son of Jonathan, Jonathan Sutton, Jr. (1797–1882), owned land at "Boothby Hill"; and the third son, James Lawrence Sutton (1806–1887),[5] who joined the Religious Society of Friends, was named for a noted naval officer and was called "of Baltimore" after 1838. His home was at "Weston," on Lake Avenue in that city. Of subsidiary interest, perhaps, is the fact that in 1865 he sold a city house at 190 West Lombard Street to this writer's great-grandfather, Dr. Edwin Chandlee.

In the region of Spesutia the second Sutton homestead was owned by the above James Lawrence Sutton. This was *Middleborough* (Fig. 231), a frame, storey-and-loft cottage located on the 216-acre property of that name, lying near "Boothby's Hill" and on the west side of Swan Creek, and surveyed in 1737 for John Hall. This place was likewise situated on the road leading to

Fig. 230(top). *Garden of Eden* or *Brick House Farm,* a Sutton home, was used for target practice. Copy of photograph taken before 1879. Courtesy, Samuel Sutton.

Fig. 231(center). Frame *Middleborough,* one of James Lawrence Sutton's properties. Author, 1939.

Fig. 232(bottom). Part of *Sorry House* foundation, Hagerstown, showing fireplace, excavated 1953. Courtesy, Washington County Historical Society.

Spesutia Creek and St. George's Parish Church. When this writer had opportunity to visit *Middleborough* in the winter of 1939, it was owned by a Baltimore saloon-keeper by the name of Pollack, and had fallen upon sorry days, as the photograph shows. The oldest portion of the four sections of the lair is at the left, adjoining a "colonnade" and kitchen, and had siding so thick that it was almost log. On the inside there was little of distinction except that the dado, as high as the chair rail, had horizontal board wainscoting.

In 1897 James Lawrence Sutton's nephew, William T. Sutton (1828–1897) left the *Middleborough* farm of 142 acres to his wife Susan.

The third Sutton berth was *Brick House* or *Garden of Eden* (Fig. 230), which before its destruction was located between Bush River and Romney Creek, and was possessed by Jonathan H. Sutton (d. 1891), son of the aforementioned Samuel Sutton of *Gravel Dash.* The "Garden of Eden" tract was originally surveyed in 1685 for Adam Burchell of Baltimore County and held 150 acres.

Although *Garden of Eden* house was smaller and lower than *Gravel Dash,* there were several resemblances between them: for instance, a porch on the kitchen wing for servants and another for quality. Many of the family must have sat on the Quaker-meetinghouse style bench which may be seen on the main piazza in the photograph.

Garden of Eden had a late Georgian façade of Flemish bond and gauged flat arches. The front doorway appears to have had narrow flanking pilasters. But no one will know what was inside the house, for it too was undoubtedly used for target practice. The destruction of early Maryland architecture and antiquities has been wholesale and continuous.

Great Carroll Plantation with Erin Background: *Clynmalira*

Named supposedly for "Clanmalier," an estate in Ireland, this Maryland place once comprised 5,000 acres surveyed in 1705 for Charles Carroll (1660–1720), who served the Free State as Attorney General. He also owned "Doughoregan Manor," a tract nearly twice as large as "Clynmalira." Daniel Carroll, son of Charles Carroll, of "Duddington," was the second owner of "Clynmalira," and Charles Carroll, Jr., the third possessor. The fourth owner was Henry Hill Carroll, of "Sweet Air," another plantation in the immediate neighborhood; and the fifth was Henry Carroll (1797–1877), builder in 1822 of the brick *Clynmalira* mansion (Fig. 234A), Carroll Road, Baltimore County.

On the approach front of *Clynmalira* a new element, the two square corner "towers" on either side, was superimposed upon a typical Georgian plan (Fig. 233) with two rooms on either side of a central passageway. In fact the cellar walls indicate that the original building (1822) was only twenty-seven feet wide on the inside and that the "towers" and portico were additions. The two-storey tiled portico with its round arches and balcony, as well as the large frame wing, are believed to have been constructed after 1892.

The front door in the portico has double leaves, with three-quarter Doric columns, and sidelights. In the elliptical transom is a lead oval with star flowers.

The garden front is typically Hangover Georgian, with central bay projecting outward eighteen inches and broken pediment with oculus above. The main door here is similar to the front door. The garden has four great "falles" with grass ramps leading from one to another. Traditionally the brick for the house was made on this plantation in the field known as the "Long Meadow."

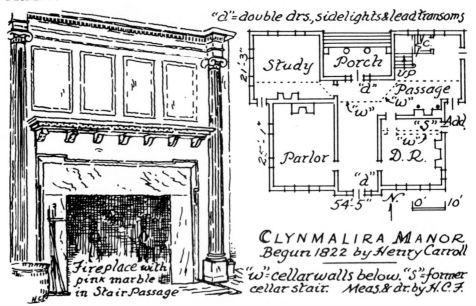

Figure 233

Inside the residence are two handsome mantels: the one, in the stair passage (Fig. 233), has a broken entablature with dentils over freestanding, fluted Ionic columns, and a pink marble facing; the mantel in the Parlor has delicate ribbons and garlands with a touch of the Adam manner, a facing of glazed yellow bricks, and small fluted Ionic columns supporting the mantel shelf. The broad stairway has a curved lower tread with balusters encircling a newel post. The windowpanes are large, averaging 12½" by 18½".

Among the numerous outhouses on the "Clynmalira" estate were two barns for wheat and hay; four stables (Figs. 227 & 234B) for cows, horses, mules, and steers; carriage houses; a pig-house; smoke house; milk house with walled-in spring; and an ice house.

For the old life at *Clynmalira*, when cooking was done before great open fires, saucepans stood on "spiders," and frying pans on live coals, the reader may refer to Mrs. J. Sparhawk Jones' article "A Childhood at Clynmalira":[6] "It was not only the house," she related, "but all that it overlooked that was loved—the distant sky line toward the south, the hills coming around toward the north, the way the shadows fell across the lawn at moonlight, the large

Fig. 234. A(top). Entrance to the *Clynmalira* mansion. "It was not only the house, but all that it overlooked, that was loved." Author, 1940. B(bottom). Cow Stable, *Clynmalira Manor*, Baltimore County, has gables ornamented with hourglass brick louvres. Note Victorian-decorated outshut. Johnston, 1930s.

Fig. 235. (Top) The middle section with gambrel roof of *Hereford Farm* was built soon after 1714. (Center) The Quarters and Spring House. Author, 1939.

Fig. 236(bottom). *Falling Green,* a Brooke home, Sandy Spring. Author, 1932.

sense of home, boundless home, *our earth.*" How many families today in their ceaseless circumgyrations of America have such a close bond with one home?

One of the dramatic moments at *Clynmalira* about which Mrs. Jones wrote happened in 1863 when the colored folks became free, and one by the name of Rose Johnson merrily descended a stair in the house while calling out, "I am free. I am free." Many of the negroes on the place later were cared for by members of the family.

Two of *Merryman:* An Ell and a Spyglass

Overlooking that part of the Gunpowder Falls now covered by Loch Raven is the site of an old Merryman plantation by the name of "Merryman's Delight," of which now only a graveyard remains. There Lt. Col. Micajah Merryman, Jr. (1788–1854), and his wife, Clarissa Harryman Merryman (d. 1879), are buried beside an obelisque, along with several others of the family.[7]

It is difficult to believe that a mansion with circular driveway, barns, stables, quarters, smoke and ice houses, log turkey house, carpenter's shop, and other outbuildings, stood on that wild site beside the Loch until about 1925. The great brick domicile itself, a long "ell" in plan, stood for over a hundred years, until its despoliation and destruction. In the short end of the "ell" was a double-decker porch; otherwise the house conformed to an early 19th-century type.

Micajah Merryman, Jr., was the son of a man of the same name who in 1776 was the first major of Col. Edward Cockey's Gunpowder Upper Battalion. The father of Micajah (I) was Moses Merryman who received in 1742 from his own father John Merryman the tract of land called "Merryman's Delight," and settled there with his wife, Sarah Glenn. This property comprised 150 acres and was patented by John Merryman (d. *c.* 1749) of "Clover Hill," on Merryman's Lane, now University Parkway, Baltimore.[8]

One of Maryland's "spyglass" houses, *Hereford Farm* (Fig. 235), named for Hereford in England, was built by John Merryman of "Clover Hill" soon after 1714. His father, Charles Merryman, was referred to in the Baltimore County land records as early as 1682, when he purchased from Thomas and Hannah Ball a 300-acre tract, "East Humphreys," located on the north bank of the Potomac River. A man noted in his own day, John Merryman, along with James Calhoun and Hercules Courtney, assisted in procuring from the General Assembly of Maryland the act for the incorporation of the city of Baltimore. Merryman became president of the Second Branch of the first City Council of Baltimore. In the carefully preserved burial plot at *Hereford Farm* are the stones of three generations of Merrymans.[9]

Originally the plantation comprised a thousand acres and included the village of Hereford. By the time it had passed to Nicholas Rogers Merryman in 1821, there were only 803 acres; and when owned by Henry Merryman, the last Merryman to have it, the property was about half its original size.

Fig. 237 (top). This is how the entrance of a well-appointed plantation-house looked in the 18th century. A view of *Trentham,* an old Craddock House, Baltimore County, which is slightly visible at far left. Johnston, 1930s.

Fig. 238 (bottom). *Gladswood,* a box-like dwelling with true pyramid roof, about 1800. HABS, 1936.

Fig. 239. The octagonal stone Bath House of the 18th century at *Trentham*, Baltimore County, has slatted shutters for privacy and a spire with octagonal base. Johnston.

Fig. 240. A(top). Here lived no checkbook farmers, but industrious and educated Quakers. *Brother's Content* was built in 1817 on "Brooke Grove," Sandy Spring. Author, 1934. B(bottom). View showing original porch with central-arched plaster ceiling. Ellis Chandlee, 1880s.

The farmhouse itself, as has been indicated, is of telescope type—the first portion built soon after 1714 comprising the middle gambrel-roofed, stone structure, with two rooms downstairs and two upstairs. A little later the stone kitchen wing was added to the west end, making an additional room on each floor. The third, and largest, section is two-and-a-half storeys high, with circular-headed dormers, and was added by Nicholas Rogers Merryman, John's son, in the 19th century. It is unfortunate that the winding staircase of this largest part was not built in the main passageway, but in an alcove where it stands hidden.

About the grounds are a large barn, a two-storey quarters (Fig. 235, bottom), a smoke house, spring house with slatted windows, all of stone, and reputed to have been built by John Merryman. A high stone wall skirts the west driveway, shutting in the lawn in English fashion. In truth, the green meadows, great trees, stone garden walls, and cluster of outhouses all help to make *Hereford Farm* resemble a farm in the Mother Country.

Brother's Content on "Brooke Grove"

This homestead on a Sandy Spring knoll in Montgomery County is unpretentious and conforms to the simplicity of life of the early Friends in Maryland—because the builder was a Quaker of long standing. In 1817 Mahlon Janney Chandlee (1790–1890), a son of George and Deborah Brooke Chandlee, descendant of a family which had lived in Philadelphia and on the Nottingham Lots (Fig. 72) in Cecil County, Maryland, erected upon a portion of the great "Brooke Grove" estate at Sandy Spring a two-storey frame dwelling (Fig. 240A), called *Brother's Content*.

The early name of the place was *Brother's Content*; but Mr. R. B. Farquahar in his *Historic Montgomery County, Maryland: Old Homes and History* (1952) chose to give the second name of the house: *Dellabrooke*.

While Mahlon Janney Chandlee, a builder, was constructing the *Brother's Content* house, he lived at *Brooke Grove,* in the neighborhood.

The *Annals of Sandy Spring* related that Mahlon Janney Chandlee, who married in 1818 at Kennett Square Friends' Meeting, in Pennsylvania, Catharine Frame, daughter of David and Sarah Harlan Frame, of *Walnut Hill* and *Brooke Meadow*, Sandy Spring, attracted attention wherever he went, because in that day of shorter people he was fully six feet tall, and he never forsook the quaint and peculiar garb of the early Friend. He was very fond of his fine timber lands and had a passion for planting groves of chestnut and oak trees.[10] In his hundredth year, when he was 99½ years old, he fell from a tree with fatal results. His gravestone lies today in the plot behind the *Sandy Spring Friends' Meetinghouse.*

From the front porch of *Brother's Content* there was a fine view looking towards the old saw and grist mill on the farm. The small, picturesque, stone miller's cottage (Fig. 241C), was once the temporary home of Mahlon's grandson, Dr. Henry Chandlee and his wife, Annie Betterton Chandlee, before

Fig. 241. A(top left). Stone fireplace in the workshop of Mahlon Janney Chandlee at *Brother's Content,* Sandy Spring. Author, 1936. B(top right). Silhouette of Mahlon's son, Dr. Edwin Chandlee (1820–66), early Baltimore dentist, whose son Dr. Henry Chandlee in his turn pioneered in X ray in that city. C(bottom). The *Miller's House* on "Brother's Content." Ellis Chandlee, 1880s.

they moved to Baltimore. Their only child, Elizabeth Betterton Chandlee, was born in 1880 in that cottage.

Ellis Chandlee, another grandson of Mahlon Janney Chandlee, remembered having watched "the logs sawn and the boys bringing corn to be ground into meal" on *Brother's Content*.[11] He further related that once he took a photograph of "grandfather" Mahlon (left) and "Beckie"—Rebecca Pidgeon, of Wadesville, Virginia,—and Albert Chandlee sitting by the front porch (Fig. 240B). This view included large lilies growing on each side of the piazza. "Grandfather," he wrote, "had a distaste for having his picture taken."

The homestead itself is plain and without much individuality. On the right of a central passageway are twin parlors and on the other side a dining room and a kitchen. The mantels and woodwork are very simple. The stairway has a rail of maple and square balusters. Upstairs are four chambers, and in the loft, two more—plenty of room for several Quaker children and visiting guests. Mahlon, who built *Brother's Content*, never knew that one of his little grandchildren there, Henry Chandlee,[12] would later become the most noted member of the family, both in this country and the British Isles.

Back of the habitation stand a stone spring house, a stone smoke house, and a workshop, partly frame and partly stone. This last outhouse, according to Ellis Chandlee, "skirted the woods," and was a spot from which "you could shoot squirrels from the doorway."

The workshop housed Mahlon Janney Chandlee's cabinet-making and smith-working tools. As late as 1936 the latter instruments were set beside the great stone fireplace (Fig. 241A); but since new owners have come into possession of the plantation, the workshop has been changed into a guest house and the tools have been scattered.

It is difficult for young folks growing up today in an industrial age to realize that a hundred years ago and before, plantation-owners had to produce nearly everything needed for life on the place. There were no department stores or shopping centers or supermarkets where you could help yourself to innumerable varieties of goods and foods at reasonable prices. In those days one had to have skills to run a mill, do cabinet-work, construct residences, plant crops, weave clothing, make shoes, churn butter, build machines and a thousand other articles and knickknacks.

The great iron gates recently placed at the entrance to *Brother's Content*, later *Dellabrooke*, are little in keeping with the spirit of the Quaker family which lived there for about a century. While the Chandlees of Sandy Spring had simple tastes—whether in home or in dress and speech,—they were educated, owned great tracts of land, and came from some of the leading families of the Free State.

Fig. 242. A(top). The west gable-end of the *Mill Pond House,* an example of Maryland-German architecture of the mid-18th century. B(bottom left). Front door with transom; (bottom right) rear doors upstairs and down. Author, 1953.

Fig. 243. A(top). Looking toward front door at the *Mill Pond House,* with great kitchen fireplace (left) and half-timbered partition (right). Author, 1953. B(bottom left). "Magazine" Cellar with stone niches and ventilation chute. C(bottom right). Detail of grooved clay undercoating for plaster. Author, 1953.

Fig. 244. (Top) Detail of the south wall of the *Mill Pond House* above the front door, showing "A" and "C," wattles, and "B," early beaded clapboards. (Bottom) Close-up of wattle-and-daub work on the inside of west gable. Author, 1953.

German Medieval Half-Timber Work and Wattles

One of the prize finds in the State is the *Mill Pond House* (Fig. 242A), built probably around 1746, on a property in Frederick County which was part of the "Tasker's Chance" holding. This habitation is Maryland-German Hangover-Medieval in style.

Land called the "Mill Pond" was conveyed by Daniel Dulaney to Jacob Stoner (d. 1767) on September 8, 1746.[13] It is believed that the dwelling here described was built there either that year or a little before. The edifice faced the old Annapolis road, no longer existing, which ran toward Emmitsburg and Woodsboro. The Episcopalian church records reveal that Stoner was in residence in 1742, probably near Frederick and possibly at the "Mill Pond." Since the mill was standing in 1746, the house must have been coeval with it.

Made on a memorable day November 17, 1953, the writer's notes of this dwelling show that it was "a house dangerous in ruins." Under the heading, "Magazine Cellar," is written: "What a place to measure alone on a winter day." The detailed drawing of the north doorway has written under it: "Here is what remains of this door, now in 100 pieces."

In places the floors had completely collapsed, or were so covered with debris that it was impossible to walk over them. Parts of the roof were gone. The small cellar was half choked with fallen objects. In short, standing in the middle of a ploughed field, *Mill Pond House* was a shambles. The biting November wind beneath a dismal sky made the abandoned fabric a spooky place in which to spend the day measuring the building and inspecting the unusual types of construction.

Jacob Stoner, the builder, was obviously a Maryland German who had erected for himself an edifice, four-square and towering, modelled after certain late medieval dwellings in the valley of the Upper Rhine. In the Free State he constructed the only known example of half-timber work and wattle-and-daub wall that remains.

In the first place the partial cellar (Fig. 247) and foundation are of field stone: sandstone boulders; the first floor comprises limestone. The second storey and gables were originally half-timber work with a filling called wattle-and-daubing (Fig. 249, top left). This is a type of basketwork made up of evenly-spaced saplings interwoven *on both sides* with split branches, as shown on our constructional diagram (Fig. 248, top). Over the basketwork on both sides were daubed layers of mud mixed with chopped straw, which helped to hold the mud together.

When wet, this daubing of clay was grooved both inside and out in square or diamond patterns by means of a comb, in order to make coats of white lime plaster stick to it (Figs. 243C & 249, top right). This plaster was especially needed on the exterior of the building in order to protect the clay daub from

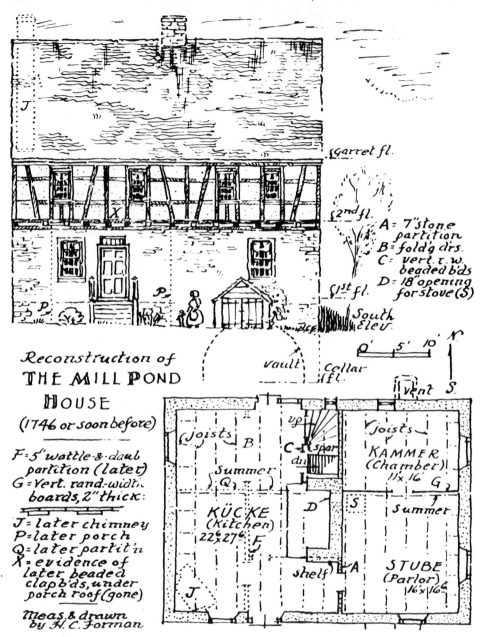

Figure 245

being washed away. Our restoration drawings (Figs. 245–247) were largely made from trying to trace out the half-timbering beneath the interior plastering, an example of which is given in the diagram (Fig. 249, top left) of the inside of the western gable.

We judge that some time before the end of the 18th century the entire area of half-timber work was covered over by beaded clapboards (see "X," Fig. 245, top), a few of which were still in place where the 19th-century porch used to stand on the south side. In the late 19th or early 20th century the old beaded

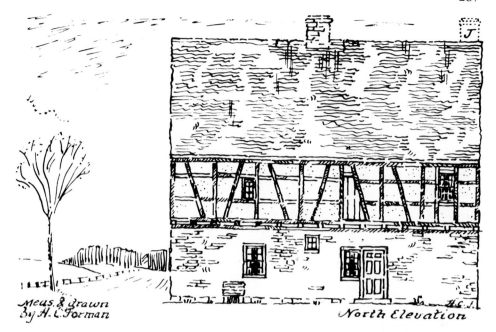

Meas. & drawn by H. C. Forman

North Elevation

Reconstruction of THE MILL POND HOUSE.

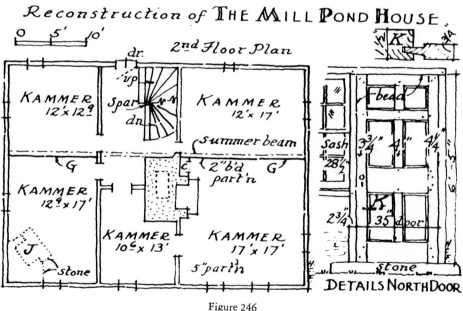

Figure 246

clapboards were removed except where the porch roof abutted the outside wall, and were replaced by novelty siding. The lines ("p") of the porch could still be seen.

The remainder of the construction work may be briefly described. Floor joists are tree trunks skinned of bark, levelled top and bottom, and laid flat. Between the joists are layers of clay and straw.

Giant summerbeams, 6½″ by 9″, run longitudinally from one end of the house to the other, upstairs and down. The roof of modern slate evidently once had wooden shingles nailed to strips.

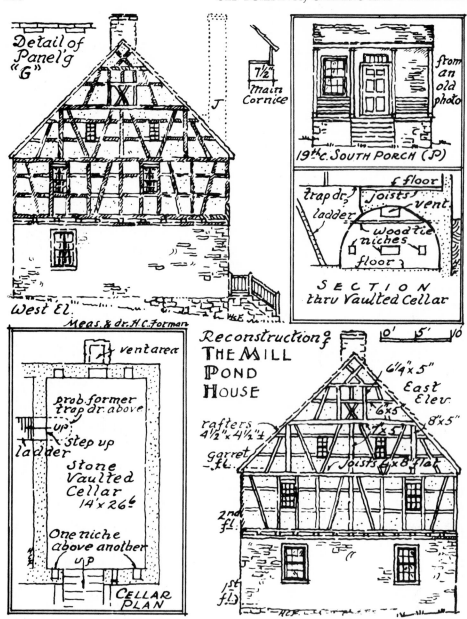

Figure 247

The "Magazine" cellar with its great stone barrel-vault fourteen feet wide occupies the space under the eastern end of the building. This storage area was so choked with debris that it could scarcely be photographed (Fig. 243B). At one end of the cellar is an outside cellarway with stone steps which may have had a gabled roof as shown in the reconstruction drawing. At the opposite end was a stone ventilation chute which also must have had some outside covering, as has been conjecturally drawn.

Access to the vaulted room was by both cellar areaway and stepladder from the floor above, and possibly by trapdoor in that same floor, for lowering goods into the cellar.

One of the interesting constructional features is the great dressed mast or spar around which the main circular staircase winds (Fig. 248) from first floor to loft. At the time of the writer's visit in 1953, the upper part of this long pole had been cut away and removed from the premises; but originally it was one piece of wood approximately twenty-three feet tall. The large rectangular treads were framed into the long spar to form triangular steps; the remainder of the treads projected at the back of the risers. So steep is the spiral that there are seven steps in a 90° turn.

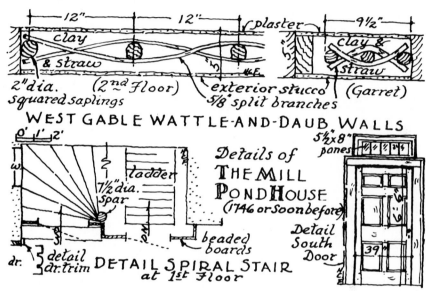

WEST GABLE WATTLE-AND-DAUB WALLS

Details of THE MILL POND HOUSE (1746 or soon before)

Detail South Door

DETAIL SPIRAL STAIR at 1st Floor

Figure 248

In its room arrangement the *Mill Pond House* follows the so-called "Quaker Plan," a scheme suggested by William Penn to his settlers in Pennsylvania in which one entered a main or keeping room with a large fireplace and a partition, near the middle of the house, and with two smaller rooms beyond. In this Maryland-German dwelling one goes in the main room, called the "Kücke," for Kitchen. Actually that was the medieval "great hall" where living, dining, and cooking were done. The stone fireplace, large enough to take a log just under eight feet long, stands in the center of the mansion and had to warm a room 27'-6" by 22'-6" in size. This was one of the largest residential rooms in the Free State, before it was cluttered up with partitions ("F," "Q," Fig. 245), folding doors ("B"), and a catercornered fireplace ("J").

Back of the great stone fireplace, which contained the "cooking fire," is an eighteen-inch-wide hole—undoubtedly an aperture for a pipe from an iron or porcelain stove ("S"), standing in the room behind, known as the "Stube" or Parlor. It might have been a five-plate iron stove from Pennsylvania, or a porcelain one, like those still extant in the Moravian settlement of Wachovia in North Carolina. The *Miller's House* at Milbach, Pennsylvania, has an opening at the rear of its large fireplace for a stove.

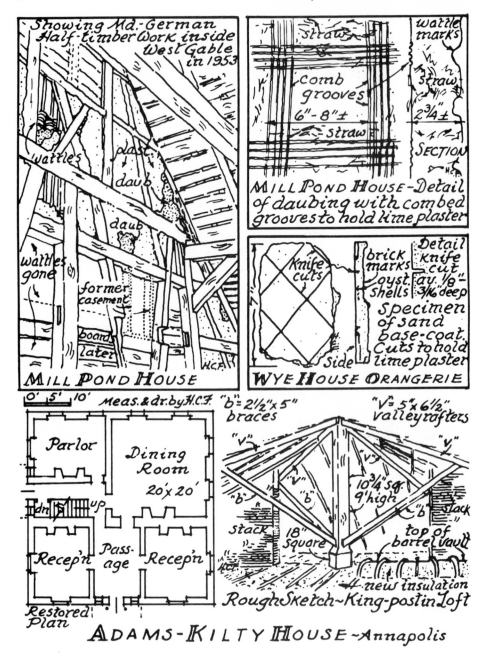

Figure 249

In the back of the "Stube" was the "Kammer" or bedchamber, which was in addition to the five chambers in the second storey. Until a diagonal fireplace was built later in one of the bedchambers on the upper floor, there was only one fireplace—that for the master chamber, directly over the "Stube."

It is interesting that in Pennsylvania the joist ends at the second floor were often continued outwards to support pent roofs across the gables or along the sides. There is little evidence to suggest that the joists at the *Mill Pond House* ever projected externally. The ones visible under early clapboards or modern novelty siding appear neatly exposed at the ends, not hacked off in a crude manner, and with small stones packed carefully in mud between them.

By the time of our survey all the windows save one had vanished, and that was a first floor sash in the east gable-end (Fig. 247). This "guillotine" window was pegged together and has an odd size for its glass pane: 10" by 13½". After all, the Germans do not measure by feet and inches. Small "guillotines" were probably used in the garret gables, and casements in two small openings on the north side of the lodging. There was one small cellar window with horizontal bars. The homestead was probably too late in date for leaded glass; at any rate, no evidence of such was discovered.

The reconstruction of the rear, or north door (Fig. 246, bottom), was put together from a door which, as before mentioned, had been knocked into a hundred fragments. On the other side, the front door had entirely disappeared, and the drawing of it is based on the north door.

The most curious outside doorway in the building (Fig. 242B, right) lies beside the staircase at the second floor. It is only 5'-9" tall; but it is twice as wide at the bottom as at the top. The right-hand side slants at an angle, following a diagonal brace. The door sill is 3½" above the floor, an arrangement indicating that the door was never used for a passageway, but for hauling in large objects which would not go up the spiral stairs.

It will be noted that the panelling is of the medieval, random-width, vertical-board type of construction, and is of two kinds: beaded boards across the staircase on the first floor ("C," Fig. 245) and plain boards, backed up by other boards, as shown in the detail "G" in the "Stube" and the chamber above it.

When the "Kücke" or great kitchen was split in two, a five-inch wattle-and-daub partition "F" was built down the length of the room, with a double-folding door arrangement "B" opposite the staircase. That is the only wattled *partition* known in Maryland.

The stone fireplaces and brick chimney, all labelled "J," were also additions, as has been mentioned. On that day of our visit, the brick stack had already disappeared, although in the garret floor was a square opening for this flue. The catercornered stone chimney could be seen below, in spite of the fact that the floor in that part of the house was too dangerous to walk on.

There have been many half-timbered dwellings discovered in Pennsylvania, Missouri, and Wisconsin. There is, for instance, the *Moravian Meetinghouse* (1742) on the southeastern slope of Oley Valley, Pennsylvania, and the *Golden Plough Tavern* (1741), York, in the same State. In Lancaster, Pennsylvania, there were dwellings with half-timbering and brick fillings on the second floor. One even had a horizontally-sliding sash. Near Millbach, *Fort Zeller* has wattle-and-daub filling between the studs. The *Bird in Inn,* Newtown, Bucks County, has wattles now showing in a glass wall panel.

As regards chopped straw and mud between the ceiling joists, we found the same feature in *The Cloisters,* Ephrata, Pennsylvania, and the *Jonathan Hager*

House, Hagerstown, Maryland. At *Fort Egypt*, built about 1725 near Luray, Virginia, we find German stone-vaulted cellars, somewhat like the single one at the *Mill Pond House.*

The particular type of homestead from which *Mill Pond House* was derived was East German or Palatinate, where the usual building is half-timbered, or framed, with plaster panels between the timbers.

The visit in 1953 took a whole day of the writer's life: perhaps what was found and recorded about the place made it worthwhile.

Sinclair Garden on the "Clairmont Nurseries"

Across Herring Run from the site of *Furley Hall* in the City of Baltimore stood *Clairmont,* a pleasant home belonging to members of the Sinclair family. The plantation-house (Fig. 250, top), which has been drawn from old and faded snapshots, was constructed in three parts. First, there was the original log section, probably built before 1800 by Robert Sinclair—the kitchen portion marked on the floor plan. Second, a large frame addition was constructed about 1840 in the Gothic Revival style on the west side of the log section, when William Corse (Course), Sr., and his wife, Deborah Sinclair—a daughter of Robert Sinclair and his wife, Esther Pancoast—went to live at *Clairmont.* This was before they purchased (1847) *Furley Hall.* Lastly, the frame outshut in the shape of a pent or lean-to, used chiefly as a dining room for the farmhands, about 1850 was stuck on the east end of the log section of *Clairmont.*

The above-mentioned Robert Sinclair was the son of William St. Clair of Baltimore and his wife, Rebecca Morton; his father, by the way, is believed to have been Robert St. Clair, "The Lost Boy," who according to tradition had been stolen from a Scottish castle and who was found in America with coat buttons stamped with the St. Clair coat-of-arms.

At any rate, the Robert Sinclair of *Clairmont,* besides owning the log house on that plantation, lived in what has been called the *Sinclair House,* a white-stuccoed brick mansion adjacent to *Clairmont.* There he established in the very early 19th century the "Clairmont Nurseries"—later called the "Clairmont and Furley Hall Nurseries,"—which grew into magnificent gardens, extensive enough to become known as containing the largest stock and greatest variety of fruit and ornamental trees in the United States. The prizes won by Robert Sinclair are noted in *Tidewater Maryland Architecture and Gardens* (p. 158).

Although General Lafayette is reputed to have visited the Clairmont Nurseries during his brief stay in Baltimore in 1824, no proof of his visit has been found. Deborah Sinclair Corse, who later became mistress of *Furley Hall,* told how her father, Robert Sinclair, took her as a child, aged eleven, down town to inspect the room prepared for Lafayette at Barnum's Hotel, and how she remembered the fine silk counterpane in that room.

The floor plans and garden scheme (Fig. 250, center) are based on the memories of those who lived at *Clairmont* at the end of the 19th century—

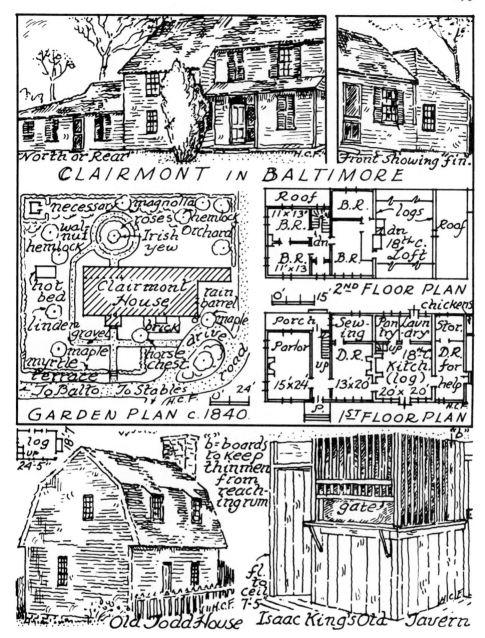

Figure 250

persons who remembered the sizes of every room, the name of every tree, and the locations of each rain barrel, doll trunk, washstand, and the like.

The park-like grounds were laid out in rectangular fashion with the front lawn set on a terrace facing South. A myrtle hedge bounded the front, and on the other three sides were hedges of arbor vitae. Contained within the log section, the Kitchen stood at the head of a slope leading to the carriage drive-way, where stood a giant maple to which horses were hitched after visitors had been unloaded from carriages before the front door. At the rear of the home-stead was a round gravel walk encompassing a bed of roses and a large yew

Fig. 251(top). At *Jug Bridge,* Frederick County, one encounters this *Toll Gate House,* with front door having a casement sash and a sliding paneled shutter. Johnston, 1930s.

Fig. 252(bottom). *Birmingham Manor,* built 1690, destroyed 1891, had a jetty and other medieval features. Copy of photograph of 1880s owned by the late Julius Snowden. Weymouth.

Fig. 253. The brick lozengy pattern on a gable-end at *Sweet Air* or *Quinn* in Baltimore County, extends from the ground to the ridge of the roof, as at *Genesar.* Two small windows have been filled in. Johnston, 1930s.

tree, grown from an Irish cutting. Covered with wisteria, the front porch had two Friends' meetinghouse benches.

Of interest was the kitchen stoop, comprising a stone slab five or six feet square, set on stone piers. Around the stoop was a brick terrace outlined with logs smoothed on top and making a step down to the ground.

The homestead itself, as the drawings indicate, verged on the plain type, in keeping with its Quaker owners. The log portion was covered with wood siding. The pent or lean-to had on its front façade what this writer has called a "fin" or sharp half-gable projection sometimes seen on New England buildings. The Kitchen, about twenty feet by twenty in size, held a dresser, table, chairs, and a "water bench." And thereby hangs a sad tale. The water supply for *Clairmont* had to be carried up a hill from a wooden pump more than a hundred feet away. Three times a day a negro helper had to carry buckets of water to the domicile and set them on water benches located just inside and

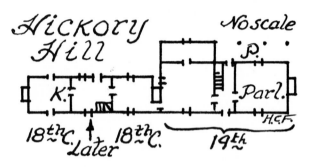

Figure 254

outside the kitchen door. At the same time the situation was ameliorated by the water from the rain barrels being used for laundry work in the wash tubs set on a bench for that purpose in the Laundry. The Pantry contained a flour barrel, sugar basket, and food safe.

The passageway had a hat rack and the stairs. On the left hand was the Parlor, about 15' by 24', with music box, side and arm chairs, sofa, table, bookcase, and flower stand. In the Dining Room were a large oval table, a rocker, desk, sofa, and cupboard. Back of the Dining Room were the Sewing Room with cupboards, sewing machine, plain table, and drop-leaf table.

The front stairway arose in a curved manner to the second floor. On the stair landing to the attic was kept an old leather trunk containing valuable silver and papers. Members of the family were under instructions that in case of fire the trunk was to be dragged out of the house. Opposite the head of the stairs at the second floor was a so-called "bath room," equipped to take only stand-up baths. It held a washstand, a hang-up area for clothes, and perhaps a chair. But then all the bedrooms had washstands, as well as clothes-bureaus.

The principal bedchamber, next to the kitchen loft, had a four-poster with a little doll's trunk beside it, a wardrobe in an alcove, chairs, a washstand, towel rack, and two bureaus.

In the attic of the 1840 part were a couple of spare bedrooms and a closet for blanket chests. The picture of the early 19th century in a little corner of Baltimore called *Clairmont* is herewith completed.

Epilogue

It was an early May morning last year. The day was warm. In the cool stillness the writer sat on the front pew of the *Middleham Chapel,* Lusby, Calvert County (Fig. 202). Hanging against the walls on either side of the chancel were two ancient gravestones with diametrically opposing views of life. One has these dispirited words:

"In Memory of Robert Addison who died suddenly Dec'r 30, 1785, aged 59 years, & 8 mos.

> How lov'd [,] how value'd once [,] avails thee not.
> To who related or by whom begot.
> A heap of dust alone remains of thee;
> Tis all thou art, and ye proud shall be.
> Life is short. Eternity how long."

The other stone reads in more cheerful vein:

"John Cook, Son of Revᵈ D. George Cook, Rector of this Parish. He dyed 5th Jan.ʸ 1759 aged 15 years & 6 mos.

> The Soul Secur'd in her Existence smiles
> At the drawn Dagger and defies its point
> The Stars shall fade away the Sun himself
> Grow dim with age and Nature Sink in years
> But thou shalt flourish in immortal youth
> Unhurt amidst the war of Elements
> The Wrecks of Matter & the Crash of Worlds."

In a late-20th-century earth beset by wars of elements, wrecks of matter, and an impending crash of worlds, young Cook's stone stands like a cheerful, hopeful beacon in darkness.

Thus we terminate this study of early Maryland civilization.

Addenda

Garden of Eden, illustrated in *Tidewater Maryland Architecture and Gardens,* was called *Serandippity.* Also it is believed to have been *Land of Promise.* The front part of the domicile has late 18th-century moldings and comprises a narrow central passage between two rooms. The stair is plain, with delicately turned newel post. On the East is a large, early 19th-century addition. The kitchen shed with quaint stone fireplace, arched cupboard, and narrow, winding staircase, was obviously built last.

Pleasant Valley was not built in 1743, according to *Early Manor and Plantation Houses of Maryland,* but in 1773. The expense book of Howes Goldsborough of *Pleasant Valley* reads as follows: "1773, July 19. To William Ashton (Bricklayer) 4. 10. 0."

Note that Robert Goldsborough (1704-1777), son of Robert Goldsborough of *Ashby House,* left by will "St. Michaels Fresh Run" [*Pleasant Valley*] "where Richard Carter did live" to his wife, Mrs. Mary Ann (Robins) Goldsborough (d. 1794).

Their son, Howes Goldsborough (1747-1797), married 16 November 1773 Rebecca Goldsborough (1757-1802), daughter of the Hon. Robert Goldsborough of "The Point," Cambridge, Md.

Thomas T. Waterman was mistaken in believing that *Pleasant Valley* may have been built by John Ariss, architect. He was also in error in stating that that house has "gable roofs hipped above the tie beams" (jerkins) and a floor plan, like the roof and plan of *Kenmore* in Virginia. See his *Mansions of Virginia,* pp. 246, 313; *The Dwellings of Colonial America,* p. 61.

Lloyd's Landing or *Mansion House Farm* are the correct names for what a tenant in 1932 called the *Old Manor Farm,* illustrated and described in *Early Manor and Plantation Houses of Maryland.*

Mrs. Arthur P. Sewell in 1956 found that Mrs. Pickersgill did have a separate kitchen outhouse to her property at 60 Albemarle St., Baltimore, now the *Star-Spangled Banner Flag House.* The will of Amos Vickers in 1800 stated in part: "I give and devise to my two nephews William Jones Dutton and Benjamin Vickers Dutton . . . my lot situate at the Corner of Queen & Albemarle Streets in Baltimore, together with the house, kitchen, and all other building appertenances. . ." In 1953 a museum was built over the site of the old kitchen.

Rehobeth in Dorchester County has been erroneously called the "Lee Mansion," but the Lees never built it nor lived there, although Francis Lee did at one time own part of the plantation. The house was constructed by Capt. John Smoot.

The *Ulm* house in Baltimore County was not over 200 years old in 1934 as stated in *Early Manor and Plantation Houses of Maryland,* but was built some time subsequent to 1765. Prior to that time Samuel Owings, Jr., was supposed to have lived with his father at the older Owings' place, *Green Spring Punch.* *Ulm* is supposed to have taken its name from the first letters of Upper, Lower, and Middle Mills.

The original name of *Asparagus Farm,* near Earleville, Cecil County, is *Frisby's Prime Choice.*

Lostock on Broad Creek, Talbot County, was the home of Peter Caulk prior to 1705. In 1736 "Peter Caulk bought from John Harrison and Eleanor his wife a parcel of land being part of land called Lostock and running 165 perches to N. E. corner of the land already the property of the said Peter Caulk in Homestead of Lostock"—thus reads an old deed.

The *Dr. Alexander Hamilton Bayly House,* High Street, Cambridge, was named for Dr. Alexander Hamilton Bayly (1814-92), an ardent horticulturist, Commissioner of Cambridge for thirty-six years, and long a president of the Town board. He was the son of Josiah Bayly (1769-1846), Attorney General of Maryland. The present owners and occupants of the house are Mr. and Mrs. Edgar Bayly Orem, representing the fifth generation of the Bayly family to live there. On June 9, 1911, the Baltimore *Sun* published a poem about their garden by the Bentztown Bard entitled, "Maryland Musings," part of which follows:

> "High Street, Cambridge, and there you are,
>   A smiling street and an olden way,
> Where shadows go by of the dames that dwelt
>   In the Dorset gardens of yesterday.
>
> And here such a garden upon the right,
>   Up from the river, still prim and sweet,
> Where Doctor Bayly, in auld lang syne,
>   Made Eden blossom in old High street.
>
> Back from the house, then the dream begins,
>   And the old box hedges its squares outline,
> Where the homely blooms of the olden days
>   In the grace of the bloomy dreams still shine.
>
> A tamarisk tree, and the smoke bush, too,
>   And the hollyhocks and the sunflower wall,
> And the nameless grace of a day that is dead
>   O'er garden and house and the hedge and all.

The friendly doctor—that must be him
   Still bending low in the shadow there
In the loved old garden that knew him well
   For his gentle pride and his constant care.

A strawberry bed, and a fig tree, fresh
   With its green young fruit and its vigorous leaf;
And the noble trees, and beyond the fence
   The ancient tombs of the parish grief."

Notes

I

1 New York. 1957.

2 Wilfong, J. C., Jr., "Maryland's Vanishing Heritage," in Baltimore *Sunday Sun,* May 10, 1953.

3 In this work the names of buildings have been italicized and the names of properties placed in quotation marks.

4 A closet with a roof of one slope beside a chimney.

5 Easton, Md. 1934.

6 Cambridge, Mass. 1948.

7 Forman, H. C., *Virginia Architecture in the 17th Century.* Williamsburg, Va. 1957. Pp. 31, 32.

8 Forman, H. C., *Jamestown and St. Mary's.* Baltimore, Md. 1938.

9 *Q.v.*

10 Kocher, L., and Dearstyne, H., *Colonial Williamsburg.* Williamsburg, Va. 1949. P. 18.

11 Radoff, M. L., *The County Courthouses and Records of Maryland.* Part I. Annapolis, Md. 1960.

12 Father-in-law of the sister of the writer's great-grandfather, Richard Townsend Turner.

13 At this writing it has not been determined whether that rammed-earth house was the one belonging to Robert Cook, of Lanham, built in 1928, or another, older one.

14 New York, 1957. P. x.

15 Chapel Hill, N.C. 1945.

16 Archives of Maryland, X, 278.

17 Baltimore, Md. 1938.

18 Radoff, M. L., *The County Courthouses and Records of Maryland.* Part I. Annapolis, Md. 1960. P. 21.

19 *Archives of Maryland.* Vol. 63, p. 239; *Maryland Historical Magazine.* Vol. 55, no. 3. September, 1960. P. 199; Vol. 33, no. 1. March, 1938. P. 26; Vol. 48, no. 2. June, 1953. P. 97; Beirne, R. R., and Scarff, J. H., *William Buckland, 1734-1774.* Baltimore, Md. 1958.

20 *Maryland Historical Magazine.* Vol. 45, no. 4. December, 1950. P. 243.

21 Plan in *Early Manor and Plantation Houses of Maryland.* Easton, Md. 1934. P. 70.

22 First noted in *Early Manor and Plantation Houses of Maryland* (1934) and described more fully in *Maryland Historical Magazine,* Vol. 41, no. 4. December, 1946.

II

1 Tilghman, J. D., "Wye House," in *Maryland Historical Magazine.* Vol. 48, no. 2. June, 1953.

2 For lack of space the writer in tracing and redrawing that fragile plat had to omit the extremities, such as the building on the north edge of the Landing Field; portions of Shaw's Creek; Chumni Creek with the notation: "This given to W. J."; the gate opposite to and across the road from the Top Road Gate; the head of Lloyd's Cove Creek; and three buildings near the above road and on the south side of it and southeast from Top Road Gate. On the survey is written: "Wye House. Scale of 40 to an Inch. J. H. 1-84 [1784]."

3 Forman, H. C., *The Architecture of the Old South.* Cambridge, Mass. 1948. P. 129.

4 The curved section of this path must have been laid out in the late 18th century.

5 A building stood in "Landing Field" on river edge just off the left-hand border of our drawing of the "Old Plat." There was another structure between field 14 and Lloyd's Cove Creek—to north of the wharf or landing.

6 January, 1933. P. 119.

7 Brochure by Mrs. Robert G. Henry, 15 July, 1947. Privately printed. Easton, Md.

8 Reproduced in *Maryland Historical Magazine.* Vol. 49, no. 3. September, 1954.

9 Tilghman, J. D., q.v. Measured drawings and details of parts of the great house are given in Chisling, E. L., "Wye House, Home of the Lloyds," in *Monograph Series.* Vol. 16, 1930.

10 Tilghman, J. D., q.v.

11 The old Library is now the Blue Room.

12 "Memorandum for Garden Tour" [of "Wye House," by M. S.]. Mimeographed sheets, 1964.

13 Vol. 16, no. 5. Published by Russell F. Whitehead. Mr. Clark omitted the fireplace and windows in the North Shed room, and put the door in East Shed room in wrong place. Both of those rooms were drawn the same width, which they are not. Also, the projecting quoins or corner blocks of the central section do not rise to the cornice, as Clark's drawing shows, because the top stones are flush with wall and do not project. The rear walls of main room are represented by only half the thickness they should be.

[14] *Captain's House* wall: bricks average 8¼" (8½") x 2½" (2¼") x 4" (4¼"); four courses make 12". Original *Orangerie* wall in East Shed room: bricks 8½" (8¼") x 2½" (2¼") x 4"; four courses make 12". Writer's field notes.

[15] In Tilghman, J. D., q.v., there was mentioned a sooty tile duct in the floor located just back of the large front windows.

[16] *Rock Hall Historical Collection,* prepared by Rock Hall Commemoration, Inc., Rock Hall, Md. 1957.

[17] Brick size in South gable-end is 9" x 4½" x 2½". Other significant dimensions: 1st floor ceiling height, 8'-7½"; 2nd floor ceiling, 7'-7".

[18] In 1722 Robert Goldsborough owned 250 acres, Thomas Gully 150 acres, William Dixon 60 acres, and John Davis 147 acres. The remaining 93 acres had been lost by water.

[19] *Maryland Historical Magazine,* Vol. 53, no. 4. Dec. 1958. P. 32.

[20] Rebuilt 1703, and used for indeterminate period.

[21] Tilghman, O., *History of Talbot County, Maryland, 1661-1861.* Baltimore, Md. 1915. Vol. II, P. 523. *Celebration of the Two Hundred and Fiftieth Anniversary of Old Third Haven Meeting House, October 23, 1932.* Easton, Md. 1932.

[22] The wing had been removed about 1861 from the head of the cove up river, and made into kitchen, rooms, and closets for the mansion.

[23] In 1802 "Botfield's Addition" included "Botfield's Endeavor," 52¼ acres; "Bite the Biter," 33 acres; part of "Ashby," 40¾ acres; part of "Tilghman's Fortune" 9½ acres; total 112¼ acres, to which were added 7 acres of vacant land, making 119¼. The tiny piece of "Tilghman's Fortune" was on the periphery of "Botfield's Addition," which in 1847 became the "North Bend" estate. Liber JL#47, folios 453-455; Liber JP#59, folios 305, 306; Liber JP#61, folio 59. Easton, Md. The "Manor of Tilghman's Fortune," 1000 acres surveyed in 1659 for Capt. Samuel Tilghman, was on west side of Tred Avon River adjoining "Ratcliffe Manor," and was not on Miles River. Liber R, folios 108, 420, 421. Annapolis, Md.

[24] Mary Ann Bartlett of "Old Bloomfield" was descended from Thomas Bartlett, blacksmith, owner of "Ratcliffe Manor," whose son John Bartlett married Mary, daughter of Richard Townsend, who came in 1682 to Philadelphia with Penn.

[25] Tilghman, O., *q.v.,* Vol. 2, P. 513.

[26] See *Maryland Historical Magazine.* Vol. 34, no. 3. September, 1939. P. 224.

[27] Forman, H. C., *Tidewater Maryland Architecture and Gardens.* N.Y. 1956. P. 55.

[28] Interior size of cellar: 14'-9" by 15'-9," although original length may have been cut off. The east chimney was flush with gable. Writer's notes.

[29] See Forman, H. C., *Early Manor and Plantation Houses of Maryland.* Easton, Md. 1934. The northern portion of "Lombardy" contained *Little Lombardy,* a decrepid early frame cottage, and *Lombardy (Apple) Orchard* of c. 1895, with a windmill plan of four back-to-back corner fireplaces —a house remodelled in 1952 by the writer.

[30] Chandlee, E. E., *Six Quaker Clockmakers,* Phila., Pa. 1943.

[31] Liber 56, folio 368-69. Annapolis, Md.

[32] Liber 4, folio 572; liber 5, folio 109, Annapolis, Md.

[33] A floor plan of the original part of *White Hall* is given in the writer's *The Architecture of the Old South* (1948), Fig. 201.

[34] Gravestone recorded by this writer: Nancy Brinsfield, d. April 5, 1868, 71st year; James Brinsfield, b. April 15, 1813, d. Dec. 25, 1873; Mary W. Brinsfield, wife of James Brinsfield, b. Sept. 15, 1814, d. April 20, 1888; Jimmie, son of Solomon and Maggie Brinsfield, d. Feb. 5, 1867, aged 12 days; Hallie, dau. of Solomon and Maggie Brinsfield, d. Sept. 10, 1870, aged 2 yrs., 7 mos., 27 days. Benjamin Denny, d. Dec. 13, 1831, 81st year; Sarah Denny, d. Oct. 17, 1816, aged 63 yrs., 7 mos., 10 days; George E. Battee, d. June 9, 1855, 32nd yr.

[35] Reprinted in part, with changes, from "The Sunday Magazine," *The Sun,* Baltimore, Md. October 22, 1961.

[36] See illustrations in *Early Manor and Plantation Houses of Maryland* (1934).

[37] Other structural details are the 3" x 3½" studs, placed two feet apart and flat against the clapboards. The rafters rest on the ends of the joists, which extend out 9" from the plates. Main sill is 8" x 12", laid flat.

[38] Remaining gravestones: Gibson W. Wright, b. Nov. 15, 1798, d. Feb. 16, 1871; Delila W., wife of Gibson W. Wright, b. Oct. 1, 1811, d. Jan. 3 (?), 1873, aged 61 years, 2 mos., 29 days; Maria K. Abbott, b. July 31, 1813, d. Sept. 7, 1868.

[39] *Maryland Historical Magazine,* Vol. 52, no. 1. March, 1957. P. 36.

[40] In 1847 Isaac Atkinson, his wife and daughters, and Wm. E. Bartlett were driving a carriage in the lane of "Locust Grove" when the horse got loose and ran away.

[41] Random-width vertical beaded T&G boards, ¾" thick, 4"–6" widths. Also note photograph of Great Room at *Locust Grove* in *Tidewater Maryland Architecture and Gardens.* P. 88.

[42] *Rock Hall Historical Collection,* Rock Hall Commemoration, Inc., Rock Hall, Md. 1957. The son of William Bradshaw died April 13, 1838, in his 55th year. William Hodges, who married Frances Bradshaw, died in 1771. His brother Robert Hodges died in 1735. Ann Humphreys, consort of John Humphreys, departed this life . . . 30th, 1820 (Author's notes).

[43] Tilghman, O., *History of Talbot County, Maryland.* Vol. 2, P. 206.

[44] *Maryland Historical Magazine.* Vol. 42. June, 1947. P. 137.

[45] See "The Clay Family," in *Filson Club Publications.* Vol. 14.

III

[1] Wm. H. Edmondson, b. Aug. 29, 1815, d. Aug. 26, 1860, aged 44 yrs. 11 mos., 28 days; John H. Edmondson, b. May 25, 1822, d. May 1, 1854; S. Joren (?), to the memory of Moses L. Edmondson, d. Aug. 26, 1843, aged 29 yrs., 4 mos., 3 days; James Edmondson, b. 1786, d. Feb. 15, 1859, aged 73 yrs.; Henrietta, wife of James Edmondson, d. Aug. 8, 1851, aged 63 yrs.; Thos. H. Edmondson, b. Oct. 18, 1820, d. Aug. 12, 1850, aged 29 yrs., 9 mos., 24 days; Mary Ann Edmondson, d. Feb. 8, 1855, aged 36 yrs., 6 mos.; Moses Hooper, d. March 25, 1814, aged 38 yrs. M. . . . 1814.

[2] In the case of early framework of House I the beading could have taken place in the 19th century, because the beams in House I loft are not beaded, but roughly adzed; whereas House II loft beams are beaded.

[3] The dimension at front of building from dirt cellar floor to bottom of first floor joists is approximately 9'-6", and at back wall, 6'-10"; at cellar cross partition, 8'-1".

[4] The first floor sash, now gone, measured 36" by 67"; the balcony sash, also removed, was approximately 32" by 48"—its sill height being 22" above the balcony floor.

[5] Maryland Historical Society, Baltimore, Md. 1949.

[6] Radoff, M. L., ed., *The Old Line State.* Baltimore, Md. N.d. Vol. I, P. 224. Mr. Orin Bullock, Jr., in *The Restoration Manual* (Norwalk, Conn. 1966), defined "restoration" in a building as putting back as much as possible into the shape and appearance which it had at a definite date or period; and stated that the validity of a restoration lies in its authenticity. The recent work at *Old Wye Church* and *Old Trinity* does not fully meet that definition, and therefore this writer has named them "partial restorations."

[7] The English cabinet-worker is reputed to have modelled the interior woodwork at *Old Trinity* on a certain church in England, *St. Saviour,* Foremark, near Repton, Derbyshire. *Old Trinity* is English, yes,—but English by way of the Eastern Shore tradition, which should be observed in any restoration. It did not have the same construction features as *John's Point. Antiques Magazine.* Vol. 78, no. 6. December, 1960. P. 589.

[8] Window dimensions: 8" x 10" panes; sill height, floor to sash, 30½"; sash, 36½" x 46½"; door and window frames, 3" wide, pegged.

[9] See Forman, H. C., *The Architecture of the Old South.* Cambridge, Mass., 1948. P. 105.

[10] Dimensions: overall foundation: 20'-2" wide; 52'-7" long. First floor to second floor heights, 9'-9". First floor chimney openings averaged 3'-0".

[11] Because of the present configuration of the box garden it appears that some of the box may have been removed when the rear wing was built.

[12] Incomplete listings: Thomas Creighton, d. Oct. 1820, aged 45; Richard Tubman, d. 1813; Nancy Tubman, wife of Richard Tubman, d. Sept. 2, 1809, aged 58; William R. Tubman, son of Richard and Zipporah Tubman, d. Sept. 23, 1831, aged 22; Richard Keen, son of Henry Keen and Mary his wife, b. April 23, 1799, d. Dec. 19, 1815; Samuel Slacum, b. 1793, d. 1818; Melley Tyler, wife of John C. Tyler, b. 1774; Mary Creighton, b. 1771, d. 1829; John Creighton, d. 1832; Charles and Emily Tubman; Nancy Gootee, d. Feb. 14, 1838, aged 64; John C. Tyler, son of Thomas and Jemima Tyler, b. May 19, 1765, d. Jan. 23, 1825; William, son of Thomas and Rebecca Wallace, b. June 2, 1782, d. July 9, 1821.

[13] Due to dense overgrowth the writer was able to record only the following names: Irene Schoolfield, wife of Elija C. Schoolfield, born Jan. 15, 1812, fell asleep in the arms of Jesus, July 20, 1895; Sarah J., dau. of G. T. and S. E. Collins, d. March 9, 1862; H. S[choolfield].

IV

[1] Vol. 58, no. 1.

[2] Hammond, J. M., in his *Colonial Mansions of Maryland and Delaware* (Phila., 1914) gave between 1690 and 1700 as the date of building by Richard Galloway.

[3] In 1960 the owner, Mr. Churchill Murray, and the writer excavated in the cellar of the Federal octagonal wing for footings of the 17th-century front porch, without success. Evidently the footings had been removed, so the length of front porch will never be ascertained.

[4] If that theory is true, then how did one go downstairs to the later mud cellar, of Phase Ib development?

⁵ In his article Mr. Kelly thinks that it was probable that this partition, making a central passage, dated about 1801-03; but it may have been earlier.

⁶ Reprinted, with changes, from the *Maryland Historical Magazine,* March, 1943. P. 56. The excavation and research work was done under a grant in 1940 from the American Council of Learned Societies, Washington, D.C.

⁷ The length of the pit is 9'-7"; width varies from 4'-8" at one end to 5'-3" at the other. The walls go down vertically 3'-7" to the floor.

⁸ It is interesting that "Charles Gift" in 1802 was the name of "Elton Head Manor." See "Henry Sewall Papers," Maryland Historical Society.

⁹ Above the sill of the second floor window in the northwest gable, the clapboards are plain (early); below the sill the clapboards are beaded (later).

¹⁰ *Archives of Maryland.* Vol. 51, P. 27.

¹¹ The graves in a thicket at *Snow Hill* read: "In memory of John W. Bennett who died June 13, 1848, aged 41 years and 6 months"; "Sacred to the memory of Isabella consort of Joseph David who departed this life January 22, 1844, aged 39 years, 'Beloved in life, Lamented in death.' "; "F 1817."

¹² See *The Architecture of the Old South.* P. 127; *Tidewater Maryland Architecture and Gardens.* P. 28.

¹³ Other stones at *Mansion Hall* are: Captain Alexander Gray, b. May 30, 1788, d. July 25, 1839; Elizabeth, wife of Capt. Alexander Gray, b. July 15, 1793, d. Aug. 6, 1857; Robert Gray, b. Dec. 8, 1792, d. Dec. 26, 1851; Elizabeth, wife of Robert Gray, b. June 1, 1796, d. Nov. 6, 1824; James F. Gray, d. Sept. 5, 1862, aged 40; Joseph C. Gray, b. May 18, 1820, d. June 1, 1880; Elizabeth, wife of Joseph C. Gray, b. Jan. 28, 1821, d. March 27, 1863; Benedictor E. Gray, d. March 13, 1866, aged 48; Mary Francis, wife of Edward L. Smoot and dau. of Capt. Robert Gray, b. Aug. 5, 1842, d. Sept. 11, 1859; Julius Miller, b. July 29, 1855, d. Oct. 5, 1855; Thomas Edmund, son of T. A. and Priscilla Smith, d. Aug. 21, 1857, aged 11 years, 4 months, 16 days.

¹⁴ See also *Maryland Historical Magazine.* Vol. 44, no. 4. December, 1949. Pp. 276, 280.

¹⁵ Stones of: D. R. McDaniel (1829-76); Martha E. McDaniel (1833-94); M. Louise (1862-90), consort of J. T. Penn and daughter of D. R. and M. E. McDaniel; J. T. Perry, son of D. R. and M. E. McDaniel, d. 1865, aged 8:

> "Our Perry smiles no more below,
> But in that world of light
> Above the clouds, above the stars,
> He lives an angel bright."

¹⁶ See also *The Architecture of the Old South.* P. 154.

¹⁷ Formerly owned about 1863 by Thomas E. Turton and his wife, Jane (Berry) Turton. Jane was the sister of Dorinda Eleanor Berry, who married Thomas Sasscer, and came to live at *Sasscer's Green* as a bride. A small child's rocking chair at *Sasscer's Green* has written on the bottom of it: "—Turton, West Nottingham."

¹⁸ Reprinted in part, with changes, from "The Sunday Magazine," *The Sun,* Baltimore, Md. October 22, 1961.

¹⁹ *Woodlawn,* often erroneously known as the Contee-Sellman place, but which is only a Sellman homestead, had its central section built in 1735 by William Sellman, although the markings in the old Flemish bond read "WA1735." Only two-thirds of this middle part exists. The largest section was constructed about 1840 by Col. Alfred Sellman.

²⁰ See *Tidewater Maryland Architecture and Gardens.*

²¹ The gravestones are: John Stanforth d. Nov. 22, 1815, aged 62; Eleanor Stanforth, consort of John Stanforth, d. Dec. 23, 1825, aged 60. Ellen Stanforth, child of John Stanforth d. Nov., 1833, aged 29. John Stanforth d. May 20, 1864, in 67th year. Ellen, dau. of John and Ellen Stanforth, d. 1833, aged 2. Benjamin Franklin, son of Levin and Elizabeth Stanforth d. Sept. 18, 1857, aged 4 years, 8 months. Benjamin W., son of Benjamin and Charlotte M. Stanforth, b. Nov. 29, 1839, d. Aug. 1, 1865. Elizabeth, consort of Levin Stanforth, b. Sept. 22, 1795. Benjamin Stanforth. . .

²² The house is 78'-10" long. The main section, the earliest, is 26'-9" long, and has a 7'-8" ceiling height downstairs and 7'-3" upstairs. The pendants or "drops" on main section are 6" long at ends and 3¾" square, with flaked edges.

²³ Certificates, TH2; Chancery Court, TBH1, folio 517; 18, folio 72; 47, folio 248; envelope 52; Wills, 38, folio 703. Annapolis, Md. *Maryland Historical Magazine.* Vol. 60, no. 3. September, 1965. P. 314.

V

¹ Other stones are: Elizabeth, "consort of the late Joshua Cockey," d. Feb. 11, 1843, aged 56; Harriet N., wife of Thomas D. Cockey, d. July 1, 1841, aged 50 ("May she rest in Peace, Amen"); Anne Cockey, b. 1840, d. aged 9 mos.; Rachel R. Cockey, d. Nov. 5, 1887, aged 73; Nicholson Lux Cockey, d. 1883; Sarah Stuart Cockey, dau. of Darby and Ann Nicholson Lux, b. 1807, d. 1874

("erected by her son Colgate"); Mary E. Cockey, dau. of Joshua and Elizabeth, b. 1817, d. 1828.

[2] A row of Sutton stones in the churchyard reads: Lora Sutton, d. Jan. 25, 1839, aged 12 yrs.; Jonathan Sutton, d. Jan. 19, 1825, aged 63 yrs., 2 mos., 2 days; Oliver H. P. Sutton, b. Sept. 30, 1813, d. July 7, 1851; Sarah Sutton, d. Dec. 3, 1824, aged 56 yrs., 8 mos., 17 days; Tobitha Sutton, d. Dec. 5, 1810, aged 8 yrs.

[3] "Fanny's Inheritance" originally had 893 acres surveyed in 1695 for Edward Boothby on west side of Swan Creek, and later belonged to Dr. Josias Middlemore.

[4] Samuel and Susan (Chauncey) Sutton's children were: 1) Jonathan H. Sutton (d. 1891) who m. Mary E. Reilly, and had Samuel Sutton of Aberdeen, Md., Leonora Sutton, William McDonald Sutton, and Ida M. Sutton, who m. William D. Trimble, of Hampton, Va.; and 2) Martha Ann Sutton, who m. 1st Samuel Sauner, and 2nd Clarence Farquaharson.

[5] The children of James Lawrence Sutton and his wife, Elizabeth M. Hewes, were: Mary Sutton (m. Townsend); Hetty Jane Sutton (m. Coale); Maltier Sutton, died at 16; Anna Sutton (m. 1862 Ezra Lippincott, b. 1836, d. 1906, of Riverton, N.J.); Sara Sutton (m. Corse); and Ellen, Lucy, Cora, Elizabeth—all died unmarried.

[6] *Maryland Historical Magazine.* Vol. 51, no. 2. June, 1956.

[7] One stone is for Hannah Lemman (d. 1840): "By long experience I have known thy sovereign power to save, at thy command I venture down serenely to the grave."

[8] Mr. Este Fisher once gave this writer a rough diagram of this plantation, but it is not complete enough for publication in a book.

[9] John Merryman (*of Hereford Farm*), d. Aug. 1777, aged 74; his wife Sarah, d. March 1775, aged 67; Nicholas Rogers Merryman; Henry Merryman.

[10] Mahlon Janney Chandlee owned: 429½ acres, the "home tract," comprising parts of "Charley Forest," "Brother's Content," and "Addition to Brooke Grove"; 238 acres, "The Old Mill Tract," comprising parts of "Addition to Brooke Black Meadows"; "The Fork"; "Gitting's Ha Ha," "Brother's Content"; 107 acres, a share of his mother Deborah's lands. Mahlon also owned with Albert Chandlee and Dr. Henry Chandlee "The Great Meadows," 840 acres on Snowden's River, lying partly in Montgomery County and partly in Howard County.

[11] Letter by Ellis Chandlee, November 8, 1931, in writer's files.

[12] Henry Chandlee (1853-1916), son of Edwin (Fig. 241B) and Cassandra Turner Chandlee and grandson of Mahlon, was born at *Brother's Content*. He earned two doctor of medicine degrees (U. of Md., 1882, and Hahnemann, 1883); was professor, registrar, and dean of a medical college; editor of a medical journal. He founded and chaired a department of roentgenology of the University of Maryland; served as radiologist of that university's hospital and of one for crippled children. With another doctor he made the first X-ray in the city of Baltimore. He was the first individual there to own and operate an X-ray machine, and had his own private X-ray laboratories at 2000 N. Charles Street; yet he was too modest to permit his name in any medical Who's Who. *The Turner Family of "Hebron" and Betterton, Maryland* (Baltimore, 1933). P. 88.

[13] Daniel Dulaney to Jacob Stoner, Sept. 8, 1746: 1) 292 acres, part of Tasker's Chance, and 2) two parcels of land (Bear's Den), part of Tasker's Chance. The beginning point of #2 was near the mouth of Tuscarora Creek and below "Stoner's Mill."

Index

Index

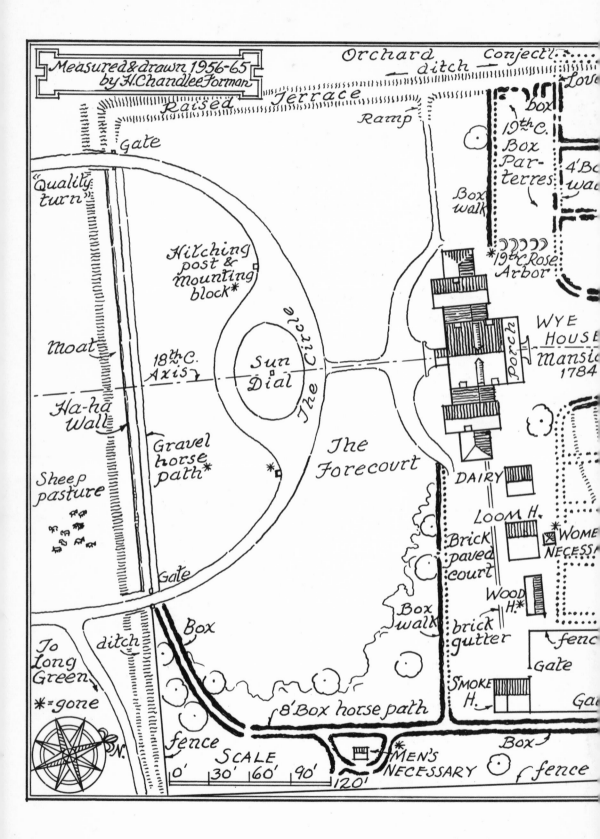